Dalit Men's Autobiographies:
A Critical Appraisal

Dalit Men's Autobiographies: A Critical Appraisal

Edited by

Bijender Singh

KALPAZ

ISBN: 978-93-5128-240-2

Price: ₹ 990

First Published, 2017

Published by

Kalpaz Publications
C-30, Satyawati Nagar,
Delhi – 110052
E-mail: kalpaz@hotmail.com
Ph.: 9212142040

Printed at: G. Print Process, Delhi

Cataloging in Publication Data—DK
Courtesy: D.K. Agencies (P) Ltd. <docinfo@dkagencies.com>

Dalit men's autobiographies : a critical appraisal/edited by Bijender Singh.
pages cm
ISBN 9789351282402

1. Indic literature—Dalit authors—History and criticism. 2. Authors, Indic—Biography—History and criticism. 3. Autobiography. 4. Dalits in literature. I. Singh, Bijender, editor.

PK2907.U56D35 2016 DDC 891.409920694 23

Contents

Foreword

The last quarter of the twentieth century saw a growing tendency of writing their autobiographies in different languages among Dalit writers across India. They have vividly described the incidents and happenings perpetrated against them, social and economic discrimination and disparities and the atrocities being committed in the name of religion which, they were unable to forget despite the best of efforts. Therefore, a peep into the active historic, mythological and Manu Smriti (Manu Code) based social structure is absolutely essential into the background of the autobiographies of Dalit literature, harassed by social dispensation, before going deep into their autobiographies. It is noteworthy that only Dalit autobiographies are under review.

Historical quintessence and facts are replete with evidence that in the ancient times, about 2500 BC, Indian aboriginals had the oldest and the richest culture, which was famous as Sindhu Valley culture. The natives of this land set up the most developed cities like Harappa and Mohenjodaro, which cannot be compared with any other country or city in the fields of civilisation and culture at that time. But around 1800 BC, the white Aryans having grey and brown eyes entered the lush green prosperous Punjab (the land of five rivers) in northern India through the Khaibar Pass, coming from different areas of Central Asia. Initially, they came in small numbers but later when they entered in big numbers and tried to settle there, hostility by the sons of the soil was but natural against them. The Aryans who had learnt many things from the natives, started indiscriminately attacking them and destroyed the glorious and proud humanistic culture of the aboriginals.

The Aryans introduced caste system to divide the locals. They created classes/groups of Brahmins, Kshatriya, Vaishyas and Shudras giving different kinds of work to each group. The Shudras were endowed with the responsibility of service to the three upper castes in the name of God and announced that nobody would disobey it. The Shudras were called Naga, Rakhsh, Asur, Dravid, Danav, Nishad, Eunuch, etc. No stone was left unturned to propagate the tradition of sacrifice of humans along with the animals and birds and to create an atmosphere of fear and terror in the society. The social dignity of half of the population i.e. women was kept at the lowest ebb, describing them as sinful....and then the supremacy was cemented by linking casteism with birth.

German dictator Hitler-1889-1945 (Mein Kampf)* had written many facts about Aryans (according to him: nomad) and Brahmans in his autobiography—*My Struggle*. For example, he had mentioned:

> If we divide mankind into three categories—founders of culture, bearers of culture, and destroyers of culture—the Aryan alone can be considered as representing the first category....The Aryan races—often in absurdly small numbers overthrow alien nations, and favoured by the numbers of people of lower grade who are at their disposal to aid them, they proceed to develop, according to the special conditions for life in the acquired territories fertility climate, etc. (*My Struggle,* Chapter 11, p.121)

It was not the end of the untold and unbearable miseries inflicted by the Aryans. They tried to destroy the natural resources of North India (Greater Punjab, Sindh, some regions of the Himalayas, Gujarat, Rajasthan, west Uttar Pradesh) with their full mite. They inflicted big loss upon this highly productive land. For example, river Saraswati is mentioned in many ancient scriptures, including Rigveda. There is no mention of this river going dry in Vedic scriptures but in Mahabharata, there is a long description about this river. Several discoveries during the last one hundred years have established that river Saraswati flowed in the dry bed of river Haakrha/Ghaggara. Scholars believe that the main reason for the drying up of the Saraswati was the change in its course by river Satluj. With this change, the river started merging in river Sindhu instead the Saraswati. They have put forth another reason for the change of course the Yamuna river (instead of flowing into the West, the river started flowing in the East, merging with the Ganges). The main reason to give out above description is to fully understand the socio-economic condition as to how the Aryans deployed every means to firmly settle down and turn the natives/locals permanently into their slaves. In the present times, Manu Smriti is active in its own way to maintain Brahaminwadi orientation permanently.

Rebellious voices among the natives against the treacherous administrative moves of the Aryan Brahmans, their inhuman treatment and the slavery started growing louder extensively. Charvaka Philosophy and Buddhism specially supported them. This proved to be a big challenge to Brahmanism. During those days, Aajivaka Darshan was prevalent among the natives. It is also true that in order to suppress and silence these rebellious movements, some of the neo ideologies and notions propagated and instigated to lead a life of lesser demands, follow the path of non-violence (Ahimsa) and be contented by considering everything as God's wish. With the passage of time, some holy men across India, pleading social equality made mind shaking poetic attacks against caste-religion in the guise of Satsang. Prominent among these saints were: Namdev, Ravidas, Kabir, Trilochan, Sadhna, Sain, Pipa among others. While their compositions preached uniformity and equality of bones, skin, veins and skeleton and the red coloured blood running in the veins of all human beings, they aroused social awakening also. For this reason, they were successful in their times in mobilising the landless, hard working classes and the artisan fraternity. The poetic compositions of these saints and holy men have autobiographical references and contemporary situations as well as historical events. It is pertinent to mention that these saints and holy men presented a resolution for Shudras and untouchables i.e. natives to shake off Brahmanical traditions and bad customs and to usher in a new society. For example, Begumpura – a city sans all pains and troubles, sans casteism, a society sans caste/class, a modern society, sans any reference to temples, an urban society, the area where no tax is to be paid or no trouble to bear with, where there is no discrimination of high or low, rather all are equals. In the concluding part of this Shabad, poet Ravidas said that he belonged to Chamar caste but was a free bird and moved in freedom with his friends and had the right to go anywhere, to a city or a village.

The full text of the Shabad (a poem), as published in Sri Guru Granth Sahib is as follows:

The regal real with the sorrowless name:
The they call it Begumpura, a place with no pain,
No taxes or cares, nor own property there,
No wrongdoing, worry, terror or torture.
Oh my brother, I've come to take it as my own,
My distant home, where everything is right.
That imperial kingdom is rich and secure,
Where none are third or second—all are one;
Its food and drink are famous, and those who live there
Dwell in satisfaction and in wealth.
They do this or that; they walk where they wish,
They stroll through fabled places unchallenged.
Oh, says Ravidas, a tanner now set free,
Those who walk beside me are my friends.

(Hawley and Juergensmeryer, p. 32,
Seeking Begumpura, p.107, Adi Granth, p. 345)

And it is also written in Adi Granth:

If Thou dost claim to be a Brahmins by the birth a
From a Brahmin woman,
Why was thy birth not from a different source? (Way, path)

Translated in English by Gurbachan Singh Talib,
Vol. 1, p. 679

— (Adi Granth p. 324)

The aforesaid poetic compositions are enshrined in Sri Guru Granth Sahib. Many scholars have opined that elucidation of the sacred text of Sri Guru Granth Sahib goes to indicate that it is pro-Dalit. Therefore, as thinker they consider Granth Sahib as Dalit Text. In other words, this great holy book rejects the false notions of untouchability and casteism and portrays spiritualism along with the half truth of social behaviour and the harsh reality without any hanky-panky in natural course seen from a human angle. Some more contemporary saints and holy men, apart from those referred to above were saint Tukaram, Chokhamela, Banka, Janabai and many more who criticised hypocrisy, misplaced belief and show business and played an important role in the development of a new social order.

In the last quarter of the nineteenth century and the first quarter of twentieth century several Dalit movements came into being with the main aim of bringing a revolutionary change in the Indian society, especially the socio-economic, religious and political situation of the untouchables. What I mean to say is that Jyoti Rao Phule (1827-1890) initiated the bonds of unity in 1868 among the untouchables by allowing the Shudras and extreme Shudras to take water from his home pond and established the 'Satiyasodhak Society'on 24th September 1873. Later he founded the Hindu Sreyobhi Vardhini Sabha Madras in 1870 and Namashudra Bengal in 1872 to bring an awakening among the untouchables about their rights. Similarly, Adi Dravida Mahajan Sabha in South India in 1927, the first Dalit Revolutionary and land reformist Ayyan Kali in Kerala (1863-1941), M.C. Raja in Tamil Nadu, Bhagya Reddy Verma in Andhra Pradesh (1888-1939), Adi Hindu Mahasabha 1926 and in North India Adi Hindu (founder Swami Achhutanand, 1839-1932), Ad Dharam Mandal Punjab (founder Babu Mangu Ram, 1886-1980), Baba Saheb Dr B.R. Ambedkar (1891-1956) who all hailed from different areas but with one uniform ideology and thinking presented their ideas before the people and the British government. They published innumerable booklets. For example, Adi Dharam Mandal published eight poetic books: (1) Adi Dukhre, published twice, (2) Sacha Pataka, published twice, (3) Achhuton ki Pukar, (4) Adi Paigam, (5) Vihar Sudhar, published twice, (6) Bharam Torh, (7) Azadi di Daundi and (8) Qaumi Alaan, etc. A total number of 50,000 copies were published of all these editions. A lot of revolutionary literature was published and distributed among the untouchables and before 1931 census, a large number of posters on creating awakening for equal rights were pasted on walls and trees.

All these aforesaid untouchable organisations and their leaders, projected in the posters and booklets that they were met out treatment like war hostages since the time the Aryans subjugated them. The aboriginals of India have no blood relationship with the Aryans.

They were not from among us nor did we belong to them. They widely propagated the essence of Begumpura Resolution of uniformity and equality in human rights for all, propounded by Guru Ravidas. Contrary to it, Mahatma Gandhi raised the banner of *Ram Raj* for *Hindu Nationalism* which aimed at removing untouchability. He wanted to continue casteism as was in vogue. Yes, in the 1931 census, a conscious effort was made to know the number of untouchables in the country. In Punjab alone, a quarter and four lakh people registered themselves as Adi Dharami, identifying them as being separate from the Hindus and asked the enumerators to write Adi Dharam as their religion in the column under religion. If we look at the data in 2011 census, we would find that there was 17 crore population of the scheduled castes in the country. In a little broader sense, in seven SAARC nations (now eight), Dalit population was 201 million. According to 2011 Census, Nepal had 4.5 million Dalits (2005 estimates), United Kingdom 50 lakhs (2011 estimates) and Canada two lakhs. Malaysia, Singapore, Bangladesh and Pakistan data about Dalit population is not available.

In our ancient scriptures, the natives were known under different names, described as above. The nomenclature changed in the modern times, as for example, Mahatma Gandhi used the nomenclature 'Harijan' (God's offspring) for the untouchables. In 1928, Desh Sevak (Punjabi newspaper) had translated the word untouchable as 'Dalit' in one of its issues which occurred in the memorandum presented to the Simon Commission. Similarly, a magazine 'Dalit Bandhu' published from Lahore came out in 1938. Its editors were Jaswant Rai and Prithi Singh Azad. Baba Saheb Dr Ambedkar used the Sanskrit word Dalit for the first time in Marathi. The use of word 'Harijan' is now banned by the court. In fact, Dalit word has great revolutionary connotation. It brings all the untouchable groups (now scheduled castes) in India, residing in any part of the country or may be belonging to any religion, caste, language, etc., under one umbrella. This word gives identity to a scheduled caste person, even if he may be having faith in any religion, Hindu, Buddha or Sikh religion.

It would be pertinent to say that Dalit litterateurs became interested in creating literature which was something new, rational, inspirational and pointed to a definite aim. The result was that Dalit movements were used as a logically sound tool. The autobiographies of Dalit litterateurs portrayed a true picture of the contemporary Indian society before intelligentsia, the world over and were successful in projecting the ugly face of the country. The bitter truth in these autobiographies, not indigent of anybody's sympathy, inspired to fight for achieving the desired goal with a revolutionary zeal and argumentative point of view.

The naked truth is also that the Dalit litterateurs, while keeping themselves in the centre stage of their autobiographies, projected more prominently the social, religious and economic conditions of their entire Dalit community. Often Dalit autobiographers wrote about the conditions which they themselves had undergone. They did not use the flowery language like the autobiographers belonging to upper castes but portrayed with logic the inhuman situations, the excesses being perpetrated against them, coercion and physical exploitation along with blind faith, fallacy, prudery, rituals and pomposity. In the present times, Dalit literature has become the mainstream literature. In other words, the tendency of the graph of traditional literature and Brahamanic biographic literature has gone down. Another fact which comes out prominently is that the claim of the Dalit literature or biography literature being written about Dalits by non-Dalits has proved to be hollow and frail as it is far from reality being outsider, full of subjugation and full of sympathy. It is not pro-social change, social justice and humanistic in any format. In this context, the following comment of the first Prime Minister of India, Jawaharlal Nehru could be pondered over in depth, which he made in a letter to Dr Rajendra Prasad on 17th November 1953 and was published in *Organizer Weekly*, New Delhi on 4th May 1997: *The Hindu is certainly not tolerant and is certainly more narrow minded than almost any person in any Country, except the Jew.*

Dalit autobiographies have been published in large numbers in different Indian languages. Majority of these are Marathi Dalit autobiographies. These Dalit autobiographies have been translated into English and many Indian languages, such as Ambedkar's *Autobiographical Notes,* Daya Pawar's *Bluta,* N.S. Suryavanshi's *Things I Never Imagined,* Narender Jadhav's *Outcaste,* Vasant Moon's *Growing up Untouchable in India,* Sharan Kumar Limbale's

The Outcaste, Laxman Bapu Mane's *Upara: An Outsider* and Arjun Dangle's *Poisoned Bread*. Tamil writer, Perumal Murugan remained in the centre of controversies for penning his autobiography type novel *One Part Woman*.

My autobiography *Changiya Rukh: Against the Night* published by Oxford University Press in 2010, portrays poverty and destitution of the Dalits in the Punjab province, which was considered prosperous. Similar expressions have been portrayed by Kannada autobiographer Siddalingaiah's *Ooru Keri,* Professor Satyanaryana's *My Father Baliah* (in English but the writer's language is Telugu).

Similarly, from the Hindi speaking areas, autobiography of Professor Shivraj Singh Bechain's *My Childhood on My Shoulders*, being published by the Oxford University Press would be out soon. Om Prakash Valmiki's *Joothan* and Laxman Gaikwad's *Uchalya: The Branded* have already been translated into English. Suraj Pal Chauhan's autobiography *Triskrit* has been translated into German language. *Apne Apne Pinjre*, an autobiography of Mohandas Naimshrai and its second part have been talk of the town. Dr Dharamvir's autobiography *Meri Patni aur Bheria* and Professor Tulsi Ram's *Murdaiya* have specially been a subject matter of discussion from several aspects.

Ghadrite and Adi Dharam founder and Punjabi poet Babu Mangu Ram's autobiography portions under the banner *Mera Jiwan Birtant te Meri Videsh Yatra* and poet Gurdas Ram Alam's autography portions, *Ravidas Patrika* and *Jantak Laher* were published in 1971 and 1985 respectively. Story writer Prem Gorky's *Gair-Hazar Aadmi*, Lal Singh Dil's *Dastan*, Sarup Sialvi's *Zalalat*, Maluk Chand Kaler's *Kore Ghare da Pani* and story writer Amarjit's *Akk da Dudh* deserve a special mention.

It is the Dalit autobiographies which had played an important role in carving out an identity for Dalit literature and established yardsticks for a separate Dalit literature philosophy and presented alternative to traditional concepts. They presented own yardsticks for the creation of an ideal society sans casteism, projecting the issues of contemporary social conditions along with caste, class, religion and race with all seriousness and humility.

The notable common feature of all these autobiographies was that their scripts differ but there is no difference in projection of situations. A similar voice of fury and rebellion for social change emerged from all these autobiographies. A study of the contemporary Dalit literature and the autobiographies of Dalit litterateurs indicate that the future of Dalit literature is quite bright, just like the Ambedkar thought in India.

Let me be highly grateful to Dr Bijender Singh, a writer and editor of great merit, who has carved a special name among the Indian editors by editing anthologies consisting of the critical articles on diverse aspects of English literature. His anthologies on Dalit literature, apart from different areas of English literature, are clear evidence of his different literary tastes and his deepest feelings to the downtrodden and the underprivileged classes despite being a non-Dalit writer. I am grateful to my esteemed friend and prominent editor, Dr Singh who he gave me an opportunity to write foreword for this book in hand. I hope and am confident that this book, edited by him, of course, would be warmly welcomed by students, research scholars, intellectuals and writers equally, like all his previous books. This book has become another feather in his cap for Dr Bijender Singh as a writer-cum-editor.

Balbir Madhopuri

Writer, Translator and Author of *Changiya Rukh: Against the Night*

(Published by Oxford University Press, India)

Introduction

> To me, Dalit is not a caste. He is a man exploited by the social and economic traditions of this country. He does not believe in god, rebirth, soul, holy books, teaching separatism, fate and Heaven because they have made him a slave. He does believe in humanism. Dalit is a symbol of change and revolution. — (Pantawane 2-3)

'Dalit' is understood as a literary metaphor, a term that could mean distinct in different contexts; a term that is played with by many; every intellectual to his understanding of the terminology and the concept or hypothesis. Scholars play with the term where all signifiers ultimately lead to an oppressed signified, a signified that would not be complete without the signifiers, without the interpretations of the signifier. The word 'Dalit,' whenever it is uttered, it seems to be a nauseating one to the ears of the people belonging to a superior class in the social context. It is generally applied to the people who are constitutively marginalised at socio-economic and politico-religious contexts. Thus, Dalit word has still become a conundrum in the minds of people and they give diverse interpretations of this word. Many people have visualised the definition of this word. According to Sharankumar Limbale:

> Harijans and Neo-Buddhists, [these people] are not the only Dalits, [because] the term describes all the untouchable communities living outside the boundary of the village, as well as adivasis, landless farm-labourers, workers, the suffering masses and nomadic and criminal tribes. (Limbale, 30)

Caste, in the modern context, is based not on the nature of works of people, it genesis is considered from their birth. The people who are born in the schedule class or backward class families are called Dalits. Arjun Dangle gives his clear interpretation when he states,

"Dalit means masses exploited and oppressed economically, socially, culturally in the name of religion and other factors" (265). However, it can be explicitly stated that any person, born in any caste who is suppressed, oppressed, tyrannised or exploited socially, economically, physically, educationally, religiously or in any other form, irrespective of gender, is really a Dalit. Many women who belong to upper caste and who are being exploited by men or who are in constant fear or pressure in their own families or in society are also Dalits. This is what is known as the phalocentric Dalitism.

With the advent of the British rule, Indian socio-economic structure was badly jolted and new avenues were opened for the global communication with the spread of English education. Moreover, social reformers, activists and saints such as Raja Ram Mohan Roy, Swami Dayanand Saraswati, Swami Vivekananda, Ramkrishna Paramhansa, Rabindranath Tagore, Mahatma Gandhi, Mahatma Phule, Dr B.R. Ambedkar, and many others also worked for the egalitarianism and equilibrium. They also tried to uproot many evils prevailing in the Indian society.

Before diving deep into Dalit literature, it would be worthwhile to give a demarcation of Dalit literature and to know the poignant position of dalits and socio-political and cultural-religious backgrounds of Indian dalits. Indian society, according to the *Rigveda*, is based on the works of people. The caste hierarchy has become a burning issue in the present context as on the basis of old system of *varna* only upper caste people enjoyed all the privileges of life. Due to the existence of unjust social order, Dalits were deprived of their fundamental rights and thus, they stood at the tassel in the social order and thus, remained marginalised at every walk of life. As a result, Dalits had no option except serving upper caste people in order to cater to the needs of their children.

Indian literature, at the very outset, had always been dominated by the upper caste people and almost all the texts of any literary value were written by writers belonging to the upper strata of the caste hierarchy. Their writings could never narrate the plights of the marginalised, discriminated and oppressed communities. Very few socially conscious writers emerged on the literary scenario that cared to voice the mute. Then the literary sphere witnessed few privileged

Dalits who took it upon them to paint the real picture of oppression with the colours dipped in the blood of the exploited. They started narrating their stories in their native languages and their co-sufferers understood their pains. They all joined hands and pledged to bring a change in their positions. English translations of Dalit autobiographies changed the way of the readers associated with these documents of sufferings. Translations not only increased the numbers of readership but made its way to the crevices where a Dalit would never have been welcomed. These narratives shook the literary scene and soon stamped a discrete place for them. Where other narratives of plight stumbled, Dalit literature stood strong and demanded a separate place for itself. The literature that sang the saga of oppression, dissolving the binaries of gender, not only targeted the oppressed and encouraged them to change but also questioned the oppressor of his vile promises. This tone of anger and dissatisfaction gave them a place that no other branch of Indian literature had acquired till date. Dalit literature today stands strong amongst the pile of canons that had ignored them and challenges them on the account of literary precision.

Almost all men and women, except a few who have emerged as writers, have their roots with the higher, higher-middle or the middle classes. All their writings have only reflected the lives of the people of their castes. They have happily ignored the lives of the discriminated Dalits as the themes of their works. It has been left to those writers who have social consciousness to write about the lives of the Dalits and to some fortunately educated Dalit writers to voice their concerns about the plights and predicaments of Dalits in their works. A more number of Dalit writers have made their presence felt through their creative pieces written in their respective regional languages. Their works have given them an indelible identity as a writer of great standing when their works got translated into English. No other works of Indian writers, based on the lives of men and women of higher, upper middle and middle class people, could attain a separate name in Indian Writing in English as the works of socially marginalised writers have got as Dalit Literature. This shows their significance and popularity as an indispensable branch of Indian Writing in English.

Bharathi Raja, the famous director of Tamil films, has highlighted the supernatural, religious, traditional and cultural living habits of the neglected people of the remote villages of Tamil Nadu as the themes of his films. But for his films, the forced life style of the isolated villages from the main stream of life would have remained in the dark. It is Ilaiyaraja, a great music director in Tamil Nadu, who has given a great publicity and life to the melodious village oriented songs through Tamil films. Similarly, the famous Tamil writer M. Jayakanthan has based his novels on the themes of the lives of the neglected lot of the village people living and has shown to the status conscious society that these people have feelings too like those of the higher middle and middle class men and women who are the protagonists of women writers of Indian Diaspora.

In the second decade of Twenty-first Century, many vibrant controversies, sometimes reflecting through Indian celluloid and sometimes through news media, appear in an open forum discussion – the stories like Bapurao Tajne's struggle for digging well have given wide publicity to the practice of Dalit repression in our society. As a consequence, Indian political life as well as literary criticism gets agitated over the inhuman treatment of class conscious human beings meted out to the Dalits. Moreover, calling one a Dalit is something more than caste exploitation because it pervades its space and connects the root of subdued voice of India. While in earlier phase the Dalit sufferings have been associated with 'sympathetic enthraldom' rather than 'empathetic care' and the voice of sufferings has been more significant than the protest. But gradually the protest becomes vibrant through Dalit autobiographies because they unmask authentic portrayal of Dalit culture and experiencing exploitation. Though those Dalit autobiographies have been written in local dialects, the uniformity of protest invents a new genre through their translations into English that celebrates the pride of Dalit identity and challenges the non-Dalit regime.

African native community in America strives to explore its authentic identity by re-asserting history and cultural identity of their own people. Similarly, Indian Dalit community renders its protesting voice against dominant caste credo and corroborates the 'dalitized history' which not only unties a new dimension of Indian literature probing the subalternist perspective of thinking but also connects with many marginalised voices across the globe. Hence, Dalit literature unveils a new study of Indian power game from Dalit point of view replacing the mainstream Indian literary canon. It has rewritten a new chapter of Indian literature first by asserting the individual and independent identity of its people who have been without history and then by remarkably transforming Dalit agonies into a voice of protest. Thus, Dalit literature pervades its purview and becomes more direct and a complete saga of Indian Dalit life. Dalit Autobiographies in reality is the liberation from exploitation through cultural, social and political rebellion.

Dalit writers held a conference in Mumbai on 2 March 1958 and decided to bring the plight of the Dalits to light through their writings. It resulted in the genesis of Dalit literature. Dr B.R. Ambedkar motivated the Dalits to "educate, agitate and unite". Later, Dalit literature started taking concrete shape in Marathi literature and henceforth, most of the Dalit works started getting translated into English. In this way, Dalit Literature first established its separate and unique place in Indian English Literature. Sharankumar Limbale expresses his view stating that "Dalit Literature is that Literature, which is written by one who is a Dalit by birth, which is filled with rebellion and rejection and which gives expression to Dalit Consciousness" (105), and Arjun Dangle gives a broad spectrum of this literature saying that it is not merely a literature, it has become a movement. He writes stating that:

> Dalit Literature is not simply Literature. It is associated with a movement to bring about change. It represents the hopes and ambitions of a new society and new people. It is a movement. (266)

Though Dalit literature has been written in many genres such as poetry, novels, short-stories, plays, autobiographies and even films have been made to spread far and wide the reality of the conditions of the Dalits, but a huge proportion of Dalit literature is found in autobiographical narratives. Dalit autobiographies and memoirs have touched the hearts of the people because they have been the authentic and first-hand portrayal of the pains, sufferings and saga of exploitation of the entire Dalit community. Many Dalit male writers have written their autobiographies in Marathi etc. regional languages. Such most notable writers and their autobiographies among them are Shankarrao Kharat's *Taral Antaral*, Daya Pawar's *Baluta*, Madhav Kondvilkar's *Mukkam Post Devache Gothane*, P. E Sonkamble's *Athavaniche Pakshi*, Uttam Bandu Tupe's *Katya Varchi Pote*, Sharankumar Limbale's *Akkarmashi*, Laxman Mane's *Upara*, Laxman Gaikwad's *Uchalya*, Keshav Meshram's *Hakikat Ani Jatayu*, Rusatm Achalkhamb's *Gavki*, Kishore Kale's *Kolhatyache Por*, Dadasaheb More's *Gabal*, Nanasaheb Zodge's *Phanjar*, and Narendra Jadhav's *Aamcha Bap Ani Aamhi.* Some autobiographies have been originally written in English and some which were written originally in their respective regional languages, have been later translated into English. Though many Dalit autobiographies have been written yet Dalit writers don't find any solution of the problem of the casteism which does not spare them till their last breath. Omprakash Valmiki rightly narrates in his autobiography *The Branded*, "Caste cannot be improved by education. It can only be improved by taking birth in the right caste." (58)

Just like the autobiographies of Dalit women writers are being used as the platform for highlighting the untold sufferings of Dalit women, Dalit men writers have exposed the atrocities meted out to them through their autobiographies. If women had not come to the field of writing and exposed the bitter reality, men writers would not have given expression of their pains and agonies. If Dalit men and women had not become writers exposing their plights at the hands of socially superior class, the literary world would have never come to know that there was a socially discriminated class in the society, going through a life of indescribable agony as voiceless beings accepting the dictum that fate cannot be tilted.

The study of Dalit men autobiographies is the main focus of this book and in the process; it markedly differs from Dalit women's autobiographies which have identified personal trauma and domestic violence as prevalent theme. Thus, Dalit men autobiographies primarily concentrate on the national issue of casteism and broadly draw the vision of social and cultural marginalisation as a whole. Instead of voicing domestic disgrace and violence, Dalit men's narratives articulate the voice of protest against caste hegemonic hierarchy and aver the uniformity of Dalit sufferings.

Dalit literature remains the illegitimate offspring of Indian literature, the child that screams for his identity but is deliberately silenced. Dalit men took the pen when society had not only thrown them at the margins but had conveniently forgotten about them. Their autobiographies tell the tale of decades' old oppression, all in the name of maintaining the sanctity of religion. The otherwise silenced accounts take refuge in this form of narrative and men unashamedly sing their plights. Unlike Dalit women autobiographies that are built around gender discrimination and double marginalisation, the autobiographies of men unveil the hegemonic suppression in the world outside that not only designates an oppressed place to the Dalit but also ensures it so.

Though any introduction can just present a small fraction of its contents, yet the readers can enjoy reading the article of this book for a proper understanding of the broad topic. They will indubitably feel pleased to note that Dalit literature has flourished steadily. *Dalit Men's Autobiographies: A Critical Appraisal* is a voluminous anthology containing twenty-four well written articles by renowned scholar critics from all over India. This has been edited, compiled and brought out by me as a sequel to my previous Dalit anthology *Dalit Women's Autobiographies: A Critical Appraisal* that has been published previous year by the same publishing house. It is a modest attempt to critically evaluate the various aspects of Indian Dalit men's autobiographies and memoirs. This anthology offers an exhaustive exploration of almost all Dalit autobiographies written or translated into English.

The first paper of this anthology is written by Professor D. Amalraj. His paper aims at exposing the religious hypocrisy of the higher caste Hindus towards socially isolated Dalit Hindus. It draws attention to the unimaginable and impracticable thoughts of the higher caste Hindus that they are only their God's chosen people and not the Dalits, and so their God has blessed them with invincible societal power over all the Dalit Hindus. It highlights how their thinking and discriminatory tactics have forced the Dalit Hindus to find haven in other religious groups. Hence, embracing either Christianity or Islam is the only option available for the Dalit Hindus to escape social oppression and suppression at the hands of their own religious people just because they are socially superior.

The second paper by Dr Manjeet Rathee attempts to explore the 'burden of inferiority' as experienced and depicted by an eminent Dalit writer, Sharankumar Limbale in his famous autobiography *The Outcaste* (*Akkarmashi*), which was published when the writer was only twenty-five years old but the burden of 'low' caste, religion and cultural inferiority that he had to live with and struggle against goes back to centuries. The paper attempts to interrogate this humiliating and poignant tale of burden along with the significant questions it raises in relation to various hierarchies and their control mechanisms, including God.

The third scholarly article is contributed by Dr D. Murali Manohar. His paper titled "Caste Hegemony or Love? A Line of Thought on *Joothan: A Dalit's Life*" is an attempt to explore how the caste line still works even in the post-modern colonial times irrespective of one is in high position or low position. The undercurrent casteism is irreversible. Marriage, education, friendship, love relationship, tradition and parental choice have the base of age old notions of caste base between Valmiki, Sarita and Kulkarni.

Dr Sakunthala A.I. has written the fourth paper of this anthology. Her paper titled "The Audible Sighs and Visible Dreams: A Discussion of Sharankumar Limbale's *Akkarmashi*" is a reflection of the traumas and the wounded psyche of the Dalits and Dalit community. *Akkarmashi* by Sharankumar Limbale depicts the meta-realistic accounts of his life as a Dalit in particular and which can be extended to the life of any individual of Mahar community in general. The text becomes an eye witness account of the horrors of the lives of the particular subaltern community. By his autobiography, Limbale wants to establish an egalitarian society which is casteless and classless, where a person is recognised as a human being not by his caste or any other differential measures.

Dr Archana Bhattacharjee herself is a Dalit activist and she has presented the voices of revolt in her paper titled "Raising Voice against

Caste Distinction and Untouchability: A Study of Narendra Jadhav's *Outcaste: A Memoir*." Her paper is a modest attempt to explore how Dr Narendra Jadhav in his memoir *Outcaste* narrates the pain, agony and pitiable conditions of the Dalit community. Narendra Jadhav faces the stigma of casteism throughout his life. At the same time, this autobiography also gives a clarion call to all the members of the Dalit community to wake up and demand a space of their own which is their birth right in the present society.

Dr Sadhana Agrawal's paper titled "Exploitation of Leather-Workers in Balbir Madhopuri's *Changiya Rukh: Against the Night*" analyses the issue of caste discrimination very adeptly and proficiently. Madhopuri's autobiography *Changiya Rukh: Against the Night* narrates pathetic plights and poor living conditions of leather-workers of his village. The roots of casteism can be clearly seen in this autobiography. Her paper explores multiple layers of exploitation in the beleaguered autobiography by a meritorious and mature writer, Balbir Madhopuri.

Dr Narendra Kumar's paper "Peeping into the Lives of Dalit Women and Children: A Rereading of Kancha Ilaiah's *Why I am Not a Hindu*" describes how the life of Dalit children and women was miserable in his caste. They had to work in their homes and fields to run their families. On one hand, Kancha Ilaiah describes poor living conditions of the people of his caste; on the other hand, he throws light on some positive aspects of his caste how the life of Dalit women is a bit better than that of the Hindu women.

The eighth paper of this anthology has been written by Ramanuj Mahato. His scholarly paper reveals the 'epistemic violence' of upper caste exploiting the marginalised section in Indian context in general and pigeonholing the dalit texts in particular. Challenging the mainstream discourse of upper caste, many dalit autobiographies interpret the new dalit discursive constellations dealing with the strategic struggle/*'sangram'* against the Brahmo-centric institution and prioritising the dalit emotions, texts unveil the true insight of dalit individual as well as dalit community. Moreover, dalit autobiographical excerpts are true documentation of Indian caste-dominated history and stories of economical, political cultural monopoly of dominating texts which consequently construct an alternative voice redefining the identity of 'Own'.

Kusum Kanger's paper titled "Problems of Maali Caste in Aravind Malagatti's Autobiography *Government Brahmana*" deals with the problems of Maali caste in the autobiography *Government Brahmana*. Dalits were given many facilities and that's why they were called government brahmana. Despite getting education, Aravind could not get out of the issue of casteism and he had to get humiliated due to his low caste. Thus, the problems of Maali caste have been explored in this paper.

Dwaipayan Mitra's paper has been placed at serial number ten in this anthology. His paper titled, "Historiography of the Dalits: G. Kalyana Rao's *Untouchable Spring*" explores how the emergence of Dalit autobiographies marks a significant change in the diachronic survey of Indian literature. The hitherto voiceless people who have been marginalised and discriminated against by Brahminical hegemony in recent time have broken down the wall of silence and asserted their own voice. These memoirs registered deep protest against various dictums laid down by the caste-rigid society.

The twelfth well-written article entitled, "Documenting the Manifold Contact Zones: An Autoethnographical Study of *Joothan*" by Anusha A.J. deals with understanding the essential Dalit ethnographic Self through a methodical analysis of Omprakash Valmiki's *Joothan*. There is a sustained effort to shed light on the characteristics of the narrative that lends it an autoethnographic nature. A patient dissection of the cultural installments of language, religion, social roles, behavioural patterns and the like has been attempted. The paper also tries to explore the institutionalised hegemonic patterns that deny the identity of the ethnic minority as share holders in the avenues of meaning making.

The next paper by Suruchi Sharma is an honest attempt to explore the pitiable plight of the Uchalya community. The conditions of Dalit women of Uchalya community were very bad and Dalit men were offered no work by anybody; that's why they were forced to steal from the markets or they had to pick pockets to run their families. Dalit women were also physically and mentally exploited and tyrannised by the upper caste people and the police. Present paper traces out how Laxman Gaikwad's education and hard-work make him a successful man in his tribe and thus, he creates awareness among others through his autobiography.

Guni Vats paper depicts the scars on the psyche of dalits in K.A. Gunasekaran's autobiography *The Scar*. Caste is the most important label of identity in the Indian consciousness. The caste prejudices govern the behaviour of the mass. Dalits have been pushed to the periphery since decades and even when they document their plight in the autobiographies it is generally read as a saga of exploitation. Guni Vats' paper attempts to change the point of view towards Dalit autobiography. It analyses *The Scar* as a document of hegemonic battlefield where the repressed use the apparatus to answer back their oppressors. The paper treats caste as a strategic apparatus for a section to exploit and rule over the other. Gunasekaran in his attempt reveals the grave realities of the apparatus and leaves the readers baffled as it exposes the filth in the folds of society. This filth needs to be cleansed before the stink engulfs the socially knit lives.

Ashok Kumar's paper aims to shed light on the Hindutva philosophy and the Shudra critique. It offers a comparative and analytical exploration of the Hindu and the Shudra traditions and rituals. Ilaiah prefers his caste and offers many reasons why he does not want to be a Hindu in his autobiography. There are some traditions in the Hindu philosophy which are criticized by Kancha Ilaiah in his autobiography. Caste has emerged as a stigma on the forehead of India and the discrimination on the name of caste has been the central focus of this paper.

Dipak Giri's paper presents the comparative discussion of two Dalit autobiographies Narendra Jadhav's *Outcaste: A Memoir* and Omprakash Valmiki's *Joothan*, though written in two different regions, languages and cultures, yet these autobiographies focus on similar theme of Dalit's freedom and emancipation from traditional caste-stigmatised society which sacrifices the interest of Dalits on the altar of tradition. This paper also tries to explore those factors which bring a radical change in Dalit's life forcing to come in action from their passivity and stillness.

Dr Deepika Rani's paper seeks to explore the hellish conditions of females through an autobiography of a male. Daya Pawar's *Baluta* is the first autobiography by a Dalit that shocked the readers. Although it is the story of Daya Pawar, a dalit that deals with the miseries of his life and struggles yet at the same times it also deals with the bitter realities of the brutal treatment meted out to wife, labourer woman, widow and it records numerous soul numbing incidents that realise us to the real condition of woman in society. Rape, sexual assault, beating and selling of wife, marginalisation, and exploitation etc. themes throw light on the pitiable plight of women in male-dominated society. The various anecdotes sign towards the bitter truth. A woman may be a dalit or not, but she is undoubtedly a woman. A word 'Woman' is enough to define her saga of discrimination. There is no need to add dalit with a woman because a woman is already handcuffed in the clutches of unjust taboos and patriarchal society. She is chained with many ropes and she is trying to get rid of them by breaking them.

Dr Deler Singh's paper deals with the short story "A Corpse in the Well" by Shankarrao Kharat which has been translated into English by Priya Adarkar from Marathi. As the story unfolds, it exposes the hypocrisy of some groups of people who crush Mahars in the name of duty. It also shows the helplessness which leaves no option for these Mahars but to follow the dictates of the society. It is not a stray incident, rather a very normal event that everyday happens in the lives of Mahars.

Dr Dipali Sharma Bhandari's paper titled, "A Critique of Casteism in Omprakash Valmiki's *Joothan: A Dalit's Life*" is the next paper that attempts to critically analyse Omprakash Valmiki's autobiography *Joothan: A Dalit's Life.* For a country riddled by the caste system, the talk about the people from marginalised communities is certainly a fresh draught of air. However, for a society which has fed on this system and nurtured it for ages, change is not too easy to come by Dr Dipali Sharma Bhandari's paper offers an exhaustive critical exploration on casteism in Omprakash Valmiki's autobiography *Joothan: A Dalit's Life*.

Dr Prachi Priyanka's paper tries to explore the voices of protest in selected men's dalit autobiographies. Dalit literature is a post-Independence phenomenon and it emerged as a protest against the exploitation and discrimination that Dalits were subjected to since ages. Dalit autobiographies are expression to literary representations and serve to organise Dalit experiences into the particularities of circumstance and individual identity. Dr Prachi's article argues how Dalit autobiographies are unlike mainstream autobiographies in their approach and manner of presentation of the socio-cultural context. Her paper endeavours to bring out different facets of their writings where they choose not to confine themselves to the author's life and hardships faced by him; but also represent the traumas and wounded psyche of Dalits and Dalit community.

The next paper titled, "Hollowness and Shadow in Siddalingaiah's *Ooru Keri*" is written by faculty of Amity University, Dr Sumitra Singh. She has tried to explore the trials and tribulations of a Dalit, who sees discrimination, alienation of the Dalit community as he was growing up. Siddalingaiah got highly inspired from Dr B.R. Ambedkar and his ideology. Education empowered him as he started studying in night schools. Through hard work also, he raised himself as an enlightened individual who not only worked for his own upliftment but also for the upliftment and emancipation of his community. This paper is an attempt to explore hidden aspects of Siddalingaiah's individuality.

The next paper titled, "Solitude as Metaphor in Y.B. Satyanarayana's *My Father Baliah*" by Dr Zainul Abid Kotta focuses on the theme of the solitude and how it operates as a metaphor in this autobiography. The metaphoric implication of solitude helps us to understand the vibrant dynamism of dalit creativity and subsequent subjugatory response of the caste highhandedness in India. The Dalits of India still fight to conquer this externally infringed solitude and they make efforts for amalgamating with mainstream social psyche, only to decipher that it is not that much easy. Dr Abid Kotta observes how Satyanarayana's memoir is a landmark in this regard.

Dr M. B.Gaijan's paper is the twenty-second paper that explores Omprakash Valmiki's autobiography *Joothan: A Dalit's Life* from different perspectives. Cultural study of the nation shows people's thinking, behaviour, social, public life, faith etc. Indian culture is the culture of hating Dalits. It becomes social habit. Considering *Joothan*, the text is evaluated from major three aspects, Dalits in rural India, Dalits in urban areas and Dalits' protest to get human identity, human dignity. The paper traces the development of Omprakash Valmiki how he emerges from his low caste as an author, activist and above all a reformer. These key points have been analysed in his paper.

The second last paper of the book is by Dr Aparna Lanjewar Bose. Her paper refutes the repetitive charge on Dalit writers that they have not accorded enough space to Dalit women in their autobiographies by showcasing the uniqueness of Kishore Shantabai Kale's autobiography *Kolhatyache Por* which is more a women centric discourse than a narcissistic self-presentation. It sits to cauterise the perverse aspects of patriarchy and presents Kolhati women in a more positive light as torchbearers of a potent cultural legacy. The crux of the entire body of Marathi Dalit writing is autobiographical. The influence of Buddha-Phule-Ambedkar renders it a pertinence and poignancy. Dismantling the politics involved in reductionist stereotyping, the writer insists on looking at such Dalit narratives more from the critical and aesthetical standpoint rather than as narratives of pain and suffering. The original quotations from Marathi have been translated for the purpose of this paper. She owes special thanks to Granthali, Mumbai for promptly sending the book to her and due to that she could draft this paper timely.

The last paper of the book is written by Dr S. Chelliah. His paper titled "Project of Poverty and Exploitation of Dalit Women in Laxman Gaikwad's Autobiography *Uchalya-The Branded*: An Analysis" highlights the exploitation of the women belonging to the Pathrut community which is best known as a criminal tribe according to the All India Criminal Tribes Act passed by the British Raj in 1871. This was a poor nomadic 'denotified tribe' which invited the hatred and revulsion of the upper caste people. The conditions of women were very miserable and they were exploited both at their home by men and outside by the upper caste people. This paper is an attempt to explore the brutal treatment made towards the women by the so-called civilised people belonging to upper caste / class people.

This book, it is hoped, will definitely get a warm reception by the students, research-scholars and teachers equally who want to get acquainted with the Dalit literature and dream to be conversant with new vistas of Indian Dalit autobiographies. It targets to nurture and boost the knowledge of the related arena of one and all, readers, writers or critics associated with this anthology.

The present shape of this book could not be visualised without the help and cooperation of many folks to whom I'm exceedingly beholden. To begin with, I extend my sincere gratitude to all the learned contributors who painstakingly forwarded their papers timely to me on the desired theme with full fresh analytical expositions. With all my heart, I would like to reiterate my profound thanks to every valued contributor.

My gratitude can never be paid to my wife, Smt. Sharmila for her deepest love, ultimate care and jam-packed perseverance for my venture; and I owe profoundly for the kind affection of my sweet daughter, Saumya. I can never be indebted for the showers of constructive and shielding blessings of my mother, Smt. Murti Devi and profound love of other members of the family. I offer my special thanks to my father-in-law, Sh. Anand Singh Barak and mother-in-law, Smt. Shanti Devi for their hands of blessings on me forever.

Moreover, I place on record my heartfelt gratitude to Mr Amit Garg, the Managing Director, Kalpaz Publications, New Delhi for his constant faith in my editorship and bringing out this book very beautifully and swiftly. I am thankful to all the employees of the production department of Kalpaz Publications for a healthy and enthusiastic communication during the composition and the development of this anthology. I am highly gratified with Dr Sony Jalarajan Raj, faculty of MacEwan University, Edmonton, Canada and Dr Soumya Jose, Faculty of English, VIT University, Vellore, Tamil Nadu, India for their judicious review of this voluminous anthology.

Last but not the least; I extend my heart-felt gratitude to my close friend, eminent Dalit writer, winner of many awards, Balbir Madhopuri who spared his valuable time to write the foreword for this book. His book *Changiya Rukh* was originally published in Punjabi in 2004 and now it has been reprinted in many editions from many publishers. This book has been translated into Hindi, English, and in Shahmukhi (in Pakistan) and it has been serialised in Punjab Express (Weekly) Punjabi in USA, Kuk Punjabi Samachar (Fortnightly) in New Zealand, Puncham (Monthly) in Lahore, Ambedkar Yug (Monthly) in Punjab, Sailab (Monthly) at Gharhshankar, Hoshiarpur, Punjab and Bits in Tehelka (Weekly), New Delhi. *Changiya Rukh* has been prescribed by UGC in the syllabus of almost all central and private universities of India since 2015 and it is in the syllabus of B.A. (Punjabi) in the University of Delhi, New Delhi. Balbir Madhopuri is the winner of the Sahitya Akademy Translation Award (2013), Gold Pen by All India Adi-Dharam Mission (2011), Lal Singh Dil Purskar (2008), Prerna Award (2004), Sarvotam Pustak Purskar (2003), S.M.S. Sahitya Award (2003), Jagroop Singh Datewas Pursakar (1999), Kaav-Pursakar (1994), Sant Ram Udasi Memorial Award (1993), Gurdas Ram Alam Award (1992) and many other honours and fellowships etc. He has been the Deputy Director (News), All India Radio, New Delhi and Editor of Yojana (Punjabi), Ministry of Information and Broadcasting, Govt. of India and he has been successfully sequestrated from his government service and presently works as the Head, Punjabi Bhawan, Punjabi Sahit Sabha (Regd.) New Delhi.

Dr Bijender Singh
Mob: 91-9992873801
Email: drbijendersingh@india.com

Notes on the Contributors

1. **Professor D. Amalraj** is a retired Professor of English. He began his teaching career at Kandasamy Naidu College for Men from October 1969. He retired in May 2004 as a selection grade faculty member. He has served as Head and Research Supervisor in the Department of English, Vivekanandha College for Arts & Sciences (W), Elayampalyam, in district Namakkal in Tamil Nadu. He has worked as a part-time Professor in the Department of English at Bishop Appasamy College of Arts and Science in Coimbatore. He has published his research oriented articles in international journals of repute. Thirty-two scholars have successfully completed their M. Phil. degree under his guidance. His areas of interest are Dalit Literature, Indian Writing in English, Diasporic Literature and Gender Studies. He has brought out many Zazzler Study Aid Series on English Literature. The revised edition of his book Research Methodology for Literary Research has been published from Innovation Scientific Research Publications, Salem in 2015.
2. **Dr (Ms) Manjeet Rathee** is a Professor of English in the Department of English and Foreign Languages, Maharshi Dayanand University, Rohtak, India since 2011. She is associated with teaching for more than 28 years. Her areas of specialisation include Modern American Literature, Media Studies and Gender Studies. Her more than 25 research articles, on Indian English Literature, American Literature, Mass Media and on various contemporary socio-cultural issues, have been published in various national and international journals, besides many articles, reviews, songs

and poems in various literary magazines like *Udbhawna, Katha Desh, Harigandha, Samya, Equality, Nav Jagran Ke Geet, Chalo Geet Gao, Mahilayon Ke Geet*. Her published books include *Violence and Women, The Concept of Absurdity and Rebellion in the Novels of Saul Bellow, Women, Media and Society: Issues of Survival and Representation, "Jab Koi Dastak Deta Hai"* and she has edited three books *Aam Aurat Ka Sach, In the Name of Honour: Live and Let Live, Gender Politics of Sexual Oppression and Rape*.

3. **Dr D. Murali Manohar** (M.Phil, B.Ed, Ph.D.) is an Associate Professor at the Department of English, University of Hyderabad, Hyderabad. He has five full-length books and ten edited books to his credit on the research areas such as Indian English Women's Fiction, Dalit Literature and English Language Teaching. He has completed two Major Research Projects sanctioned by UGC, New Delhi. He has published extensively in various national and international journals.
4. **Dr Sakunthala A.I.** is presently working as an Associate Professor of English at M.P.M.M.S.N. Trusts College, Shoranur, Palaghat, Kerala. She has 28 years of experience. She has done her M.A. from University of Kerala, M. Phil. from Madurai Kamaraj University and Ph.D. from CSJM University, Kanpur and pursuing for D. Litt. in Dalit Studies at Bharatiyar University, Coimbatore. She has published two books *Image of New Woman in the Fiction of Anita Desai and Margaret Atwood* and *Dalit Voices in Indian Poetry: A Study of Malayalam and Marathi Poems*. She has presented papers in various National and International Conferences and she has published 18 articles in various International Journals with ISSN.
5. **Dr Archana Bhattacharjee** is an Associate Professor and Head in the Department of English, Kakojan College, Jorhat, Assam which is affiliated with Dibrugarh University. She did her M.A. in English Literature from Gauhati University and M. Phil. from Vinayaka Missions University, Tamil Nadu. She has presented around seventy papers at various

national and international seminars and conferences both within and outside the country. She has published more than thirty research papers also in various journals and books. She is the joint editor of an ISSN journal "Emerging Echoes." She is also in the Editorial and Advisory Board of four international journals. She is TEFL certified from Wisconsin English Second Language Institute, Madison, US. Her areas of interest are Gender Studies, Post-Colonial Writing, Indian Writing in English and British Literature. She also works as a social activist for the people of backward tea community in Assam who are dalits and grapple with various problems.

6. **Dr Sadhana Agrawal** (M.A., Ph.D.) is an Assistant Professor of English at Maharani Laxmibai Govt. College of Excellence, Gwalior (M.P.), which is one of the best known colleges of Gwalior - Chambal region affiliated to Jiwaji University, Gwalior, (M.P.). She has more than 30 years of teaching experience of English Language and Literature. She has attended various National and International Seminars/Conferences and presented her scholarly papers there. She has published 42 research papers in National/International reputed journals/books. She has completed two Minor Research Projects in English sanctioned by UGC/CRO Bhopal. Her areas of interests lie in Indian English Literature, American Literature, British Literature and English Language Teaching.
7. **Dr Narendra Kumar** is a Principal at Stani Memorial P.G. College, Jaipur, Rajasthan. He has worked at many reputed institutes at different capacities like an Assistant Professor, Head of Department and Principal like Shankara Institute of Technology, Sri Balaji College of Engineering & Technology, J.D. College of Technical Education, Jaipur and Rajasthan P.G. College, Chirawa, Jhunjhunu, Rajasthan. He has published his papers in many international journals and edited anthologies. He is a multi-talented personality who has many degrees at bachelor, master and doctorate level like B.A., B.Sc., BJMC (Journalism), MBA (HRM and

ITM), M.Sc. (CS), M.Ed. (CE-UK, USA) Ph.D. in three subjects—English, Education and Management. He has good command on English, Hindi, French, German and Russian equally. He has guided many Ph.D. and M. Phil. candidates and has evaluated many theses and dissertations.

8. **Ramanuj Mahato** is a lecturer in Chitta Mahato Memorial, Jargo under Sidho- Kanho-Birsha University, Purulia (W.B.). With excellent academic background, he did his M.A. from Banaras Hindu University, Varanasi and he has qualified in UGC-NET thrice. He has already published his articles in many national and international journals and anthologies from renowned publishers. His areas of interest are Cultural Studies, Indian English Writing, Dalit Literature, Diasporic Literature and Post-colonial Literature.
9. **Kusum Kanger** is an Assistant Professor in B.A.R. Janta College Kaul, Kaithal, Haryana. She is a Ph.D. Research-scholar in NIMS University, Jaipur. She has earned her M.Phil. from Kurukshetra University, Kurukshetra. She has presented and published her papers in many national and international seminars and conferences. Her papers have been published in many national and international journals and edited anthologies.
10. **Dwaipayan Mitra** (CBSC-NET & JRF, West Bengal SET) is an M. Phil. Research Scholar at Jadavpur University, West Bengal. He has completed his M.A. from Rabindra Bharati University. He is a budding scholar who has keen interest in research. He has attended many UGC-sponsored seminars. His areas of interest are Postcolonial Studies, New Literature, American Literature and Indian Dalit Literature. He has published his papers in a few anthologies.
11. **Anusha A.J.** is a Guest Faculty at the Department of English, All Saints' College, Trivandrum. She is a University Rank holder in MA English Language and Literature from the University of Kerala. Her interest lies in the arenas of Cultural Studies, British Drama and Film Studies.
12. **Suruchi Sharma** (UGC-NET) is an Assistant Professor in R.K.S.D. College, Kaithal, Haryana. She has done her P.G.

from K.M.V. College, Jalandhar, Punjab. She is pursuing Ph.D. from NIMS University, Jaipur. She has presented her papers in many national and international seminars and conferences. Her papers have been published in many national and international journals and seminar/conference proceedings and several edited anthologies.

13. **Guni Vats** is a Ph.D. Research Scholar at the University of Lucknow. She is a keen reader, an enthusiastic writer and dedicated researcher who takes immense pleasure in looking at diverse aspects of life from a psychoanalytical bent. She loves to experiment with themes, subject and writing styles. She is keen to research on the Indian women writers and carves a niche for them in the predominantly masculine world. She has few publications to her credit which include a paper in the labyrinth journal, five papers in book publications, a story and a poem published in online journals.
14. **Ashok Kumar** (M.A., M. Phil., UGC-NET, SET) is an Assistant Professor (Guest Faculty) at Govt. College, Nagina, Nuh, Mewat. He has completed his M.A. from Osmania University and M. Phil. from CDLU, Sirsa. He has qualified UGC-NET in June 2012 and State Eligibility Test for Assistant Professorship for the states of Maharashtra and Goa in 2015. His areas of interest are Indian Writing in English, Diaspora Studies and Gender Discourse.
15. **Dipak Giri** [M.A. (Double), B.Ed., UGC-NET] is a teacher of English from Cooch Behar, West Bengal. Currently, he is working as a Guest Lecturer of Netaji Subhas Open University Study Center at Cooch Behar College in West Bengal. Previously he served as a Part-Time Lecturer in Cooch Behar College (Cooch Behar), Vivekananda College (Jalpaiguri) and Thakur Panchanan Mahila Mahavidyalaya (Cooch Behar) in West Bengal and also served as a Guest Lecturer in Dewanhat College (Cooch Behar) in West Bengal. He is a critic and a scholar and has contributed several research papers in books and journals. His area of studies includes Post-Colonial Literature, Indian Writing in English, Dalit Literature, Feminism and Gender Studies.

16. **Dr Deepika Rani** (M.A., M.Ed., and Ph.D.) has rendered her services as a Lecturer in English in Dashmesh Girls College, Badal and D.A.V. Sr. Sec. School, Malout, Punjab. She has eight years teaching experience. She is a bilingual poet, a critic and a reviewer. Her publications include many research papers, poems and reviews. She is a member of an international e-journal, 'The Expression'. Her areas of interest are Indian English Writings, Postcolonial Writings, Feminism and Dalit literature. Her active participation in National and International Seminars has enriched her knowledge. She has won many prizes in academics as well as in cultural activities at various levels.
17. **Dr Deler Singh** is presently working in School of Humanities and Social Sciences at Thapar Institute of Information Technology, Patiala, Punjab. He has teaching experience of more than five years at UG and PG level. He has presented papers at national and international seminars and conferences. His papers have been published in various national and international journals.
18. **Dr Dipali Sharma Bhandari** is an Assistant Professor in English Literature at SGGSJ Govt. Degree College, Paonta Sahib, Himachal Pradesh in India. She has obtained her doctoral degree in Translation Studies from H.N.B. Garhwal University, Srinagar, Garhwal. She has presented research papers at various national and international seminars. She has published her articles/papers in many national, international journals and books.
19. **Dr Prachi Priyanka** is an Assistant Professor at Sharda University. She has contributed her short stories in various anthologies like *Crumpled Voices, You, Me n Zindagi 2, Social Potpourri, Strings of Love, The Zest of Inklings, Blank Spaces* and *Minds at Work 3.* She enjoys weaving articles on various topics ranging from art criticism to book reviews and relationships to recipes. Her articles, stories and poems have been published in online magazines and international journals. Dr Prachi writes with equal ease in Hindi and her poems and stories are published in magazines and books like *Kavyashala* and *Sirf Tum*. Conflicts and

contradictions that emerge in human relationships fascinate her to the core; and her writings are often spilled with varying shades of experiences that intrigue her.

20. **Dr Sumitra Singh** is an Assistant Professor at Amity University, Noida, Uttar Pradesh. She is Editor of International Research Journal of Humanities, Engineering and Pharmaceutical Sciences. She holds her Ph.D. in Afro-American Literature. She has presented her research papers/ articles in various national and international conferences/ seminars and workshops. She has published many papers in various national and international journals of repute. She is also associated with various Community Outreach activities.
21. **Dr Zainul Abid Kotta** is an Assistant Professor and Head in Postgraduate Department of English at Government College, Malappuram, Kerala, India. He has been a Syndicate Member and Academic Council Member of University of Calicut, the largest University in Kerala. He is a research supervisor at the Postgraduate Department of English, Government College Malappuram and eight research-scholars are working under his supervision. He is chief-editor of *International Journal of Advanced Research* (www.ijar.net.in). He is a regular contributor to research journals and his edited work *Modern Prose and Drama* (2014, 2015 and 2016) is published by Oxford University Press, New Delhi.
22. **Dr M.B. Gaijan** is the Head, Department of English, Samaldas Arts College, Shri M. K. Bhavnagar University, Bhavnagar, Gujarat. He has been teaching English Language and Literature at U.G. Level since last 25 years. He is also a visiting faculty for P.G. Department. He is a Ph.D. guide. He is a counsellor of Dr Baba Saheb Ambedkar Open University, Gujarat and IGNOU. He has also worked as the coordinator of IGNOU. He has presented more than 60 papers in various national/international seminar/conferences especially on Dalit Studies, Women Writings, ICT, Diaspora Literature and Indian Writings. His more than 58 papers are published/ reprinted in reputed journals/books. His poems and translations are also published in Gujarati/Hindi and English.

He has contributed four books. He is the member of the editorial board of the journals, "*Shyamal*", "*Hayati*", "*Unheard Melody*" "*Sangharsh e-Journal*" and "*Creative Space: International Journal*". He is the author of "*Dalit Literary Tradition in Gujarat: A Critical Study*". His co-edited books are "*Dalit Literature: A Critical Exploration*", *Pristine Land: Gujarati Dalit Literature*", "*Indian Women Writers: A Critical Reinterpretation.*" Dr M. B. Gaijan is a poet, critic, translator, editor and teacher. His translations are published in Hindi and English. He has guided and evaluated M.Phil. and Ph.D. theses. He has chaired the sessions in different conferences.

23. **Dr Aparna Lanjewar Bose** (b. 1971) is an Associate Professor in the Department of English, English and Foreign Language University, Hyderabad (A Central University). She is a trilingual writer, poet, translator and activist. She taught English Literature at University of Nagpur for seven years and then for a decade at the Postgraduate teaching Department of Mumbai University before joining EFL University, Hyderabad. She specialises in American Literature, British Literature, African American Literature, Revolutionary and Marginal Literatures and Contemporary Women's Writings. She also has a degree in law. She participated as a resource person in several major national and international platforms both in India and abroad. Her study tours, research and social activism led her to visit severally countries like Germany, France, England, Switzerland, Sweden, Zimbabwe, South Africa and Thailand to speak on both literary and social concerns. Widely travelled both in India and abroad, she was invited as a member of the Sahitya Akademi's writers and scholars' delegation to Moscow and Istanbul at the Moscow International Book Fair 2009. She has published several papers and three books which includes a collection of her book of poems in English titled 'In the Days of Cages'. Her collection of Hindi-Urdu poems titled "Kuch Yu Bhi" and a collection of translations from Marathi to English titled "Red Slogans on the Green Grass" also have been published.

She is primarily a poet who writes poetry in Hindi, Urdu and English. She is the daughter of renowned Marathi poet and critic Dr Jyoti Lanjewar.

24. **Dr S. Chelliah** is a Professor, Head and Chairperson of School of English and Foreign Languages, Madurai Kamaraj University, Madurai, Tamil Nadu, India. He did his M.A. in English Literature from Madurai Kamaraj University, Madurai and he got his Ph.D. Degree in English from Madurai Kamaraj University, Madurai after his committed research pursuit at American Studies Research Centre at Hyderabad. He has published more than 50 papers at various National and International Journals and he has served as Chief Guest/Guest Speaker/Special Invitee at various National, International, UGC Seminars and Conferences and also served as An Evaluator/Adjudicator for Ph.D. Dissertations at various Universities. He has served as Dean for Curriculum Development of Madurai Kamaraj University, Director for Board of Studies Section, Director for Spoken English Institute of Madurai Kamaraj University, Co-ordinator for CBCS Wing, Liaison Officer for SC/ST Cell of Madurai Kamaraj University and Member of Board of Studies of Both UG/PG of Pondicherry University, Manonmaniam Sundaranar University, Bharathidhasan University, Trichy, Bharathiar University, Coimbatore and Gandhigram University and an Examiner of various Colleges/ Universities both PG and M.Phil. levels and also Co-ordinator for UGC Remedial Coaching Scheme for SC/ST/ OBC and Minority Categories.

1

Religious Conversion as Escapism from Social Discrimination – A Study of Laxman Mane's Autobiography *Upara: An Outsider*

PROFESSOR D. AMALRAJ

Every country in the world considers those who are born and brought up on its own soil as its natives. It does not discriminate its people on the basis of their difference in spoken languages, faiths and social statuses. It gives equal rights to all its natives to live in dignity and provides avenues for educational and professional advancement for their individuality and independence. If both man and woman of one country immigrate to another country for their livelihood, they are always treated as outsiders because they are not the natives of the country. The Blacks in America first began their discriminated lives as slaves because of their colour in the white society. Now they have become African Diaspora in America and established their identity as indispensable one to the growth and development of America. Despite their indispensability to American development, many whites in some nook and corner of America enjoy meting out discrimination to the Blacks whenever possible. The Blacks are physically stronger and so they are not afraid of suitable reply to the whites in the form of retaliation.

However, the happenings in the lives of many of the natives in India are something indigestible, uncivilised and inhuman just because such natives, though Hindus, belong to the untouchable social class known as the Dalits. This class comprises people belonging to scheduled class, and hill and nomadic tribes. Though the Dalits follow the same religious faith and enjoy equal educational advancement and professional status like those in the middle, upper-middle and the higher social class Hindus, they stand discriminated, isolated and marginalised. They do not have guts to follow retaliatory measures to protect themselves as they are kept always at the mercy of the privileged people. Moreover, all the constitutional and human rights of India are only for the sake and so they fail to protect this socially exploited class. Apathy of the governments both at the centre and the states has paved the way for these people experiencing untold and indescribable experiences of humiliation; injustice and rejection in all fields of human endeavour and at all levels. Their "agony is [not to be] abated" (qtd. in Kirby-Smith, 1997, p.15) as long as the negative mentality of the advantaged class continues to remain stronger than ever.

All social workers talk of equality among all the natives of India. They hate Indians discriminating other Indians on the basis of the differences in caste, religion, region, and profession. The politicians and the government promise that they will abide by the constitutional and human rights so that all Indians in India can live in dignity and equality. The irony is that their work stops with mere talks and promises because the majority of the politicians are from the powerful middle, upper-middle and higher class. As law-makers, they are more willing to break the established laws and human rights for their selfish ends than following them for the betterment of all the Indians. Hence, the living conditions of the Dalits not only remain unchanged but also they are becoming worse and worse as the days go by. The Dalits have the strong feelings that if they remain as Hindus, they will neither be allowed to live in dignity nor to mingle with the other Hindus nor to enter into the temples of worship nor to walk through the streets where the privileged Hindu class has their dwelling places. They will not have any permission even for their dead people to have decent burial. They are meant only for menial works such as cleaning the public toilets and the towns and villages. Therefore, they are always forced to identify themselves with the people of their caste wherever they are either in educational institutions as students or as teachers or in working places as colleagues. They also feel shy, uncomfortable and afraid of ill treatment whenever they are in the midst of the people of other castes. Thus, they don't have any individual identity to assert their rights to live in equality with others. Most of the Dalits have reconciled themselves to their fate as an unfortunate class. They have also remained unaware of the ways and means of escape from their exploiters.

The feminists of both the genders voice their concern only for the empowerment of women of middle, upper middle and higher class, but they do not care about that of the Dalit women. Hence, it has been left only to the Dalit writers to protest against the privileged social classes for keeping their men and women as untouchables and bring their isolated life to the knowledge of the reading public through their writing. But for their exposure of the discrimination of the Dalits through literary works, the world humanity would not have come to know of the greater disparity prevailing among the Indians. Shashi Bushan Upadhyaya has stated that "the Dalit writings are only for the Dalits, of the plight of the Dalits for the consumption of the reading public, and written only by the Dalits and not by any other writers who are not Dalits by birth" (qtd. in Deepak n.pag).V. Kavitha in an abstract to her article titled *Subaltern Autobiography: Challenging the Canon* has underlined the important roles the Dalit writers have played in bringing out the plight of the Dalit community in a civilised Indian society:

> The sufferings of the marginalised people will be understood in a better and suitable manner only when they are transported in written form by the Dalit writers. This process of writing provides a space for these marginalised writers to voice not only their victimisation by writing autobiographical works but also that of their entire community through the portrayal of the lives of both men and women in their fictional works. (p. 221)

Many Dalit men writers have written autobiographies besides poems and novels in their respective mother tongues. Many of their works have been translated in English too. Through their autobiographies, they have narrated their real life struggles against the society dominated by the higher strata of society. Their works speak volumes of their sufferings due to discrimination, exploitation and humiliation of all types. They have also been very open in expressing their views against the caste apartheid and their modus operandi to establish that they are in no way inferior to the other classes who think of themselves as superior beings. Laxman Mane is one of such writers of the discriminated category. In the beginning:

> Laxman Mane had no pretensions to become a writer nor was he [interested or] engaged in any literary activity. He started writing to inform the world of his bitter experiences of endless struggle, oppression, exploitation and agonies as a Dalit. His unending struggle started from his childhood and it reached its peak after his inter-caste marriage. (Ranjanickar n.pag.)

Almost all Dalit writers have been determined that conversion has been their only escape route to freedom, recognition, dignity, equality, respect, and brotherhood. They have also found Buddhism as the only religion in which all people are considered as one and the same creations of God and treated with equality and as independent individuals. What has been denied to them in Hinduism has been given to them in Buddhism:

> Buddhism preaches equality, non-violence, morality and dynamism to its followers. It diagnoses causes of misery and sorrow among them and teaches cure for suffering and methods for enjoyment of eternal bliss. It motivates its followers to believe in themselves by preaching that everyone is only the master of his destiny. No gods and goddesses can solve one's problems unless one works hard with purified mind and good intentions. Unlike other religions like Hinduism the centre of Buddhism is human being and his problems and it can alone liberate them. (Sri Dhammanand n.pag.)

Laxman Mane's autobiography *Upara: An Outsider* bears testimony to his endless predicament as a discriminated Dalit man and to the causes of his conversion to Buddhism. What has happened while writing this autobiography has been stated in his foreword to *Upara* by the writer Laxman Mane himself:

> He had relived whatever tortures he has seen, undergone, suffered and experienced in the past and he had the limited intensions of illuminating that slicer of life, which he had considered was and is indeed unknown to many in its stark reality. He wanted society

> to get acquainted with the sufferings of homeless people and do something substantial and constructive for them. (qtd. in Goswami p. 129)

In the united India, the natives have been uniquely classified into forward, backward, most backward communities, scheduled class, and hill and nomadic tribes. There is a greater variety among these natives in their cultural habits, religious beliefs, spoken languages, relationships, attitudes, behaviour and treatment. Each and every community, class and tribe maintains its individual identity intact by following its own established conventions. Apart from these recognised caste classification, there also exists a strange class among the native Indians. This class does not come under any of these accepted caste categories. Nobody cares about and thinks of this disadvantaged group and its existence. The irony of human life is that this group is composed of people of all the castes and faiths. The people in this group do not have any individual identity of their own because they are homeless, friendless and deserted ones, leading their lives on the pavements. They do not attach themselves to any religious groups. Neither does each one look worried about to which social status he or she belongs. They know that they are unwanted and neglected ones of the society and that they are earning their daily bread only through begging. They do not care about any castes and religions. They are seen standing outside all the places of worship such as Temples, Churches, Mosques et cetera (etc.) with their begging bowels for alms from the people of all the faiths and castes.

All the Indian natives who have individual identities as classified groups on the basis of castes follow different religions in which they have strong faith. Hinduism, Christianity, Islam, Buddhism, Sikhism, Jainism and Judaism are some important religions in India. Hinduism is the religion followed by the majority Indians whereas other religions with comparatively limited set of followers are considered as the minority ones. The caste disparity is more dominant and explicitly displayed in Hinduism than in any other religious groups. There is no equality and human consideration even among the people of different social statuses that follow Hinduism. The worst affected groups in Hinduism due to caste discrimination are the scheduled class, and hill and nomadic tribes. These categories come under one common class called the Dalits and they are treated as the untouchables. Even the pet animals in the houses of the higher class caste Hindus enjoy more equality and priority than these people in the society. Sulaiman Razi has explained the bitterness of caste system in Hinduism:

> Caste system is one of the evils of Hindu religion that still exists in the society. It is nothing but isolating the low castes from the society. It divides the people within the Hindu fold. The condition of the low caste people has been very miserable. The low caste people have suffered and continued to suffer the Brahminical oppression. The people belonging to upper middle class and middle class also follow the path of the higher caste Brahmins in discriminating the low castes as untouchables. (no pag.)

The discriminated Hindu Dalits have no other option except seeking solace, comfort and shelter in other religious groups to escape exploitation and humiliation at the hands of the higher caste Hindus. They feel that in such religions they are respected as equally dignified people. All the Hindu outfits make hue and cry against the conversion of the Dalit Hindus to other religions. They want all the Hindus to remain as Hindus forever. They also force those Dalit Hindus, who have gone to other religions, to come back to their Hindu fold. The irony is that they expect the Dalit Hindus to be Hindus but they are not prepared to treat the Dalit Hindus as their equal with due respect. They always consider the Dalit Hindus as the outsiders to their higher caste Hindu community. Their views look like contradicting the concept and the true spirit of Hinduism. Their contradiction in their thinking and behaviour is all because of fanaticism of certain higher castes Hindus. For their selfish interests, they simply look like having forgotten the fact:

> Hinduism is a universal religion. Its primary emphasis is on universal brotherhood. It views the world as one family. It believes that man is divine in nature and the realisation of that supreme truth is the primary aim of all human activity. But it is unfortunate that for a very long time till this day, this religion of great antiquity has been in the clutches of a few privileged castes like Brahmanism. (Jayaraman, n.pag.)

However, the Dalit Hindus remain indifferent to the empty cry of the higher caste Hindus against the conversion. They know well that the life is a choice and they are forced to choose the better choice to escape from the prevailing worst situations in Hinduism. The better choice for them lies only in embracing either Christianity or Islam or Buddhism instead of remaining in Hinduism with endless torture of discrimination. But at the same time, the conversion is not like their falling out of the frying pan into the fire. It is a kind of blessing in disguise for them to have chances for their betterment and better treatment in the society. Of all the Dalit factions, it is only Kaikadi tribe, which is the most affected not only by discriminatory tactics of other higher social classes but also by the self-exploitation of their own tribe. It is only the wearer knows where the shoe bites and similarly it is only the Dalit men like Laxman Mane who know the bitterness of the human life for having been a suppressed and oppressed ones. Laxman Mane's autobiography *Upara: An Outsider* narrates the exploited and discriminated life of the entire illiterate Kaikadi community. The root cause of its wretchedness lies in its status of illiteracy. It also shows how his conversion to Buddhism has paved the way for him to come out of the wretched and cursed life as a Dalit and to start his life anew as a dignified human being.

Laxman Mane belonged to a marginalised nomadic tribe Kaikadi in Maharashtra. His Kaikadi community had neither any permanent place for its living nor any permanent work for earning regular income for its livelihood. It was always seen moving "from one place to another place for generations, loading its hearth and home on the backs of donkeys" (Upara, 1997, p.15). All Kaikadis were unskilled people as far as farming was concerned and so no landlords were interested in employing them for farming work. In groups, they camped in their respective huts, erected outside the villages by the side of the roads. They stayed there for days together and sold their hand-made products such as the cane-baskets, stalks and brooms. Then, they moved to different villages with all their belongings and members of their families. They earned their daily bread by selling their products to the villagers. They never cooked and when the elders went out for selling the products in order to earn their daily bread, their children also began going out in order to beg for food from the houses in the villages:

> Kaikadis lived on the Ukirda [garbage ground]. They had no house because they had no economic stability. They had no position in the society, leave alone social status or prestige. They were the people surviving on the borrowed crumbs of food, often stale and leftovers collected through begging or bought with the help of small money earned by selling stalks or brooms [foka] and often facing starvation and hunger…living mutely and silently without any kind of murmuring or protest. (qtd. in Punalekar, p. 498)

Whenever they went out of their community village to far off places or returned, they should inform their village chief of it as per their customs. They should also give an account of their belongings before their leaving and after their arrival as per the rules formulated in their community village.

The people of other castes always found fault with the Kaikadis for anything and everything just because they were untouchable nomadic tribes. One woman belonging to the other caste happened to see Laxman Mane's donkey having ruined her haystack. Boxing his ear, she started scolding his entire community, saying, "You lazy bum! Your donkeys have ruined my haystack and you are busy pissing into your own mouth! Oh! You beggars! May you die! You are a plague on our village!" (Upara, p. 18). Some villagers were always suspicious of the presence or the movements of these people in the villages. They considered them as born criminals. Whenever a Kaikadi family was leaving the village after its stay, the duty of checking their belongings to ensure whether the family had not had any stolen things in their belongings was entrusted to Dagdya Ramoshi, an ex-untouchable cum village servant. Laxman Mane's family could not escape from this humiliation at the hands of Ramoshi. When Ramoshi had stopped his father to check his belongings, his father fell at his feet and pleaded with him not to do the checking. However, Ramoshi was adamant and began checking Laxman Mane's father's bags saying, "I have to search all your bags. What do I know about you? Beggars that you are! Who knows whether you have stolen anything from someone in the village?" (Upara, p. 29). Laxman Mane had to stand watching his family being tortured for being a Kaikadi. He felt ill at ease and cursed himself for his inability to protect his father from humiliation because he was just a small boy.

The Kaikadi community did not care about existing rules in the traditional society but it followed its own rules, culture and tradition. It was against the intellectual advancement of its people through education of all types from the basic to the advanced levels. It was for every eligible bachelor to marry only Kaikadi girl within its tribe. It was not only against love marriage but also against inter-caste marriage. It allowed every Kaikadi to have more than one wife but almost most of the married men were monogamous. Just like every Kaikadi Hindu being treated as an outsider by his own Hindu upper castes, any Kaikadi, if he or she violated the rules of the Kaikadi community, was also treated as an outsider by his or her own community. It had its own Jat-Panchayat to mete out justice to its people. All types of its judgments were binding on them whether they were just or not and whether the Kaikadis liked them or not. The children going to school was against the law of the Panchayat. Just like its people being kept at distance by all other higher castes, the Kaikadis would be kept in isolation by their own community if they raised a word against the judgement of the Panchayat.

Moreover, the presence of the Kaikadis in any functions of the other castes was considered inauspicious and so they were neither invited nor allowed to attend. Moreover, Kaikadis never took part in any kind of functions at the houses of the other castes even if invited. Once, Laxman Mane attended the marriage of the other caste because of the invitation of the bridegroom who was his friend. A villager who knew about Laxman Mane happened to see him eating along with others at a wedding ceremony. He should have kept quiet till Laxman Mane had finished his eating but he did not. He burst out his feelings at Laxman Mane in the presence of all by saying, "Son of a Kaikadi, a low caste! Have you taken leave of your senses? Get up and get out!" (Upara, p. 107) and thus he had humiliated Laxman Mane in the presence of his friends and other Maratha children. Knowing full well that it was his mistake, Laxman Mane had left the dining hall quietly and without completing his eating. While leaving, he felt greatly hurt and thought about the attitudes of the people there because, "no one intervened on his behalf. His shirt became damp with his tears. He left the place quietly and slept in the house allotted to the family of the bridegroom. Nobody had inquired about him. Nobody asked him anything" (Upara, p. 107). On hearing the incident, his father got angry at his son and beat him too.

The Kaikadis were prone to stealing things they wanted for their livelihood. This habit continued to haunt them whenever they were in need of something for their daily bread. If they were caught red-handed while stealing, the punishment meted out to them was severe and they used to be greatly humiliated and disgraced in public too. The higher caste people took the laws in their own hands and punished the Kaikadis without showing any semblance of mercy and pity. Even the family of Laxman Mane was not free from this habit. Laxman Mane was a direct witness to the happenings to his parents after having been caught pilfering canes:

> [Laxman Mane's] father was being pushed ahead by a small crowd. Mother was behind him. She had no blouse on. She was wearing father's shirt. Her sari was torn. Father had only his dhoti on. One could see black and blue lashes all over his body... Mother was wailing loudly and father was consoling her. (Upara, p. 61)

On seeing the humiliation of his parents, he was burning with anger and helplessness. He saw his mother falling at the feet of the man who captured her while stealing cane and begging him to let her go home. In spite of all pleadings, they were arrested and imprisoned for two days.

Every act of humiliation meted out to Laxman Mane's family in public got imprinted in his mind indelibly. He thought of a way out to escape discrimination permanently. At once, he realised that it could be possible only through education. If he was educated, he could become someone important in the society. Other caste people would not look down upon him but consider him with respect for his educational advancement. If his educational advancement brought him dignity in the society, all the Kaikadis could look forward to their educational advancement and attain dignity in the society.

Mahatma Jyotirao Phule also strongly felt that education was the panacea for almost all types of social and religious discriminations. He stated:

> Without knowledge, intellect was lost; without intellect, morality was lost; without morality, dynamism was lost; without dynamism, money was lost; without money, Shudras were degraded (demoralised). All misery and disasters in human life were due to lack of knowledge and it was only education that would provide knowledge that everyone would be in need of for his civilised life. (qtd. in Sutradhar, p. 2168)

Through his advancement in life, he could be on par with the higher caste Hindus in status. His father also knew about the value of education. He did not want his son to suffer exploitation like other Kaikadis for being illiterate. So he brought his son to a school for admission. The school master made fun of Mane's desire for education and discouraged him with humiliating words, "You funny guy! Do nomadic beggars go to school?...If they study, who will weave our baskets? Nothing doing! You want to study, huh!" (Upara, p. 36). However, Laxman Mane got admitted.

No student in his class allowed Mane to sit near him. The school teacher asked him to sit near the door. He had to sit without any book, a slate, and a pencil and he just listened to what his teacher taught. All the students were afraid of establishing physical touch with him because he was a Kaikadi and an untouchable. Since Mane looked dirty in appearance and his way of speaking his Kaikadi language appeared funny, his class mates started teasing him. As he was very firm in his advancement in life through education, he did not care a bit about teasing. He was very regular in attending school without mingling with his class mates. His determination to prove to the society that he was not inferior to the other caste students in educational status did not let him down. By doing odd jobs outside his school hours and braving all obstacles and humiliation, he completed his matriculation successfully.

If a family is too poor to provide further chances for its son for his pursuit of graduation in a college after matriculation, its God will not fail him and some friends will be of a great help to its son's desire to be fulfilled. The same thing happened in the life of Laxman Mane. His father expected him to be a teacher after matriculation but some of his friends from Maratha community helped him to pursue graduation in Arts. During his college days, girl by name Shashi from the Martha community fell in love with him and wanted to marry him. The moment she came to know that Mane was a Kaikadi and not a Martha; she was hesitant. But his friends and Professors convinced Shashi and made her marry him. His actions like getting educated, falling in love with a girl and entering into inter-caste marriage were against the laws of Jat Panchayat. He established his individuality among all Kaikadis and proved that he was not either for self-exploitation by his own community or for humiliation by other community. He had lived up to his life's desire by violating the cruel norms of his community and that of the Martha through his inter-caste marriage. No sooner did he marry Shashi than her community people started showing signs of uncontrollable anger at Laxman Mane. He looked frustrated and began cursing the higher caste Hindus:

> I piss on the social system that bluntly refuses to consider me as a human being. The Martha girl has married me willingly though I am a Kaikadi and untouchable. The law of the land is not against our inter-caste marriage but my Jat Panchayat and Martha community are. It is only my caste Kaikadi that is against me. I feel boiling with rage and I am not able to do anything except shedding tears in helplessness. (Upara, p. 178)

His friends came to his rescue again and assured him and his wife of their protection. They gave them hope and trust that as long as they were with him and his wife, they need not be afraid of any harm.

Even after education and inter-caste marriage, Laxman Mane's humiliation by the higher caste Hindus did not stop. His self-respect was taken for granted. He was not given any house for rent for his living with his wife. Being a Kaikadi, he did not have a native village of his own like other untouchables from the communities of Mahar and Mang. The entire life of his community rested on the back of its donkeys. The places wherever they had their huts erected had become their places of living temporarily. The moment Laxman Mane had moved to the city after his education and marriage, he felt relieved of all the tensions caused by suppression and oppression for being an untouchable. He wanted his community to know itself such as its weaknesses and strengths. He desired that all should get educated and move to the cities for their civilised and respectable lives. As a Hindu, he hated Hinduism because his religion failed to honour him as an equal human being. His wife was no exception. Her reply to the some elderly Hindu women why she did not observe certain Hindu rituals after her marriage was like slapping them on their faces:

> I am not observing the fast like any other Hindu woman. Though I am a Hindu still now, I do not share your views of Hinduism. I do not have faith in the Hindu rites and rituals. Since I do not have any belief in rebirth, I do not want to be a hypocrite. I am not sure whether I will get the same man as my husband in all of my seven future rebirths. (Upara, p. 202)

After moving to the city and becoming a social worker, he created awareness in the minds of the Kaikadis that as human beings, they were in no way inferior to the higher caste Hindus and they were actually and equally superior. As long as they continued to be Hindus, they could neither escape discrimination nor keep their self-respect intact nor get social justice. The only way lying open to them for their decent living as human beings in the civilised society was their option for conversion to Buddhism. His embracing Buddhism along with his followers was the result of his complete rejection of inhuman Hinduism and its way of treating fellow beings as untouchables. He had proved thinking of those in higher castes wrong through his life that they were not alone God's chosen and anointed people on earth but all the human beings in spite of their differences in social status.

Man cannot make others good without being himself good first. He should practice himself first what is good before he preaches it to others. Unless he changes himself according to changing situations, he cannot bring in changes for the good of all and sundry. If he does not have any feelings of fellowship, he cannot create conducive environment for happy togetherness of people of different cultures, faiths and social statuses. India is for all the natives of India and not for one elite group. Men like Laxman Mane are Indians too and their name should not be 'Discrimination.' If Hinduism does not prevent its followers of higher social class from torturing fellow Hindus on the basis of their birth and caste, Indian soil cannot but be another Pandemonium on earth.

Works Cited

Dhammannand, Sri. *Buddhism Today: Buddhism and Present Life.* 6 May 2006. Web. 26 May 2016.

Deepak, K.P. "Dalit Literature After Independence." *Literarism: The Republic of Letters.* 2013. Web. 25 March 2016.

Goswami, Lalita C. "The Anguish of a Dalit: A Study of Laxman Mane's Upara: Of an Autobiography in Marathi." *Indian Literature.* 31.2 (1988): 129-138. Print.

Jayaraman, V. "Preface: Hinduism and Caste System." *Hinduwebsite.com.* n.d. Web. 26 May 2016.

Kavitha, V. "Sabaltern Autobiography: Challenging the Cannon." *Research Journal English Language and Literature (RJELAL).* 2.1 (2014): 221-226. Print.

Kirby-Smith, Henry Tompkins. *A Philosophical Novelist: George Satyana and The Lost Puritan.* America: SIU Press, 1997. Print.

Mane, Laxman. *Upara: An Outsider.* trans. A.K. Kamat. New Delhi: Sahitya Akademi, 1987. Print.

Punalekar, S. P. "Dalits, Dalit Consciousness and Sociology." *Social Sciences: Communication, Anthropology and Sociology.* ed. Yogendra Singh. New Delhi: Pearson Education India, 2010. Print.

Ranjanikar, Ashwin Purushottam. "Marginality and Oppression in Dalit Autobiography with Special Reference to Laxman Mane's *Upara: An Outsider.*" 29 Sept. 2011. Web. 25 May 2016.

Razi, Sulaiman. "Caste System in Hinduism." *Truth about hinduism.* 5 June 2015. Web. 27 May 2016.

Sutradhar, Raman. "Dalit Struggle for Education: With Special Reference to Barak Valley." *International Journal of Science and Research (IJSR).* 3.12 (2014): 2167-2171. Print.

2

Limbale's *The Outcaste*: A Poignant Interrogation into the 'Burden of Inferiority'

DR MANJEET RATHEE

The emergence of Dalit literature in the 1960's, with its unique blend of 'pathos and protest,' has not merely exposed the ugly realities of caste exploitation in all its magnitude but also brought to the fore the underlying currents of seething anger and restlessness that had always been an integral part of the agony of exclusion and humiliation of the marginalised sections. It has been a literature of protest against the established system based on hierarchy and injustice and it has attempted to expose the conservatism and hypocrisy of the higher castes. A predominant spirit of rage and rebellion against caste inequalities and social injustice, with yearning for a life of dignity and equal opportunities, has been a 'defining feature' of all kinds of Dalit literature, which includes the literature of "the most oppressed and exploited sections of the caste system" (Omvedt. xi.) In the words of Farah Siddiqui: "Dalit literature is not simply a body of disparate texts that address similar themes of marginality and resistance. Rather, it is a living, breathing literary movement that is intent on establishing itself as an integral part of the field of Indian literature." (*European Academic Research*, 5910) This anxious yearning to be recognised as 'humans' gained central significance with the advent of Dalit autobiographies in the 1980s since they expressed the anger and humiliation of the deprived in a more direct and explicit manner. The ugly facets of the lived reality of various Dalit writers as expressed in their autobiographies with all the latent layers of rage and agony, served to establish the urgent need to re-look into the discriminatory and inhuman processes of marginalisation due to 'tyranny' of the dominant structures of hierarchy, power and control. As G.N. Devy puts it, these autobiographies were not merely personal documentation of the trajectories of their individual lives and painful experiences, but can best be described as 'social epiphanies' in the sense that they brought to Marathi literature "a larger canvas for depiction of the social, cultural, and political processes of marginalisation." (*The Outcaste*, xxii) Present paper attempts to focus upon the 'burden of inferiority' as experienced and depicted by an eminent Dalit writer, Sharankumar Limbale in his famous autobiography *The Outcaste* (*Akkarmashi*), which was published when the writer was only 25 years old but the burden of caste inferiority that he carried was centuries old.

Sharankumar Limbale is a prominent Dalit writer, activist, editor and literary critic, who has written in several literary genres and who has more than forty books to his credit. He is best known for his autobiography *The Outcaste* (*Akkarmashi*), an acknowledged masterpiece written in 1984 and translated since then in many other Indian languages and in English. In writer's own words: "I have always lived with the burden of inferiority. And this book is a tale of this burden." (Limbale, xx) This is a burden of being born and brought up not only in a caste, which in Hindu religion and caste hierarchy, occupies a lower and inferior socio-cultural status, but to be condemned to be born as an illegitimate child and hence an outcaste. Born out of 'relationship' (which he calls 'rape') of an untouchable 'Mahar' mother and a high caste 'Patil' father, the writer is doomed to lead an impoverished life of 'a half caste' since he was neither accepted by his father and his high caste community, nor by his own community that humiliated him calling him 'akkarmashi' or a half caste. The writer narrates with agony: "My mother is an untouchable, while my father is a high caste from one of the privileged classes of India. Mother lives in a hut; father in a mansion. Father is a landlord; mother landless. I am an *akkarmashi* (half caste). I am condemned, branded illegitimate." (ix) Thus, the burden of inferiority not only relates to 'a lesser born' identity of a low caste but is multiplied due to his fractured identity of being 'a half caste' because of the humiliating unacceptability by his father and his whole existence getting reduced to that of being an illegitimate child. While his mother 'Masamai', deserted by her husband, Ithal Kamble, accepted to live openly with Hanmanta Limbale- his legal father just as a kind of 'revenge' since it was because of his evil intentions that her marriage and life with poor farm worker Kamble was 'ruined' and the caste council forced her to divorce her husband, yet the fact that she could not regain the status of a wife and was confined to being Limbale's 'whore' wrecked the writer's life beyond all imagination. He interrogates with impunity: "Why did my mother say yes to the rape which brought me into the world?...Why did she allow this bitter embryo to grow? Which family would claim me as its descendant? Whose son am I, really?" (37) The fact that he was all along excommunicated and ostracized due to his 'half caste', a burden that affected even his prospects of marriage and subsequent adult life, tells volume of the burden that had to carry almost like his alter ego. The anguish of a wounded heart is clearly visible in the 'Author's Note," when he says: "My history is my mother's life, at the most my grandmother's. My ancestry doesn't go back any further." (ix) The question "who am I" which has haunted the writer like a nightmare throughout his life, therefore, becomes all the more significant in the light that he had "no inherited identity at all" since he had "neither a father's name, nor any religion, nor a caste." (59) Though this search for individual identity goes beyond all kinds of barriers but as Amartya Sen says in his book *Identity and Violence: The Illusion of Destiny* that such 'identity-based' thoughts and interrogations, as it is in the case of Dalits, "can be subject to 'brutal manipulations'" and can invite "violence and terror from aggressive opponent groups that have a different identity and set of competing interests" (Sen, 16-17). Sharankumar Limbale, who grew up with most bitter experiences of such 'brutal manipulations,' had to bear the tyranny and backlash of opponent upper caste groups and communities in its most inhuman and explicit ways.

This burden and agony of exclusion begins right from his birth when his very first breath 'threatened' the moral fabric of a caste ridden society. Since his father did not acknowledge him as his offspring, he had to grow like 'Karna in the Mahabharata.' While in school in his early childhood, there were separate games and separate playgrounds for high-caste village boys and for students belonging to Mahar community: "We played one kind of game while the high-caste village boys played another. The two games were played separately like two separate whirlwinds." (2) Even the tree under which Mahar boys and girls were made to sit after playing was different and 'tattered' and they had to be contented to sit in its 'broken shadow.' They were made to carry out menial kind of duties in the school like smearing the floor and walls of the school with cow dung paste. They were forbidden to enter the temples and though children in general are considered to be the 'flowers of God's abode', this did not apply to them and they grew up like the 'garbage' which the village throws out. The deep sense of humiliation leaves its mark right from his infancy, as he is constantly made to feel like a thrown away material: "We had grown up like aliens since our infancy. This sense of alienation increased over the years and to this day my awful childhood haunts me." (5) During the recess times in the school, the upper caste boys threw stones at him calling him 'Mahar' which made him 'anxious.' Even the water from the wells and the rivers reminded him of his inferior status, with water at the lowest end of the river meant for his caste and community. It is ironical that people could buy and accept liquor from Mahar caste but not water. What more, the barber too got 'wild' at him and refused to shave his head. The writer questions: "How could this barber, who used to shave buffaloes in the village, refuse to shave my head?" (22) The kind of lowly work that the people of his caste and community had to perform for the villagers also added to his tale of burden. This included, apart from sweeping the village streets and collecting alms to dragging the dead animals, skinning them and eating their flesh. They were not allowed to enter inside the temple and were supposed to offer their prayers from the steps outside only, since their entry was supposed to make even the gods 'impure.' The writer again raises fundamental questions: "What kind of God is this that makes human beings hate each other? We are all supposed to be the children of God, then why are we considered untouchable? We don't approve of this God, nor this religion, nor this country because they ostracize us." (62) He felt so deeply offended at the constant insults hurled upon him in one form or the other that the seeds of revenge begin to sprout in his heart against the individuals, structures and symbols of the caste system. He, along with his friend wanted to rape Shobhi, an upper caste girl who had humiliated them for being impure and untouchables, in order to take revenge, but they were afraid of the consequences and were well aware of the atrocities heaped against all the Dalits under such circumstances. Yet the burden of being considered as 'born inferior' went on piling up to such a horrible extent that even the cobbler beside the bus stand refused to repair his footwear on recognising that he was a Mahar and he had to put them back on his feet unrepaired.

The situation, however, begins to change after the writer enters the college after completing his high school education and spends a major part of his time in the company of the bright students. The self-esteem derived from education gave him a sense of pride and confidence. He confesses "we hated the very idea of untouchability. With our education, there grew in us a sense of pride." (76) However, as the writer confesses, the high caste people did not like this new born feeling of pride since they didn't want us 'to enjoy any self-esteem'. Yet the Dalit students having realised the 'unusual strengths' of the self-esteem, were now in a position to protest against the insults heaped on them. With the joining of the larger struggle for dignity, the youth, for the writer, began to assume 'a new meaning and significance' and any kind of atrocity against the Dalits made him restless. However, it was difficult to wipe away the discrimination prevalent for ages in social and cultural life and in the minds and consciousness of the people in a short span of time and the writer falls victim to the worst form of humiliation at the time of his marriage when many proposals were not merely rejected but he was humiliated to the core due to his half caste and 'impure' blood. It happened in the case of sweeper's Janabai's daughter, who was proposed to him by one of his childhood friend Mallya. Janabai went wild with anger when she came to know about the writer's birth and began to hurl abuses at him. He narrates painfully: "Janabai's words pierced my heart. I felt I was being flogged in a market square." (88) He had to undergo the same kind of piercing and shocking agony yet once again when his childhood friend Mallya's sister's proposal was refused on the same grounds that he was not of 'pure blood.' And all this happened in spite of the fact that the writer and Mallya had been intimate friends right since infancy and Mallya's mother had always liked him. Finally he was married to Maryappa Kamble's daughter Kusum and in exchange to his own marriage, his sister Nirmi was made to marry Maryappa Kamble's son, but he again had to face similar insults after the marriage since his mother-in-law refused to send their daughter till he got a job and kept calling their family 'rotten' and impure. And the burden continued even after his job when his caste followed him 'like an enemy' and in a town like Latur, with huge buildings and bunglaws, he could not find a single room to live, since "every town and person was caste conscious." (106) The writer underlines with agony and pathos: "This casteism has dehumanised everyone." (106)

The writer interrogates this burden of inferiority not merely in terms of caste but also in terms of religion, in terms of rigidity of conventions and above all in terms of the abject and humiliating poverty which has almost defined his essence and reduced his existence to a lesser human being. The tale of burden, especially related to the writer's identity, becomes further complicated by the fact that he was brought up by a grandfather like figure who happened to be a Muslim, namely Mahmood Dastagir Jamadar, who lived with his grandmother, Santamai: "Does this mean I am Muslim as well? Then why can't the Jamadar's affection claim me as Muslim?" (38) His grandfather, whom he called 'Dada' had to tolerate all kinds of tortures and humiliation because of his religion including losing his job as a night watchman with the village council and even the risk of being killed in a frenzy during Hindu-Muslim riots in 1947. On being discovered by the soldiers that he was a Muslim, it was the village chief Jagannath Patil who somehow saved him with great difficulty. Dada's loss would have left him all the more 'homeless.' Dada had always loved him as his own child without any kind of religious or caste-based hindrance and yet that was not acceptable to the society and its rigid conventions. The writer poses a most pertinent question: "Is it man who is a hindrance to religion or is it the other way round? Is the premise of religion greater than man's? Is religion made for man or man made for religion?...Can't man exist without religion and caste? (39-40)" This is how the 'given' factors of caste and religion are negatively used by man for their own vested interests and for keeping the structures of power and control intact. It was Dada who, being the only earning member, fed their family through his 'daily wages' as a porter and helped in every other way like their own family member. There was no discrimination whatsoever in Dada's heart and mind on the basis of caste or religion, so much so that the writer felt as if Dada was his 'real father.' He was not related to them through blood in any way, yet "I felt that somehow we were of the same flesh and blood." (58) Whereas Dada's affection never 'smelt' of religion, yet the social codes and conventions always reminded him of Dada's religion not only being different but also being 'inferior.' Even writer's grandmother, Santamai, whom he loved more than her mother, was seen with suspicion since she lived with a Muslim and he had to painfully hide this fact from his friends and acquaintances for fear of being all the more isolated and ostracized. The 'hideous' reality of his Dada being a Muslim negatively affected all his prospects whether it was marriage, employment or getting a room on rent. The family of his in-laws felt humiliated due to his relationship with a Muslim. Even his father-in-law Maryappa Kamble, whom he had repeatedly helped with money, could not tolerate this fact and tells him bluntly: "You say that you are a relative of that Muslim. You are the cause of humiliation for us among our own caste...You must have some self-respect, otherwise don't enter our house." (101) This naturally was highly insulting for the writer and he could never understand why a Muslim cannot be his relative just because of a different religion. That was the reason why he could not endorse and believe in Hindu rituals and even his marriage was solemnised according to Buddhist rituals. It was painful for him to see people engaged in 'bloody carnage, riots and crusades' just because they belong to different religions. He asserts: "If you cut out his religion a man is still a man. So why doesn't a human being from one religion love a human being from another? Why does religion hinder them? Why is man imprisoned by conventions?" (102) As Gail Omvedt opines that caste in India works "not only an open conquest and subordination but also on deception and religious illusion." (*Understanding Caste*, 2011:24) The autobiography is a powerful assertion of human values independent of caste and religion. It strongly denounces all kinds of rigidity and retrogressive elements in the name of orthodox traditions and rituals and places love, humanitarian values and relations above everything else. Such traditions which divide and separate people on the basis of caste, colour or religion should be re-looked and re-defined. The whole life of the writer is turned into a disaster because of the retrogressive traditions related to the high caste people. It was because of Hanmanta Patil that his mother was divorced and had to live with him with the humiliating status of a 'keep'. The writer says with great anguish: "This is almost a tradition- a Patil, always a big landowner, has a Dalit woman as his whore. There is at least one such house in every village. Children born to such a whore have no legal father…" (59) His mother, after being deserted by his father, Hanmant Limbale, was kept by another Patil and thus the 'the tyranny of sex' continued in the name of tradition. The writer compares his fate and identity with that of Karna from Mahabharata because like Karan, he too had to bear the burden of tradition which left him drifting with the 'flow of the river.' Mahatma Phule, a great scholar and philosopher who spent his whole life for the upliftment of lower caste people, severely criticised this age old caste system and dominance of retrogressive traditions through the books like *Gulamgiri* (Servitude) and *Brahmananche Kasab* (Skill of the Brahmin) and propounded the spread of rational thinking which alone could lead to emancipation.

The cruelty imposition of some of the most regressive traditions is most vividly reflected in the use of two separate tumblers at Shivram's tea shop- one for upper caste people and another cup and saucer for low caste customers since they didn't want Dalits to enjoy any self-esteem. The writer painfully describes that "the cup and the saucer outside Shivram's tea shop were an insult to our entire community." (76) There was separate aluminium tumbler for them even to drink water from and water was poured into it from a distance to avoid any kind of direct touch with the 'low caste' individuals. Whereas some of the 'low castes' like Rambaap passively accepted it as 'a long tradition' handed down from forefathers, the writer along with his friend Parshya decided to 'go against the village customs' and lodge a complaint against Shivram to the police: "But some day we ought to rebel. How long can we mutely suffer all this?…Some time we ought to reject all this." (76) However, the constable too, being an upper caste and a regular customer of Shivram shop, instead of helping them, threatened them with dire consequences if they dared complain against Shivram and the entire village and Maharwada got enraged against the two of them for having gone to police station. Yet, the seeds of rebellion that had taken roots into their hearts, were bound to sprout and show their might. Various customs like the whole village getting united against Maharwada at the sight of a dead animal and beating them badly and ostracizing them for a few days, enraged the writer beyond all tolerance: "We had reached a dead end. Such humiliation was agonizing."(78) When his grandmother Santamai told him stories of great injustice against them like instances of Dalit women being beaten like slaves and even undergoing sexual harassment at the hands of the farmers whenever they were discovered grazing the cattle or for grass in their fields, it assumed the proportions of an epic: "Santamai's tears were like an epic. Her agony contained the potential spark of a great war." (79) Giving it a historical linkage, he compares his grandmother Santamai to Jijabai narrating stories of valour to Shivaji. Various mythical, historical and religious similarities are poignantly used in the autobiography to trace the linkages of the past injustice to the ongoing struggle: "My agony was not limited to myself alone. Injustice done to me was not just today's phenomenon but had a long history. ..My agony was also the agony of Lord Buddha." (79) The writer is ashamed at the continuity of such a culture which differentiates between human beings on the basis of birth and is terribly angry 'at its customs.'

The fire of hunger and its socio-cultural ramifications further add fuel to it and make him so helpless that he had no experience of any kind of life 'beyond bread' and 'beyond hunger' till he got his job after completing his education. The writer had entered the college with 'seventy generations of utter poverty' behind him and it is this deep accumulative pain of 'detestable poverty' that makes the burden of inferiority so difficult to handle. For someone, who always felt 'half-fed' or under-fed and who survived on the 'leftovers' by the rich and the high caste which he calls 'nectar', the 'politics of hunger' tends to acquire extraordinarily alarming proportions. The pain multiplied on the occasions of weddings or other customary village gatherings when the guests were warmly invited in and he had to wait outside 'swallowing his own saliva' till being called in towards the end when all others had finished. The fire of satisfying the 'huge cauldron' of starving stomach often turned them into a beast 'selling' their dignity and honour for the sake of stomach: "A woman becomes a whore and a man a thief. The stomach makes you clean shit, it even makes you eat shit." (8) Writer's grandmother used to eat 'bhakari' made from the 'jawar' picked out of the cow dung and hence it always 'stank of dung.' Eating it was like actually eating dung only: "Santamai was used to eating such bhakari. It was like pushing garbage into a furnace, feeding its fire." (11) The fire of hunger made his elder sisters, Nagi and Nirmi steal eatables from the market and experience all kinds of exploitation because of the curse of starvation right from the moment of birth. He questions the ethics and morality around starvation: "We knew we shouldn't steal, but then how could we feed ourselves? Who steals out of habit? The poor steal for the sake of hunger. If they had enough to eat, would they steal? Black-marketeers become leaders, whereas those who are driven to steal by hunger are considered criminals." (21) This 'famine of hunger' borne out of affluence of the influential sections and generations of accumulated poverty of the poor and the deprived, makes them undertake all kinds of lowly jobs and bear up with various kinds of affronts. Since his grandfather, the only earning member of the family, was a porter, so bus stand was like a home to them and "every bus meant bread and butter for us" (41) A bus that did not carry passengers enough to provide with the work of carrying luggage was like the 'foetus of a barren woman.' Most of the time, majority of his family members went hungry and survived on a glass of water only. They fed themselves and lived in the open behind the bus stand and since it was too little a space, he was warned every night by his grandmother not to stretch his legs while he was asleep.

The whole autobiography revolves around the pathetic conditions of hunger and the quality as well as the quantity of 'bhakari' that they could afford each day. The writer repeatedly asserts how they were hungry 'most of the time' and could afford just a single 'bhakari' which they had to distribute amongst themselves like a thief or a beggar distributing alms at the end of the day. Under such deprived conditions, the issue of satisfying hunger becomes the most significant social and political issue and 'bhakari' is what matters to them the most. In what can be considered as one of the most powerful assertions on the politics and ethics of hunger, the writer expresses his heart's agony:

> Bhakari is as large as man. It is as vast as the sky, and bright like the sun. Hunger is bigger than man. Hunger is more vast than the seven circles of hell. Man is only as big as the bhakari, and only as big as his hunger. Hunger is more powerful than man. A single stomach is like the whole earth....The world is born from a stomach, so also the links between mother and father, sister and brother. (50-51)

The pain of poverty and limitless hunger reduces his life to that of a junk that he and other family members gathered from the garbage and the writer often wondered if he weighed at least as much as the junk he had gathered throughout the day: "On the one hand there was the garbage, on the other, our hunger. The junk was sold by weight. I felt our hunger should be weighed instead of the junk..." (74)

The issue of hunger began to acquire different dimensions with higher education and heightened sense of awareness. Helplessness was gradually substituted with anger and resistance against the unequal structures and discriminatory conditions that kept them on the fringes. The fire within began to burn with more and more intensity: "I burned within. Our poverty was detestable. I wanted to rebel against such humiliation." (82) Life and issues 'beyond hunger' began to attract him as he came into contact with the organised struggle against the prevailing inhuman conditions and to achieve social justice for the disadvantaged and the marginalised became an overpowering concern. The writer admits: "While studying in a college I was mentally aflame. I was growing amidst a conflagration. The roots of the movement were settling more firmly. Injustice towards us was assuming a new meaning." (83) It is the awakening of this collective consciousness and identification with the joint plight of Dalit community at large that made him 'introspective.' As the writer identifies himself as 'a writer of the movement' writing a literature of 'pain and struggle,' it is this agony and humiliation that makes him burn with anger at any news related to atrocities against Dalits. Full of new hope and youthful energy, his blood 'flowed like hot lava' through his body and he grew more and more impatient with the existing inequalities and disparities. With his growing awareness, he could even discern the futility of retrogressive traditions within his own community. He begins to question why such customs like dedicating one's children to God are laid down and practiced by Mahars and backward communities only. The journey of his life had reached a point where there was now the urgent need for an outer as well as inner struggle. This acute identification with a larger and collective cause gave him abiding strength and confidence to fight against every form of injustice and stand for the dignity and honour of every deprived caste and class. The final questions raised at the end of the autobiography clearly depict the evolutionary journey of the writer from a helpless 'half caste' illegitimate child bent under the burden of inferiority to a confident and mature intellectual and social activist fighting for social justice and emerging victorious in his belief in human dignity and self-respect for all. It is an ongoing struggle and hence the introspection and search for right answers continues: Why this labyrinth of customs? Who has created such values of right and wrong, and what for? If they consider my birth illegitimate what values am I to follow?" (113) In the light of the above analysis and poignant interrogation of burden of caste, religion and rigidity of regressive customs and traditions, it can be easily understood why Sharankumar Limbale feels the urgent need for creation of 'a separate aesthetics for Dalit literature' (*Towards an Aesthetics of Dalit Literature)*, an aesthetics based on the 'real experiences of life' of all the categories who have been oppressed and marginalised and ultimately merging into a common literature of larger human aesthetics based on human values and social justice beyond all discriminations.

Works Cited

Farah Siddiqui. "Dalit Literature: Issues and Trends" *European Academic Research*. Vol. I, Issue 12 / March 2014: 5905-16. Print.

Limbale, Sharan Kumar. *The Outcaste (Akkarmashi*). Translated by Santosh Bhoomkar. New Delhi: OUP. 2003.

Limbale, Sharan Kumar, Alok Mukherjee. *Towards an Aesthetics of Dalit Literature: History, Controversies and Considerations*. Canada: Orient Longman, 2004: 1-176. Print.

Omvedt, Gail. *Understanding Caste: From Buddha to Ambedkar and Beyond*. New Delhi: Orient Blackswan Pvt. Ltd. 2011. 7-24. Print.

Phuley, Jotirao. *Slavery*. New Delhi: Gauram Printers. Sangharsh / Struggle. 2008. Print.

Sen, Amartya. *Identity and Violence: The Illusion of Destiny*. New Delhi: Allen Lane. 2006: 16-17. Print.

3

The Audible Sighs and Visible Dreams: A Discussion of Sharan Kumar Limbale's *Akkarmashi*

DR SAKUNTHALA A.I.

Dalits are being exploited physically, mentally and socially in the caste-ridden society. Though India is politically free with her own constitution proclaiming liberty, equality and fraternity, spearheaded by a Dalit himself, Dr B.R. Ambedkar, it is still difficult for backward classes to lead their lives peacefully. Dalit literature is an arduous endeavour from the canonical to the marginal, from mega-narratives to micro-narratives, from the virtual to the real and from self-emulation to self-affirmation. Dalit intellectuals operate their modes of resistance creatively in Dalit literature, the most powerful being Dalit autobiographies.

Autobiographies are generally written by eminent personalities towards the end of their lives and who have much to evidence before the world, while Dalit autobiographies are penned at an early age when the author is neither distinguished nor eminent but noted for its depiction of a poignant past that has affected the history of a community. The difference between autobiographies written by mainstream writers and Dalits is significant. Unlike autobiographies written by mainstream writers, Dalit autobiographies are not confined strictly to the author's life or hardships faced by him and the happy moments in his life though it is narrated in first person. It is the reflection of the traumas and the wounded psyche of the Dalits and the Dalit community. According to Ashok Boyar, "The Dalit writers have to be a spokesperson of his community. He carries the burden of his society on his shoulders. He is a bard and he can even be the prophet to lead his people to the Promised Land" (64).

Sharan Kumar Limbale, the Marathi poet and literary critic, has written more than forty books, but is well known for his autobiographical novel *Akkarmashi*. It was first published by him at the age of twenty five in 1984. It was translated into English by Santosh Bhoomkar as *The Outcaste* in 2003, and got published by Oxford University Press. The title *The Outcaste* signifies the position of Limbale in contemporary Indian society of 1960s. The word 'Akkarmashi' is a Marathi word which means a person whose birth is illegitimate or one who is an outcaste, impure, incomplete. Society calls him 'akkarmashi', a half caste, an impoverished man, because Limbale was born as the illegitimate son of a higher caste Patil and a landless, poor untouchable mother who belongs to the Mahar caste.

Akkarmashi depicts the meta-realistic accounts of his life as a Dalit in particular and which can be extended to the life of any individual of Mahar community in general. In an autobiography, the normal trend is to 'glorify' the self and boast about the extraordinary quality of oneself. But that changes at the hands of a Dalit. When he writes, it's about denial of opportunities, about being forced to live a life worse than an animal's. The self becomes the representative of all other Dalits who were crushed and kept down because of their Dalit identity. Their entire life narrative gains a representative quality and imparts the true feelings of the sting they have suffered. The protagonist of the autobiography is, of course, the writer himself, but his personal experiences, instead of being mystically unique and individualist, encompasses the general condition of the whole Dalit community. In the text, the narrator moves back and forth between the individual 'I' and the collective 'We'. "The experiences of exclusions and ostracisations of both the self and the community are the creative and critical sources used to create testimonies of caste-based oppression, anti-caste struggles and resistance offering a distinct world view" (Rege, 14).

The author describes how an innocent Dalit couple Ithal Kamble and Masamai are discriminated and exploited by the upper caste landlord Hanmantha Limbale, for whom the poor couple used to work day and night. Hanmantha ruined the poor family and it led to the separation of Ithal Kamble and Masamai forever. After the divorce Masamai was forced to remain a keep of Hanmantha and gave birth to Sharankumar Limbale.

More than the shocking life of the Dalits, where one suffers in groups, what affects Limbale is his isolated stigma of being an 'akkarmashi.' Limbale is reminded now and then by the society- his position within the position less group of outcastes. Birth defines the identity of a person in a very first stage, but Limbale believes that his birth is the curse for him because he was born out of an illegitimate sexual relationship of his mother with Hanmantha. Limbale writes: "My birth must have threatened the morality of the world. With my first cry at birth, milk must have splashed from the breasts of every Kunti. Why did my mother say yes to the rape which brought me into the world? Why did she put up with the fruit of this illegitimate intercourse for nine months and nine days and allow me to grow in the foetus? Why did she allow this bitter embryo to grow? How many eyes must have humiliated her because they considered her a whore? Did anyone distribute sweets to celebrate my birth? Did anyone admire me affectionately? Did anyone celebrate my naming ceremony? Which family would claim me as its descendent? Whose son am I, really?"(*Akkarmashi,* 36-37).

He laments, "a man is recognised in this world by his religion, caste or his father. I had neither a father's name, nor any religion, nor a caste. I had not inherited identity at all" (59). Is not this lack of inherited identity, his real identity? The stigma of an 'akkarmashi' hurls around it intolerable humiliations. The narrator is someone more inferior to a Dalit. It is surprising to note that he is an untouchable among the untouchables. His identity is that of an 'akkarmashi' and this is what the narrator tries to present through the many episodes of his life.

The text becomes an eye witness account of the horrors of the lives of the particular subaltern community. The insurmountable challenge faced by Limbale and other Dalits as young children is hunger. He writes:

> Every bus meant bread and butter for us. We waited at the bus stand for a bus as a prostitute waits for her customers. The moment I saw a bus at a distance, I became excited hoping that this bus would provide at least a few annas and Dada could buy me a cup of tea (41).

The writer has dwelt on this basic need of man over and again throughout the book, philosophising on the need of food: "God endowed man with a stomach. Since then man has been striving to satisfy his stomach. Filling even one stomach proved difficult for him. He began to live with a half-filled one. He survived by swallowing his own saliva. He went for days without eating anything. He started selling himself for his stomach. A woman becomes a whore and a man a thief. The stomach makes you clean shit; it even makes you eat shit" (8). Through this autobiography, Limbale has revealed a world of poverty and discrimination in which the Dalits had lived for thousands of years. He raises some valid questions to be answered by people who consider themselves civilised and modern: "How is a person born with his caste? How does he become an untouchable as soon as he is born? How can he be a criminal? (54).

The most exploited lot of the downtrodden was the Dalit women. They were twice tyrannised, first by their husbands, and secondly by the high-caste people. Limbale writes about his mother: "My history is my mother's life, at the most my grandmother's. My ancestry does not go any further. My mother is an untouchable, while my father is a high caste, from one of the privileged classes of India. Mother lives in a hut, father in a mansion. Father is a landlord, mother landless. I am an akkarmashi. I regard the immorality of my father and mother as a metaphor for rape. My father had privileges by virtue of his birth granted to him by the caste system. His relationship with my mother was respected by society, whereas my mother is untouchable and poor. Had she been born into the high caste or were she rich, would she have submitted to his appropriation of her? (47).

The motherhood of Sharan's mother creates problems for his marriage also. His mixed caste becomes a hindrance for his marriage.

No one is ready to accept Sharan because he is neither a pure Mahar nor a pure Lingayat. With a government job and education to cushion him, Limbale still finds it difficult to get a wife. A single attempt at bride-viewing ends in disaster. At one point the reader suspects Limbale to be satisfied with any woman for a wife. He does not make a choice. He gets a wife out of sympathy and his occasional bribing his would-be father-in-law with alcohol. He writes: "The girl I married needed to be a hybrid like me to ensure a proper match. A bastard must always be matched with another bastard. No one else will marry their daughters to a bastard like me" (98).

However, Limbale does not succumb to the pitiable existence but acquires liberation and freedom from his purgatory of caste through education. The knowledge he had acquired from books, had taught him to think differently. He understood that the sufferings of their lives were based on the false concept of superiority. Limbale's social protests and the subsequent redemption serve as inspiration for other members in the community to use education as a tool to overcome their economic and social conditions.

Dalit literature represents a powerful, emerging trend in the literary field. Dalit literature began as a voice of protest against an unjust social order. Today, it has attained the status of a creative literary world, reflecting the plight of the marginalised people of the world, and highlighting the struggles of the human spirit against the age-old oppressive practices. In the changed circumstances, Dalits are getting education and are becoming aware of their rights. The policy of reservation ensures jobs for the educated ones. Towards a conclusion, it is well observed that an autobiography is the awakening consciousness of Dalit identities from his marginalisation. It can be said that it is an urge for the liberation of humanity from all kinds of suppression. Like the other Dalits, Sharankumar calls for humanism, humanity for Dalits. By his autobiography, he wants to establish an egalitarian society which is casteless and classless, where a person is recognised as a human being not by his caste or any other differential measures.

Works Cited

Boyar, Ashok. "Making of a Dalit Writer." *Journal of Literature and Aesthetics* 8 (2008).

Limbale, Sharan Kumar. *The Outcaste: Akkarmashi*. Trans. Santosh Bhoomkar. New Delhi: Oxford University Press, 2005.

Rege, Sharmila. *Writing Caste/ Writing Gender: Reading Dalit Women's Testimonies*. New Delhi: Zubaan, 2006. Print.

4

Caste Hegemony or Love? A Line of Thought on *Joothan: A Dalit's Life*

DR D. MURALI MANOHAR

If anyone has thought that there is no importance to caste as far as love between a girl and a boy in the twenty-first century/ contemporary world is concerned, let himself/herself read this autobiography written by Omprakash Valmiki entitled *Joothan: A Dalit's Life* (2003). There are views airing from different sets of people where there is no casteism, discrimination and untouchability.

Falling in love is natural between the opposite sex individuals. Sometimes it is calculative. Sometimes it is successful and sometimes it is a failure. The backgrounds such as caste, religious, social, economic, political and cultural are some of the reasons for success or failure as far as love relationship are concerned.

In this paper, I would like to analyse the caste background which plays a barrier for the failure of love relationship at the budding stage itself. It also analyses how the caste hegemony still works in the post-colonial and post-independent situation.

Omprakash Valmiki comes up in his life having faced with atrocious caste discrimination right from his school level to college level. He has been made to sweep the school classrooms and campus premises as a child who was supposed to study along with his peer group. Valmiki's father happens to see his son sweeping the school premises instead of studying. The purpose of sending Valmiki is to study not to sweep like him. Valmiki gets inspiration from his father when he questions the headmaster Kaliram and shouts at him in front of all teachers and students for the act and punishment based on caste identity. The discrimination is to show that he belongs to sweeping community. Therefore, he has been made to sweep the school premises. It is after all his family profession. This was the answer that the father of Valmiki gets from his village elders, when questioned. Despite this discouragement, one thing that registers in Valmiki's mind is that though in a village scenario the marginalised people cannot raise their voice against upper castes but Valmiki's father did raise and questioned the headmaster.

Secondly he gets discrimination in awarding marks at his plus two level by the Chemistry lecturer in his college when it comes to the award of lab marks. The teacher fails him because he could not fail in the public exams but he could fail in the lab as the marks are in his hands. The dropout of Dalit students in schools, colleges and universities is precisely because of these caste- hegemonic reasons.

> I was unable to conduct any experiments during that whole year. Not only did I do very poorly in the lab tests in the board exam, I also got low marks in the oral, even though I had answered the examiner's questions quite correctly.
>
> When the results were announced, I was among the failures. I had good marks in all other subjects except Chemistry. I had failed the lab tests. (Valmiki, 65)

Thirdly, he has been teased by his classmates about his dress and asked him to give address of the tailor so that they could also get stitched from the same tailor. It is to ridicule his dress sense and the poverty with which he has been brought up in his life and in turn make him run away from the school. Valmiki expresses:

> One day, just as I was coming out of the English class, a boy from another section waylaid me. He had three or four other boys with him. They began to make fun of me. One of them began to pull down my pants, 'Which tailor did you go to? Give us his address too.' The other boys were laughing loudly. I wanted to get away from them but they would not let me go. Some were pulling at my pants and others at my shirt. I entreated piteously,

> 'It will tear...please let go.' They laughed heartily at my rural accent. One of them asked, 'Which village has your majesty arrived from?' Their mockery stung me deeply. (Valmiki, 69)

Many a Dalit students face this as a hindrance, blockage and discourage for their studies. Luckily, Valmiki was strong hearted who could come over all these humiliations. He had a strong will power and escape from the "caste" as his father keeps reminding him to.

Having seen the education system and discrimination he has lost faith in this traditional education system. What I mean my traditional educations system is doing B.Sc/B.A/B.Com which does not bring any job unless one tries for State Service Commission/Union Public Service Commission. Therefore, he moves on to technical education. He feels the caste hegemony prevails all over right from primary level to higher level. Thus, he moves on to say:

> I abandoned my college education when I got admitted to the Ordnance Factory, Dehradun, as an apprentice. I knew absolutely nothing about the work before my induction into the factory. All I knew was that I did not want to go into the line of work that my ancestors had been doing for thousands of years.
>
> I had written to Pitaji, informing him of my decision to leave college and learn this technical work in a government factory. He was delighted. He kept saying repeatedly, 'At last you have escaped "caste"'. But he did not know till the date he died is the 'caste' follows on right up to one's death. (Valmiki, 2003: 77-78)

The caste system has been making Valmiki to look for a job than continuing the studies. The biggest fear is that he should not fall back to his family tradition. The studies were not educative for a person like him even if he wants to continue. The peer group is also not encouraging rather discourage more in the way of teasing. How can a person like Valmiki concentrate on studies? The result of his search for job while doing apprentice is in the following:

> AFTER A YEAR'S TRAINING at the Ordnance Factory, I sat in a competitive examination and was selected. I was to go to Jabalpur for further training. I would spend two years at the Ordnance Factory Training Institute, Khamaria. This selection had opened new doors for my 'progress'. (Valmiki, 81)

Omprakash Valmiki is good at literary and cultural activities. His friend Patil had another friend called Ramesh who introduces a Brahmin named Vinayak Sadhasiv Kulkarni who have become close friends in a place called Ambernath. They often meet in Kulkarni's flat. The interesting thing about Kulkarni is a lover of non-vegetarian food, being a Brahmin. Traditionally, culturally and socially he cannot eat it at home as he is a Brahmin but not an orthodox Brahmin. Therefore, he goes to the mess of Valmiki and Patil and eats on their account. As a result, Valmiki's monthly mess bill is escalated. Never mind. Kulkarni has a daughter called Savita. It looks like Kulkarni is interested in Valmiki because he has a surname called Valmiki which is associated with Brahmins in Maharasthra. Kulkarni is a Marathi Brahmin especially Pune Brahmin.

Kulkarni has a responsibility of getting married his daughter Savita. Kulkarni's wife is also interested and both of them like and encourage their daughter to fall in love with Omprakash Valmiki. Valmiki has a central government job and Savita's life will be settled. Two Brahmins can be together. The plan is to invite Valmiki to their place on the occasion of Diwali.

> A day before the Deepawali festival, on chaturdashi, Mrs Kulkarni invited me to their home. That, too, at four in the morning. When I asked Patil about it, he had burst out laughing. I had not understood the reason for his laughter and when I demanded an explanation, he said, 'Enjoy yourself. Mrs Kulkarni is going to bathe and massage you with fragrant oils.' (Valmiki, 94)

The mistaken identity is about the caste of Omprakash Valmiki. Valmiki personally sees with his own eyes how a Dalit Professor is treated when he visits Kulkarni's place. This incident makes Valmiki alert about the caste consciousness of that family.

> One day, I met Professor Kamble at the Kulkarni's place. Kulkarni and Kamble were deep in conversation about Marathi plays. Patil and I were listening to them quietly. Mrs Kulkarni came in with the tea. While drinking my tea, I noticed Kamble's cup. It was different from the cups offered to the rest of us. I asked Sudama Patil who nudged me to be quite. On our way back, I asked him

> again. At first he tried to be evasive, but finally he said, 'Maharashtra Brahmins, that too, from Poona, they don't allow Mahars, to touch their dishes. That's why their dishes are kept separate. Mrs Kulkarni had come to take the used cups of everybody else, but Kulkarni had taken Kamble's cup inside.'
>
> As I listened to him my ears started to boil as though someone had poured mercury into them. 'Do they treat all Dalits like that?' I had wanted to know. (Valmiki, 95)

Even our hero Valmiki has been treated like an upper caste person as they do not know that he is a Dalit. Professor Kamble who thought that he was treated royally is not true. There is casteism. A professor has been treated inhumanly with a sophisticated touch of untouchability. They have not said that you are an untouchable. Yet they have said. Though Kamble is a professor, in the Kulkarnis family's opinion is that he is not. His cup is separate in a modern untouchability. It is a modern two cup system that has been meted out to a professor. The other side is not a professor but only a person who is interested in Marathi plays. The turn comes to Valmiki now. After seeing Kulkarni's treatment for Kamble he is in a fix and defensive:

> I did not care for love and respect gained on the basis of a lie. I remained mired in turmoil. Lost in my inner battle, I did not visit the Kulkarnis for several days. Savita had come to the hostel after having waited in vain for my visit. I wanted to talk to Savita frankly. But it wasn't possible within four walls of the hostel. I said to Savita, 'I need to talk to you...Alone'.
>
> 'Alone...Why?' she had replied mischievously, her eyes dancing.
>
> 'Hm...'
>
> 'Let us go to the temple tomorrow.'
>
> 'But won't your mother be there with you?' I objected.
>
> 'No, I will come alone,' she assured me.
>
> After Savita left, I told Patil that I was going to let Savita know everything. Patil tried to stop me; he said, No, don't do that. It will cause a storm.'
>
> But I had come to a decision. Things should be cleared up. I would face whatever happened. (Valmiki, 96)

Having experienced the discrimination in his life he should not be in the mask of caste identity and conceal with Saivta. He wants to make it very clear to Savita about his identity and let her lose interest in him. It does not matter to him. He is thick skinned about such discrimination. He has self-respect about his caste. Though his friend asks him not to reveal his caste identity, Valmiki decides to be crystal clear. One must have courage to be and to make such a decision. The following conversation will jolt Savita:

> Suddenly Savita made out as though she had remembered something, 'Oh, I had almost forgotten, weren't you going to tell me something?' Her eyes grew large as she gazed at me steadily. For a moment I felt I would not be able to do it.
>
> Gathering my courage, I said, 'That day when Professor Kamble came to your place…'
>
> Before I could finish Savita interrupted with, 'That Mahar…SC?'
>
> The way she said it made me flush with anger. 'Yes, the same…' I replied bitterly.
>
> Surprised, Savita asked, 'Why are you thinking of this today?'
>
> My voice hardened, 'You had given him tea in a different cup?'
>
> 'Yes, the SCs and Muslims who come to our house, we keep their dishes separate,' Savita replied evenly.
>
> 'Do you think this discrimination is right?' I asked. She felt the sharp edge in my voice now.
>
> 'Oh…Why, are you mad? How can we feed them in the same dishes?'
>
> 'Why not? In the hotel…in the mess, everyone eats together. Then what is wrong in eating together in our home as well? I tried to reason with her.
>
> Savita defended the discrimination as right and justified by tradition. Her arguments were infuriating me. However, I remained calm. According to her, SCs were uncultured. Dirty.
>
> I asked her, 'How many SCs do you know? What is your personal experience in this regard?'
>
> She fell silent. Then I asked her, 'What do you think of me?'

'Aii and Baba praise you. They say you are very different from their preconceptions about U.P. people,' Savita cooed.

'I had asked for your opinion.'

'I like you.' She leaned on my arm.

I pushed her away and asked, 'OK…would you like me even if I were an SC?'

'How can you be an SC?' she laughed.

'Why not, what if I am?' I had insisted.

'You are a Brahmin,' she said with conviction

'Who told you that?'

'Baba'.

'He is wrong. I am an SC.' I put all my energy into those words. I felt that a fire had lit inside me.

'Why do you say such things?' she said angrily.

'I am telling you the truth. I won't lie to you. I never claimed that I am a Brahmin.'

She stared at me, totally shocked. She still thought I was joking with her.

Savita appeared grave. Her eyes were filled with tears and she said tearfully, 'You are lying right?'

'No, Savi…It is the truth… you ought to know this.' I had convinced her. (Valmiki, 97-98)

Savita never expected that her parents would be wrong in choosing a life partner for her. She thought that she was going to marry Valmiki. When Valmiki enquires about Professor Kamble she never thought this conversation would lead into revealing of true identity of Valmiki. She vehemently expresses her negative attitude about Dalits, Muslims and the tradition with which she has been brought up by her parents. She follows her family and caste hegemonic tradition. That is why Savita could forget Valmiki as her boyfriend very easily. The reason is that the parents have taught about different social milieu but brought her in the same caste hegemony thus her response for Professor Kamble "that Mahar". Ambedkar has already appealed to the upper castes to leave this caste business in marrying the daughters and sons. He had appealed in his article

"Annihilation of Caste" that the next generations have to be equipped with inter-dining which did not happen between Kulkarni and Professor Kamble. Even if it happens with the contagious caste discrimination there is a lot of hypocrisy. Ambedkar had also appealed for inter-caste marriage in 1940s. It has not happened. It still continues. The caste hegemony never dies including at the matter of love and marriage.

Works Cited

Ambedkar, B.R. "Annihilation of Caste". *Writings and Speeches*. New Delhi: Dr Ambedkar Foundation, 2014. Print.

Valmiki, Omprakash. *Joothan: A Dalit's Life*. New Delhi: Samya, 2003. Print.

5

Raising Voice against Caste Distinction and Untouchability: A Study of Narendra Jadhav's *Outcaste: A Memoir*

Dr Archana Bhattacharjee

India's caste system assigns individuals a certain hierarchical status according to Hindu beliefs. Traditionally there are four principal castes (divided into many sub-categories) and one category of people who fall outside the caste system – the Dalits. As members of the lowest rank of Indian society, Dalits face discrimination at almost every level: from access to education and medical facilities to restrictions on where they can live and what jobs they can have. The discrimination against the Dalits is especially significant because of the number of people affected there are approximately 167 million Dalits in India, constituting over 16 per cent of the total population.

Dalits have been oppressed culturally subjugated and politically marginalised. The principles of untouchability and 'purity and pollution' dictate what Dalits are and are not allowed to do where they are and are not allowed to live go or sit; who they can and cannot give water to eat with or marry, extending into the minutia of all aspect of daily life. More than 165 million people in India continue to be subject to discrimination, exploitation and violence simply because of their caste. In India's 'hidden apartheid' untouchability relegates Dalit's throughout the country to a life time of segregation and abuse. Caste-based divisions continue to dominate in housing, marriage, employment and general social interaction – divisions that are reinforced through economic boycotts and physical violence.

According to Milton C. Albercht, "The relationship of literature and society has been variously conceived. Three general assumptions are that literature reflects society and culture and its serves as a means of social control, and that it influences attitudes and behaviour of people in ways considered in some respects desirable in other undesirable. (http://www.jstor.org/stable424?2088)

The reflection theory maintains that literature reflects society and culture. From the perspective if we view Dalit literature it may be considered as a mirror reflection and justified articulation of ill starred marginalised section of Indian society. Sharan Kumar Limbale (2010) argues that Dalit literature is aimed at raising the consciousness of the Dalit masses, and making them aware of their conditions combining Marxism and Ambedkarism. He suggests that writers play a significant role in the political and ideological contestation involved in making a humanist society.

The primary motive of the Dalit literature is the liberation of Dalits in India, which is based on presentation of reality. Therefore, authenticity and liveliness is the essential feature of Dalit literature.

Kanval Bharti (2004) maintains that Dalit literature has created a unique perspective in so far as earlier literature suppressed the question of caste and untouchability. Particularly it seems to that progressives writers represented caste primarily as a question of class. Consequently, the question of Dalit subjectivity was not recognised. This opens up multiple registers of discrimination. The uniqueness of Dalit literature lies in bringing this new subjectivity into literature.

The revolutionary movements of Rajarshi Shahu, Maharaj, Mahatma Phule and Dr Babasaheb Ambedkar woke them up from their slumber and made the Dalit aware of their identity and their position in the society. They how sought education to help them articulate their oppressions, marginalisation's and humiliation. Those who were empowered through education took to literary writings and by 1960's there was a flow of Dalit writing in the form of poetry short stories drama and autobiography. Almost all these, autobiography became favourite genre to express Dalit experiences before the world. These autobiographies very explicitly portray the surroundings of Dalit and their social behaviour of Indian society.

Dr Narendra Jadav's *Outcaste: A Memoir* represents the life of untouchable world. It is an expanded, rewritten version in English of Dr Narendra Jadhav's *'Ancha Baapthan Amhi' (Our Father and Us)* published in Marathi around ten years ago. There, Damodar Runjaji Jadhav's story was reproduced almost exactly as he has scribbled it in his dairies. The language was rough the idiom rural and the narration unselfconscious. The language of *Outcaste* is refined, its structure consciously schematic and its narration flaunt.

The story of Sonabai, the author's mother is a valuable addition in *Outcaste*. She did not write like her husband but Jadhav has presumably constructed her story from the things that he had seen and heard. The Marathi version 'Amcha Baap Aan Ambi' was a best seller which was first translated into French named as 'Untouchable' by Fayard and later also published in other European languages. This paper will examine the journey of three generations of a Dalit family and their struggle against all conventional caste codes followed by the society and religion.

The autobiography *Outcaste* explores the world that Jadhav lived and struggled in through the eyes of his family. It is narrated from the perspective of his father, a mother himself and his teenage daughter. It traces the journey of Damu, the author's father from a small village, Ozar in Maharashtra to Mumbai written in the form of a memoir, the novel bears testimony to the success of a Dalit family in the course of a single generation.

The autobiography is a thought providing piece of writing that compels us to wake up and accept the inhuman harsh reality of a social order that treats human worse than animal."

In his Author's note Jadhav describes Damu as "Damu was not a leader but he refused to define himself by circumstances and aimed at shaping his own destiny" or "Damu had no formal education.....yet he steered his children to educational heights and inculcated in them the spirit of excellence" or "Damu was not a guru....but he taught his children to believe in themselves and retain human dignity" or "Damu was often humbled. Yet he maintained, goats are special offerings, not lions" or "Damu was an ordinary man, they said….but he did an extraordinary thing: he stood up against the tyranny of the caste system." (Jadhav, 6)

In the opening pages of *Outcaste* we find Damu engrossed in his Yeskar duties (village duties to Mahars) in his native village, Ozar. We see Damu running in front of the Mamledar senior revenue official, announcing his arrival. Later, Damu was asked to guard the dead body of a woman found floating in the well. He was not allowed to go home to inform his wife and also to have his food. He is forced to stay near the well and the tragedy does not end here, he is also abused and insulted. The next day the Fauzdar (a police officer) comes and asks Damu to get into the well to draw the corpse out. Damu refuses to do this work because she is not allowed to touch the dead body of an upper caste woman. Narendra Jadhav says, "The caste system is so deeply ingrained that change can, at best, be cosmetic. The caste system was disposed by God and not by mortals. It has such a powerful sanction behind it that no laws, no reform movements, and no revolution will ever change it completely." (Jadhav, 34).

For neglecting the order Damu is beaten up by the Fauzdar. But Damu never gives up and he says: "In spite of these inhuman traditions, I am not going to abide by such traditions. I am a man of dignity and I will not got go from house to house begging for Baluta. What are all of you going to do? Kill me? (Jadhav, 10)

Disgusted with the degrading behaviour of the so called upper class people, Damu decides to leave the village with his family on that very night and leaves for Mumbai in search of a better life. Damu had to struggle a lot in his new environment and worked at various places too like the Railways, the Port Trust and in Textile mills to earn his living. He also participates actively in the Dalit Movement at the call of Dr B. R. Ambedkar. He also takes part in the Nasik Temple Entry Movement in 1930 in Mahad Satyagraha in 1927, in the Buddhist conversion movement in 1956, Ambedkar's funeral procession and a lot of other activities of the Dalits. Damu refused to be cowed down by all the odds in his life. He had always declared himself as the master of his will. He also encouraged his children to be ambitious and succeed in life through education and concentrated effort. The character of Jadhav is that of an assertive self made Dalit in the text. He inherits the philosophy of his father and asserts "If others look down on me in their belief that my caste is low. It is their problem, not mine. I certainly don't need to torment myself over it. I pity them for they are the victims of their own obsolete prejudices" (10). Dalit identity gave Damu's family confidence and pride to reject their ascribed status as low caste Mahars. The transformation of Damu was possible only because he dared to leave his village in search of a new identity in Mumbai. The Dalit Movement led by Ambedkar also inculcated within him progressive views helped and developed in him a sense of self worth.

> Truly, we sensed a change in the way we carried ourselves. We proudly proclaimed ourselves Dalit. With our chin up, and we looked everyone in the eye. We began to lose our former servility, associated with being born in low caste (Jadhav, 12).

Throughout the narration runs the clarion call of Dr Ambedkar, which unites all Dalits, "Educate, Unite and Agitate". This slogan had a deep impact in Damu's mind and he went all out to make sure that his children did not remain illiterate like him and received the best education that he could afford. He also tried to empower his wife through education which was unheard of in those days. In return his wife supported him in all his endeavours and praised him highly for his in prejudiced attitude, tolerant behaviour and respect shown towards her, "He never drank, never abused me. Best of all, he never raised his hand to me." (13).

All Damu's earlier sacrifices and struggle to live with dignity and self-respect from 1920 till his death in 1989 proved worthwhile as he managed to save his children from the clutches of casteism, social stigma and economic backwardness through education.

In *Outcaste: A Memoir* Narendra Jadhav tries to show the interpersonal relations between low caste people and upper caste people. It delineates the dark facet of Indian society which allows the practices of untouchability due to which the Dalit men and women are maltreated and humiliated by the upper class people down the ages. Their struggle to create an identity of their own is similar to the movement of the American Negroes during the sixties and the South African Blacks who had the victim of racial discrimination.

Strange through it may seem, but it is true till date. Surname still that in certain areas determines a man's social status, his wealth (intellectual also) his daily life and behaviour. It is the 'cross' that every Sudra has to bear since birth without visibility but having weight enough to make him socially collapsed, economically crippled. Narendra Jadhav's *Outcaste: A Memoir* very explicitly traces the awakening of Dalit traversing three generations, and their aspirations to escape persecution meted out to those belonging to their community.

The remarkable journey of Damu and Samu from a small village at Ozar in Maharashtra to the city of Mumbai is a symbolic one, showing how the Dalits are slowly emerging from their subjugated status to a position of power through their own efforts and endeavours. Damu's struggle against caste oppression, untouchability and poverty gives a true picture of the Dalit experience. But his uncompromising spirit fuelled by the Ambedkar's slogan – "educate, unite and agitate" filled him with just and energy to overcome all hurdle and educate his children and encourage them to reach heights of academic excellence and become role models for other Dalit youngsters.

The message that the author tries to pass on through this memoir is that in modern India dignity rests in the mind and hearts of people and that archaic prejudice do not really matter. As Amar Nath Prasad so rightly opines, "Yes, even a Dalit or an untouchable can became an engineer or a doctor or a lawyer or a Professor if he is given proper education and proper facilities. God never makes any difference between touchable and an untouchable between the poor and the rich between the rough and the sublime. The minds of all men are almost equal" (Prasad, 199).

Works Cited

Bharati, Kanvil. *Dalit Vimarsh Ki Bhumika*. New Delhi: Sahitya Upakrama, 2004. Print.

Jadhav, Narendra. *Outcaste: A Memoir*. New Delhi: Viking, 2003. Print.

Jadhav, Narendra. *My Family's Triumphant Journey out of the Caste System in Modern India*. New Delhi: Publisher Scribner, 2005. Print.

Limbale, Sharankumar. *Towards Aesthetics of Dalit Literature: Histories, Controversies and Considerations.* New Delhi: Orient Blackswan, 2010. Print.

Prasad, Amar Nath, "Arundhati Roy: A Novelists of the Dalit and Deserted", ed. Dr Amar Nath Prasad. *Indian Novelists in English. Critical Perspectives.* New Delhi: Sarup and Sons, 2000. Print.

www.tribuneindia.com/2003/20030928/spectrum/book-1.btm

http://www.jstor.org/stable 424?20888424

6

Exploitation of Leather-Workers in Balbir Madhopuri's *Changiya Rukh: Against the Night*

Dr Sadhana Agrawal

According to Varna system Indian society was divided into four categories on the basis of their works—Brahmins, Kshatriyas, Vaishyas and Shudras. Among these Brahmin and Kshatriyas belonged to the upper castes. Brahmins performed the acts of worshipping and the Kshatriyas were the ruling people. In the present era, there are no Kshatriyas but this position of the ruling has been taken by the politicians and many parties have been constructed. Vaishyas were the commercial people but Shudras were the lowest of the low and they were degraded in the society. In modern era, Indian society has been divided into various castes and communities. This dividing has become a root cause of many problems for those who belong to low castes or have economically backward status. Financially weak people had to engage in unclean and dirty professions which were not adopted by the economically rich people. Leather workers and the Valmikis were from the fourth category who had to do the work which was not done by the financially rich people. These people were mostly uneducated as these people were not allowed to study and their duty was merely to clean the dirt but later due to awareness and the efforts done by the Dalit activists and social-reformers; these people also started taking formal education. After getting education, these people also created awareness through their poetry, autobiographies, plays and novels. Amongst these, Dalit autobiographies gained the momentum and this form of narrative got widely accepted in the scholarly circles due to authenticity of the events and the closer appeal to those people who had to suffer the tyrannies, atrocities and miseries of the upper caste people due to their backward status.

Balbir Madhopuri's *Changiya Rukh: Against the Night* is the first Punjabi autobiography that narrates the moving pictures of caste discrimination. 'Changiya Rukh' means a tree that has been trimmed, lopped or slashed so that it may not grow according to its natural growth; it may grow as the gardener or the farmer wants it. Through this metaphor that writer wants to portray that the leather workers of his village were those people whose growth was monitored by the upper-class people and they could not prosper according to their wish. Ravi Bhushan observes about it:

> *Changiya Rukh* is a powerful testimony to the suffering, angst and attempt at rebellion of the dalit community of *chamars* in Punjab but it is something more. It is this something, which makes it significant as a literary work. It is a lively chronicle of a host of people, each significant and memorable, not as a representative of a caste in one part of the country but as an individual. (Bhushan, 03)

Balbir Madhopuri is a versatile writer who has written many books and he has also worked as a deputy director of News in All India Radio apart from his job as an editor. He presently works as the Head, Punjabi Bhawan, Punjabi Sahit Sabha, New Delhi. His village is situated in Punjab as he himself writes in his autobiography, "Actually, Madhopur in district Jalandhar is one of the villages located in the *mand*—the land where the river Beas once flowed." (01) He further tells about his village:

> This is what my birthplace is like… My village is not very big. It has a population of about twelve hundred. Nor it was very old, only about 250 years old….The common land is 17 acres and this includes the lanes and ponds of the village. There are thirty wells in the fields. But how much land the untouchables have? Almost nothing! (05)

The autobiography *Changiya Rukh: Against the Night* has many very touching themes and even the opening of it makes the point clear when Dalit leather-workers of their communities are not allowed to drink water from the common wells which were used by the upper caste people and that's why they had to be dependent on the well which were reserved only for Dalit people. The quest for water of these people has been shown in the opening words of the autobiography:

> Sim sim paniya
>
> Qugi tihai aa...
>
> (Ooze o water, ooze/ the dove is thirsty...) (Madhopuri, 01)

Through these words it is clearly indicated how the author and his friends would dig shallow holes in the earth so that they might get water from these pits to drink. There were the seeds of untouchability and caste discrimination in the village that's why there were separate wells in the village. Madhopuri writes this situation in these words:

> The village appeared to be one, but every group had its own drinking well. Later some Muslims also settled in the village and bought land for themselves. They did not practice untouchability against the dalits, but this could be because many of them had once belonged to the untouchable and artisan castes. (2)

Dalits have to suffer the real trauma of caste discrimination as they have to face this discrimination and insult directly. Balbir Madhopuri has had a very bad experience in his village that's why he drops his Hindu surname and adopts the name of his village instead of his surname. Dr Ravi Bhushan also writes in this context:

> In *Changiya Rukh*, the author documents the inner turmoil to which Dalits are reduced whenever they have to conceal their caste identity. We observe instances of how, sometimes, the Dalit people themselves internalise the view of caste-Hindu society and develop a feeling of inferiority. Simultaneously, Balbir reveals how he was so upset with his Hindu-sounding surname that he dropped it and instead took up the name of his birthplace Madhopur. By expunging one identity, and taking on another, he succeeds in rejecting an entire history of oppression. (Bhushan, 5)

Untouchability and caste discrimination is not the problem of a single village in present time also and these problems were rampant in Balbir Madhopuri's village also. The Jats of the village would not like the low caste people and they felt jealous for these people. Balbir Madhopuri depicts in this autobiography how the low caste people were bound to beating if they wear neat and clean clothes:

> If a low-caste boy were to come out in the lanes of the village, all bathed and dressed in new clothes, his hair combed, one or the other of the Jats sitting under the trees would get up and throw mud on him. If he protested, he was sure to be beaten up. If an untouchable appeared in the village dressed in the new clothes, he was certain to be given a beating on the pretext that the low castes were trying to become the equals of the higher castes; no one knew or could predict when such an incident would occur and where. (Madhopuri, 02)

The life of the Dalits in Madhopur was very bad. Dalits were reprimanded for the trifles as is narrated by Madhopuri in this autobiography. The poverty, hunger and the unemployment are the root causes for all this:

> 'Give these Chamar brats a shout and drive them off,' the Jat bhai of the *gurudwara* would say to whosoever stand near him and on the occasion of Sangurd—the first day of the Indian solar month—or Gurupurub—the birthdays of the Gurus, when he saw us standing on our toes and clinging to the bars of the window, as he distributed the Prasad to the congregation....We would all run away, in the flicker of an eye, trampling the jootis that lay strewn outside the *gurudwara*. But as soon as he turned the other way, we would be back at the window, exactly like we had been earlier. (Madhopuri, 11)

Dalit boys were considered just like animals and the upper caste people will call them names as is narrated in this autobiography. The Jats would use uncouth language for them and the Dalit boys had no any alternative but to tolerate it, "You can't control this litter. I myself will drive them away, the mother's —,' and he would jump up mouthing an obscenity, which we all completed in our minds." (12)

Hunger, poverty and unemployment make a man humiliated and disrespectful. The leather-workers of Madhopur were very poor and the Jat Bhai would scold them at *gurudwara* when it was their turn to get the Prasad. Madhopuri narrates this incidence in these words:

> 'Haven't I told you "again and again" you low castes, to sit patiently in one place!' Yet we contrived to stand stretching out our small hands cupped together, to receive the Prasad. He would throw it into our palms without bending, but we were sharp enough to catch it before it hit the ground. At times, a child did fail to grab it on time, and it would fall on the ground, driving him to the verge of tears. And before he could pick it up, Daboo the dog, lying in wait for a chance like this would gobble it up. (12)

The deplorable plights of the dalits and their hunger have been described in almost every Dalit male's autobiography. Sharankumar Limbale has to eat the grain of road side cow dung, roadside banana peels, and the flesh of dead animal. Laxman Gaikwad had to eat the roasted rats and pigs. Om Prakash Valmiki's *Joothan* and Laxman Gaikwad's *Uchalya: The Branded* are its perfect illustrations. The hunger drives the Dalit people thieves as they found no any other way to earn their livelihood. In *Joothan* they are forced to eat Joothan and in the *Changiya Rukh* Dalit boys feed on the Prasad of the *Gurudwara*:

> The only difference between the well-dressed boys and girls inside the *gurudwara* and me was that I had only one pair of shorts to cover my nakedness, and I was darker than them....The crack in the wall of our mud-house would widen, and the roof would almost collapse. Amidst all this, the innocent face of a young girl of my own age, who had come from her mother's paternal village, and who had been close to tears when the dog has eaten my share of Prasad, would flash before my mind's eyes. (12-13)

The grim pictures of penury can easily be seen in Dalit narratives. *Uchalya: The Branded* also has many such illustrations and Balbir Madhopuri also describes how Dalits were busy in their bread and butter that they were not able to give full attention on their kids. He writes, "My clothes were washed only on Sundays. I sat behind the wall of the trough and picked lice from the folds of my clothes.

My mother would scrub my feet vigorously, as she bathed me at the well, saying, "Just look at the layers of the dirt!"(24) Himanshu Sharma also observes in this context:

> The theme of deprivation, exploitation, poverty and social exclusion are dominant in *Changiya Rukh*. It is set in the village of Madhopur in Punjab and it tells how the life of the dalits is miserable and pitiable and they have to lead a life of humiliation, suppression and socio-religious discrimination. When there is a question on his caste or he is humiliated for his caste, he himself considers pruned or lopped. (Sharma, 220)

Dalits are expected to do all those tasks which cannot be performed by other caste people. In *Changiya Rukh* Khusia, Bhima and Piari carried carcasses because this work could be performed only by those people who were the lowest of the low. Such a charterer is Bhaka from Mulk Raj Anand's novel *Untouchable* who had to clean all kind of dirt. In this autobiography, Madhopuri narrates that leather-workers performed this act:

> They tied the hooves of the dead animal together and passed a hold through them, which they then carried across their shoulders, so that they could walk easily and comfortably. The animal hung upside down, and swung from side to side, its ears and neck shaking with every step. (25)

Sometimes four or five Dalit people would carry the larger carcass. This was a very obnoxious work that only these people could do. That was one of the several reasons that dalits were called untouchables by the upper caste people. Untouchability was prevalent in the village as is described in these words:

> It had often noticed that whenever we used the tap, any Jat child who used it after us would wash the tap thoroughly before drinking from it. This often made me wonder what was wrong with my hands that others had to wash a tap after I had touched it. Was it because I had touched the animals? They, too, had often twisted the tail of the same live animal! (25)

Dalits lived their lives like animals without any respect for them. They had to listen the words, "Which bitch gave birth to you? Stop, or I'll cut you into pieces!" (41) The upper caste people were the masters of their life because their economic status was good because they owned lands, "No one says anything to those who harass us day and night! Do we not belong here that they have made life so difficult for us? They scold and terrorise us all the time. Merely because they have land, they have become our god!" (32) Dr Ravi Bhushan writes about lives of dalits in these words:

> Madhopuri uses the metaphor of Changiya Rukh to describe the Dalits' lives, robbed from traditions and slashed and dwarfed by the society. This book is a reflection of Indian society, customs and her social order. The author has used his literary skill very nicely. Words are interwoven gently, prose reads like poetry. The events are described in a well manner and catch the imagination of reader. The humiliation of Dalits is a bolt on any civilised society but this humiliation does not look like, that sort of thing due to the response of Indian society. (Bhushan, 06)

In the conclusive remarks, it can be said that the life of the leather-workers in Madhopur village was very bad and they had to face multi-layered exploitation at different layers. Despite the efforts done by Indian governments and the Dalit activists, slight change have been noticed in the position of dalits in rural areas while in the cities affluent dalits also have to face a few problems. Khsushi Saroha observes that the worst position of dalits was found in Maharashtra and Punjab is the least affected state:

> At such instances, it seems like that the shared sorrow demolishes the barriers of language and geography between these unprivileged men. From my findings, all I can conclude is that while Maharashtra stands the lowest with regards to caste-based discrimination; and Uttar Pradesh if at all, does only slightly better; it is Punjab that has always given a comparatively habitable environment to the Dalits and continues to do so. (Saroha, 237)

Works Cited

Bhushan, Ravi. "Balbir Madhopuri's *Changiya Rukh* - A Critique of Dalit Identity and Politics." Edited by M.S. Thirumalai. 11.3. (2011): 1-8. Web.

Sharma, Himanshu. "Prejudicial Caste Hegemony in Balbir Madhopuri's *Changiya Rukh: Against the Night.*" *Indian Dalit Autobiographies:*

Marginalised Voices. Ed. Singh, Bijender. Authorspress, New Delhi, (2015): 219-225. Print.

Khushee Saroha. A Regional Study of Dalit Autobiographies from Maharashtra, Uttar Pradesh and Punjab. *The Criterion*: *An International Journal in English.* 5.2. (2014): 228-238. Web.

Singh, Shweta. "Representation of Dalit Women in Dalit Men's and Women's Autobiographies." *The Delhi University Journal of the Humanities and the Social Sciences*. 1.1. (2014): 39-47.

7

Peeping into the Lives of Dalit Women and Children: A Rereading of Kancha Ilaiah's *Why I am Not a Hindu*

Dr Narendra Kumar

Dalit literature is a record of pains, sufferings and anguishes. In other genres such as poetry, play or novel, there may be a fancy of imagination of a writer but in the autobiographies the narration is real and that's why Dalit autobiographies touch the heart of a reader. Many male autobiographies have been written in Marathi and other regional languages because many Dalit writers did not feel comfortable in other than their regional language due to their weak educational status. Moreover, those who were capable to write in other languages, they also did not want to shed their roots. That's why many Dalit autobiographies were written in regional languages and these were later translated into other languages. Though female Dalit writers have written their autobiographies but the clear, bitter and comparatively, the bitter narration and naked depiction has been done in male Dalit autobiographies because male writer did not felt much embarrassed to use the real language they had to listen from the people surrounded. Kancha Ilaiah is one of those writers who have narrated the pains of the *maalis* (gardeners) of his caste.

Kancha Ilaiah's autobiography *Why I am Not a Hindu* is a critique on the Hindutva philosophy. He has narrated in this autobiography how there are many traditions prevalent in the Hindus which he calls derogatory. He criticises the life-style and selfishness of the Brahmins. He compares that the condition of Brahmin women is not good and comparatively the women of his caste live an independent life.

The position of women in the Indian society is not hidden from anyone. They have to remain dependent on the men who are the bread-winners for the family. Dalit women are, in this way, exploited at their homes as well by the society. Omprakash Valmiki describes the poor plight of Dalit women. He narrates in his autobiography Joothan, "All the women of the village, young girls, older women, even the newly married brides would sit in the open space behind these homes at the edge of the pond to take a shit. Not just under the cover of darkness but even in daylight." (Valmiki, 01) But now with the advent of education, girls also have started getting education and in this way there is now responsibility of both home and earning to them. Dr Amandeep observes in this context:

> These women live life at three levels: society, family and self. At each level there seems to be a multiplicity of self-images. She considers herself powerless at the level of society because of her lack of education. At the same time, she is conscious of her equality to men at this level as a political or religious entity. (Amandeep, 329)

Kancha Ilaiah depicts in his autobiography that the people of his caste were so poor that even boys, girls and women had to do the domestic chores or they had to work in the fields. There was no any focus on the education of children. Dalit children faced the problem of untouchability and humiliation in schools. The upper caste teachers looked down upon them and they cleaned the school premises from Dalit children. Such teachers were afraid that if Dalit children would get education, they might dominate over them. Jitan Ram Manjhi, a politician and 23rd Chief minister of Bihar, said about the caste system in India:

> The caste formed the basis for a high degree of polarisation in access to knowledge and means of production....The instrument used for perpetuation of socio-economic differentials was the separation of work from knowledge and power. The working class was denied the access to education as it was considered a privilege of few upper castes. The denial of education was essential to prevent them from acquiring rights in productive assets..." (Manjhi n. pag.)

It was the thinking of even teachers that they did not want Dalit children to get education and Dalit children had to face many problems in getting their education. Bama, Urmila Pawar, Kumud Pawde, P. Sivakami etc. Dalit women autobiographers faced many problems in their life. Thus, dalit women have always been kept under pressure so that they may not get power and reign over the upper caste people. Dr S.D. Sargar writes in this context:

> Dalits formed the lower strata in Indian social structure. Hence, they were denied each and every opportunity by the upper caste Hindus. All the efforts of Dalits for getting education were strongly and unanimously opposed by the upper castes for social and political reasons. The upper castes were afraid that if the lower castes are allowed to get education, they will ask for their share in power. (Sargar, 1-2)

Kancha narrates that he was forced to clean the school. He was not the only student who faced this problem. Omprakash Valmiki's teacher also ordered him to clean the school and punished him. There were different roles assigned to the boys and girls of their caste. There was training for the boys and girls separately. The boys had to do their ancestral works of sheep grazing and they were trained for many things related to sheep. Kancha writes:

> I was introduced to the specific language of sheep and sheep-rearing tasks. I was taught the different names of the sheep—*bolli gorre, pulla gorre, nalla gorre,* and so on. I learnt about the diseases that the sheep were afflicted with, how a delivery should be 'midwifed', how young ones should be handled, which was the best green grass for rearing the sheep. Goats required special treatment as they were to be fed with tree leaves (goats do not eat grass). (03)

The boys of his community had to help their parents in some works. They had to shear the wool from the sheep and this task seemed to be very difficult to them. Kancha Ilaiah narrates about this difficult task:

> One of the most difficult and expert tasks was shearing the wool from the sheep's body. The scissors had to be handled with such care that they cut close but did not cut the skin of the sheep.

> All this was part of the expertise of a sheep-rearer, and we were carefully educated in all these tasks. (03)

Likewise girls were also trained in many domestic chores. They had to work in the fields. Their mothers would take them in the fields and trained them in the field related activities. They had to bear the burden of bringing up their younger brothers and sisters and cooking was also handled by them:

> The elder girls were taught, even as they turned three, how to handle a younger brother or sister. Holding a three-month-old baby requires skill and care, more so when the arms are those of a three-year-old girl....By the age of twelve or thirteen (by the time she has reached puberty) a Kurumaa girl is supposed to know the basics of cooking. She begins with lighting the hearth and learning to handle it. (03-04)

Kancha tells that Dalit children were much frank sexual activities also. Such things were common in their caste and most of the learning in this regard was done in the fields. Even the women also had extra-marital relationships but their relationships become public very soon. Even the children also knew about such affairs. He writes that such things were very rare in the Hindu families but for their community it was a very common discussion:

> If any Dalitbahujan woman has a relationship with a man who is not her husband, the relationship does not remain a secret. The entire *waada* discusses it. Even the children of that family come to know about it. Particularly when the father and mother quarrel, every aspect of life becomes public. No quarrel hides inside the house. For the children the house is a place of pleasure and of pain but it is all in the open. Male children learn about women and about sex in the company of their friends, in the cattle-rearing grounds or sheep-feeding fields. All kind of sexual trials take place in the fields. (05)

The people of Ilaiah's caste lived a carefree life and they were not bounded for anything. They always lived in the present. Kancha writes that they just believed in their present birth and there was no any place for the sins, charity, rebirth, hell or heaven. Thus, this world was a battle of actions for them, "But there is no *swarga* (heaven) and there is no *naraka* (hell). All the dead live together somewhere in the skies." (07) Dalit children were innocent and they had to know the tyranny of the casteism when they were admitted in the school. Kancha Ilaiah commends a few things about his caste that widows lived a respectful life in his caste, "I remember many young widows in my village who were the team leaders of agrarian operations as they were the most respected persons" (8) while in Hindus widows had to burn in the pyre with their deceased husbands or they had to live a very ordinary life without any charm and taste. Kancha feels proud that he is born in such a community where widows are not burnt alive like Hindus do. He writes, "Similarly, when we read that Hindu women ought to die along with their dead husbands I was extremely happy that our women do not have to die like that. I was so glad that we do not belong to such a religion because if suddenly my father were to die my mother would not have to die also. If she so desired she could get me a stepfather." (16) In Hindu families, child marriage was prevalent as an evil and after the death of a married man, his wife was either burnt or she had to wear white clothes. Such women had to live a very austere life. In Dalit families, women would easily get divorced if they did not feel contended in their in-laws' home, "Seeking divorce from an irresponsible husband is as much a sanctioned social act as performing marriages. In my childhood, when I read about Savithri struggling against the death of her husband, because otherwise she would become a widow, I was very happy that our women do not have to struggle like her." (16) There was discrimination in the village on the name of caste and Dalit children were considered untouchables and ugly. The upper caste children and the lower caste children lived different lives:

> Children are trained not to get involved in production-related tasks, which Brahmins condemn as 'Sudra' tasks. Similarly their friendship with Dalitbahujan children is censured. 'Upper' castes speak of Dalitbahujans as 'ugly'. 'Sudra' is an abusive word; 'Chandala' is a much more abusive word. 'Upper' caste children are taught to live differently from Dalitbahujan children, just as they are taught to despise and dismiss them. (09)

Dalit children and the upper caste children had a different life-style. In Dalit families there was much open environment but for the

Hindus sex was a private matter and it was never discussed in their families.

> Discussion of sexual behaviour is a taboo in Hindu families. Mothers are not supposed to talk to daughters about their sexual experiences. The father's atrocities against the mother cannot be discussed in Brahmin or Baniya families. But this is not so in our families. The father abuses the mother right in front of the children and the mother will pay back in the same coin then and there. The children are a witness to all that. In Hindu families the father can abuse the mother, but the mother is not supposed to retort. (09)

It is generally seen in some villages of India that women are kept under pressure and they are not allowed to perform the activities outside their houses. They just do the work of cooking, cleansing and other chores which can be performed only at homes. Jayanta Banerjee writes about Dalit women, "Doubly oppressed as a Dalit and a woman in Dalit patriarchal society, the women find a psychological defence-mechanism in taking recourse to 'possessions' by Gods, Goddesses and evil spirit. The sturdy father-in-law, drunkard husband and venom spitting mother-in-law all virtually come and fall under the feet of a possessed woman." (Banerjee, 337) Kancha tells that Hindu women lived almost such kind of life. He tells that Dalit women had a life of liberty and they were not as restricted as Hindu women. Dalit women drank and smoke but nobody thought negatively about them. These women could do what they liked for them. Kancha Ilaiah narrates it in these words:

> An ideal woman in a Hindu text is one who does not eat and drink in the presence of older women and men of all ages. A woman is not supposed to smoke and drink even if the man is a chain-smoker and the worst drunkard. But in our homes no one talks badly about a woman who smokes or has a drink. All our women drink toddy or liquor along with our men. Our women smoke *chuttaas* (cigars made with leaves and tobacco) at home and in the fields. They try to be at least notionally equal to men in all respects. (18)

Works Cited

Banerjee, Jayanta. Tracing the Fragments of Unwritten History: Indian Dalit Personal Narratives in the Light of Folklore and Indigenous Culture. *Research Journal of English Language and Literature (RJELAL) A Peer Reviewed (Refereed) International Journal* http://www.rjelal.com. 3.2.2015.:331-340.

Ilaiah, Kancha. *Why I am not a Hindu: A Sudra Critique of Hindutva Philosophy, Culture and Political Economy.* Kolkata:Samya, 2012. Print.

Manjhi, R. *Education of Dalits: Beyond Literacy.* www.google.co.in

Amandeep. "Feminist Atrocity in Minoritized Literature." *International Journal of Language, Literature and Humanity.* Volume II, Issue III, July 2014. 328-335.

Valmiki, Omprakash. *Jhoothan: A Dalit's Life*. Kolkata: Samya, 2003. Print.

Sargar, S.D. "Dalit Autobiography and Education: An Analytical Study." *The Criterion: An International Journal in English*. 2.4. (2011):1-8.

8

When the Dumb Learn to Speak: (Re)-Reading Four Dalit Autobiographical Excerpts Recognising the 'Alternative Narrative' of Protest through (Re)-Defining the 'Own' Identity

RAMANUJ MAHATO

> "And it is as important for Dalits to tell their stories as it has been for colonised people to write their own histories"
>
> – Arundhati Roy (Anand 2003: 16-17)

Having strong and ponderous support for the backward section of society Roy expresses her angst upon Indian caste system where equality is supposed to decline due to the lack of 'own histories' that preserve the identity of the indigenous particularly marginalised section. Certainly the backward communities have their own identity and cultural ethos which are pertinently preserved by their 'own histories' representing their bonafide tale of struggle/*sangram* against the dominantly repressive authority. As Post-coloniality allows a space "for the colonised to write their own histories" (Anand, 2003: 16-17). Dalit movement in post-independence India also unleashes a new dimension and interpretation of Indian caste-bound society where upper caste dominates the lower and 'untouchable' castes and employs the epistemic domination by partial and hierarchal narratives. Hence things fall apart and the centre of grand narrative cannot hold; consequently those 'untouchables' discover the means 'strategic narrative' to protest, to challenge, to create a scope for alternative voice of micro-narratives and understanding the 'history from dalit'. Thus, the agitations and the stories of dalit rebellions are reflected though dalit autobiographies though their own language which is free from Brahmin hegemony of 'Vedas' and mainstream historiography. Arjun Dangle writes about dalit autobiographies:

> In these autobiographies, relating to different periods of time and set in different levels of society, we see varying facets of dalit movement, the struggle for survival, the emotional universe of dalit life; the man-woman relationship; the experiencing of humiliation and atrocities; at times, abject submission, at other times, rebellion. (Dangle, 1992: *Introduction* ix)

Strengthening the theme of humiliation, exploitation and submission, dalit autobiographies also acutely focus the stories of rebellions and subversion of existing narratives through multi-layered meta-narratives. Though the concept of autobiography is basically associated with the depiction of self-experiences of the author in term of his own recreation as well as leisure or personal events recollected in tranquillity but dalit autobiography adds special dimension by visualising the sufferings of dalit world and documenting the socio-political history of caste-centric India. Moreover the role of autobiography differs while it penetrates deeper corroborating the historical context of India and creates a new perspective of "dalit-graphy" voicing 'own' identity of the community and "dalit ecriture". (Singh, 2015: 137)

Exploring the insight of dalit sufferings, this paper seeks the authentic voice of dalit community and true picture of contemporary India under the veil of individual story of humiliation and exploitation. Four significant autobiographical excerpts/ dalit prose are selected to analyse the acuteness of trauma in dalit life – Shankararo Kharat's "A Corpse in the Well", Daya Pawar's "We are Kings!", Sharankumar Limbale's "The Bastard" and P.E. Sonkamble's "This too Shall Pass". Those dalit narratives assert the real and horrendous history of dalit society which challenges the mainstream autobiographical cannon and prevailing oppressive discourses. The stories of their personal life give voice to the dumb and offer strength to resist the violence and insult of dominant upper caste; those stories simply assert that stories never die rather turn the individual voice as a history of the community and culminating it, Om Prakash Valmiki says, as an "inspiration to our future generation" (Mukherji, 2003: xxviii). But dalit writings by other non-dalit writers sometimes fail to understand the intensity of their trauma and often ignore the acuteness of dalit humiliation and lacks 'dalit point of view' of 'self-discovery'. Thus, connecting the true cord of dalit world those autobiographical excerpts represent and validate the 'alternative' discourse of 'dalit-graphy' to confront the regime of non-dalit oppressive discourse. In many literary texts dalit exploitations cover the main theme but they remain mere a story of untold voice of pathos instead of unlocking their proclamation for justice, for identity, for equal rights. In fact 'dalit-graphy' reveals the story of individual as well as social subjugation and naturally pathos turn into protest against the physical and psychological domination.

To analyse Shankhararo Kharat's "A corpse in the Well", an excerpt from the complete autobiography *Taral Antaral*, the contemporary dalit history of Mahar community gets unlocked and connects the narrater's own miserable plight with the painstaking glimpses of marginalised Mahar community. Centring on narrator's personal life in connection with his Anna (father), the story projects the glimpses of oppressions, humiliation and sufferings. But the complexity of story is perceptible when oppression is manufactured in the society by the dominant system of authority which is overt in nature – a constable being the agent of that exploiting system executes oppressive order to Anna to take out the dead body from the well, "What are you waiting for, Mahar? Jump in." (Dangle, 1994:3) – but another structured violence is operated by caste-dogmatism and untouchability which has strong and deep root in India that is basically covert in nature but it contaminates the social inequality and results naturally physical violence. Anna being an untouchable of Mahar community accomplishes his duty to guard the corpse but he is not allowed to touch the body of a stranger of upper community. As M.L. Shahare writes up, "The Mahar also known as Veskars, meaning watchman" (Shahare, 1988: 3) is basically involved as night guard. Hence Anna denies to fetch the dead body from the well and speaks out, "How can we touch it? What would the heirs of this corpse have to say?…'The heirs will say', 'Where we dead, that you touched our kinsman's corpse?'" (Dangle, 1994:3). This confirms the resistance of Anna to pursue the order of higher hierarchy. Though he finally submits himself to the harsh order of the constable but her son (narrator) again arises as a voice of protest. The narrator becomes castigated as little 'worm' and 'bastard' but he challenges the dominant discourse of oppression by his own alternative discourse of slang words to curse the constable. Those unarticulated, suppressed curse assert their existence as a significant entity of the society. Kharat not only criticises the orthodox caste system and but also the dominant authority and systematic rule which preserve the claustrophobic caste hierarchy. The story appears as a story of 'self discovery' which exposes Mahar is alien at its own home and 'self criticism' is another perspective which genuinely seeks to explore the root of slavery of Mahar community. In fact, the narrator learns to speak, to curse, to challenge and to marginalise the mainstream discourse by dismantling the social and literary cannon. But the struggle of a dalit is for justice that has motivated to criticise even dalit's own tradition and hereditary servitude. While in this story the narrator comes to help Anna and urges to eat '*bhakri*', Anna reveals the truth "Once you're saddled with the village duty, you'll be stuck with it for life! That's the tradition! That's our doom!" (Dangle, 1994: 2) In fact, Kharat accepts that fact that a dalit is 'dalit' in every aspect because of poverty and humiliation and dalit is bound to remain in the periphery until social and economic consciousness awakens about their own identity. Though in several contexts dalit autobiography is supposed by many that "there is little connection between Literature and increasing voice of the Mahars" (Paswan, Sanjay and Pramanshi Jaideva, 2002: 17-18) but it seeks to explore a tentative narrative that would not imitate strictly any western literary form rather penetrate the folk tradition of Indian life by denoting a study of 'alternative' parallel historiography.

The extensive research on Daya Pawar's "We are Kings!" as a significant autobiographical excerpt from *Baluta* marks an exquisite combination of individual protest and social documentation and overlaps the sufferings and pride with a strange taste of alternative discourse challenging the mainstream historical approach.

'*Dalitiya Sahitya*', as Professor Aravind Malagatti defined and ramified, projects 'own identity' of dalit community with their exhaustive detail in many aspects like folk culture, mythical anecdotes and oppressed pride. In Pawar's work "a lamenting cry for liberation breaks out" (Paswan, Sanjay and Pramanshi Jaideva, 106: 2002) and makes a conspicuous study of the Mahar-dom which is 'imprinted' in his soul as Pawar says, "It lingers with me forever." (Dangle, 1994: 13) Here dejected and cursed tradition of Mahar life is glorified in great extent; and the granting of fifty-two rights emphasises their "glorious traditions" (Dangle, 1994: 14) as an evidence of alternative historiography. Emerging as a story of protest, "We are kings!" asserts the bold and defiant attitude of Mahar people who have endeavoured to create their own history of 'strategic narrative'.

> There is a story about a village where the Mahars, tired of their ill-treatment, set out to leave for ever. The villagers stopped their Mahars at the boundary, mollified them and brought them back with all due honour.
>
> The villagers probably feared that if there no Mahars in the village, there would be some great calamity. That was the incident. So the Mahars and the villagers never let their mutual tensions go to a snapping point (Dangle, 1994: 16).

Mahars have their own myth of greatness and honesty confirming the superiority of their caste and creed; the story of a young man who pleases the king with his loyalty and trustworthy attitude resulting fifty-two rights which is "a deed of gift...handed down for generations, and everyone had great pride in this tradition" (Dangle, 1994: 13). Pawar here reinforces the significance of Mahar community that challenges the dominant historiography and subverts the existing myths by creating their own historical myth:

> The king has a young and beautiful daughter who has to be escorted to Delhi. In those days there was a thick jungle on the way, and no vehicles. This Mahar, too, is young and he is robust. After he has left the king's daughter at her destination and returned, a suspicion is voiced against him in the durbar. The charge is that he has probably raped the girl on the way. Now, the Mahar has left a little wooden box with the king before his

> departure, saying, 'It is something valuable of mine; return it when I come back.' The young Mahar now asks for the little box to be opened. In it is his penis, cut off before he went. The king is pleased with his loyalty, and tells the young man, 'Ask for whatever you want.' (Dangle, 1994: 14).

In this excerpt "a little wooden box" and "penis, cut off..." (Dangle, 1994: 14) emblematises the power relation between the king and Mahar community. Another story of subversion is revealed through the exploitation of an old widow who gave patti (taxes) to the Brahmin clerk but he tactfully accused her in the crime of embezzling the village patti; and it gives a metaphorical implication about Mahars' challenge to the Brahmin phallocentric ideology. Pawar expresses another reality that various caste conflicts between Mahar and villagers, Mahar and the Chamar household reflect the contemporary picture of Indian caste war. Contemplating the caste conflict, Pawar draws the inner reality that Indian caste hierarchy employs complex power relation as Chamar household often gets marginalised by Mahar community unfixing the existing dominance theory – that upper caste only dominates the lower – and seeks to explore another face of Mahar life as described "the whole village was terrified of them." (Dangle, 1994: 16) The use of "Soma Mahar", a variety of poison, is another face of their defiant identity and it is used to fight back against the oppressor. Finally, the *mamlatdar* (District official) who was once from Mahar community is discovered as a converted Christian. His appearance as a significant representative in the Maharwada strengthens the struggle/ *sangram* of Mahar people for justice and social recognition. In fact, the story proclaims 'Mahar is the king' of their own will and deed:

> We are kings!
> Kings of what?
> Kings of ourselves! (Dangle, 1994: 17)

Another significant autobiographical excerpt "Bastard" from Sharankumar Limbale's *Akkarmashi*, is true representation of dalit life with deep repulsion and sorrow and it encapsulates dichotomy of society that dalit women though is untouchable, forced to be fulfilled the lust of upper caste as Limbale says, " A man can chew up and spit out as many wads of betel as he likes. If a woman does so, it only stains her honour. Once you've had her, she's spoilt fruit. (Dangle, 1994: 49) Hence it is connected with the ghettoisation of dalit community and the process of isolation marks alienated identity confirming their physical, psychological and political deprivation. In the social backdrop of 1970s and 1980s, Lambale depicts the sordid reality of caste segregation by the exploitation of Mahar community in Maharashtra. The story of "Bastard" which in Dangle's words, "a severe jolt is given to values concerning relations between men and women, and the family structure" (Dangle, 1994: *Introduction* ix) acutely portrays the childhood experiences of the narrator and reveals the subtle aspects of alternative historiography which has a unique ability, according to Limbale "to raise the reader's consciousness of fundamental values like equality, freedom, justice and fraternity." (Limbale, 2010: 120). Here his identity as an *'Akkarmashi'*, which in Marathi means 'impure of blood' is delineated with sarcastic note that how he is turned into a abandoned child. Being born of a high caste (Patil) father and low caste (Mahar) mother, Limbale expresses painful account of his life that his identity as an illegitimate or fatherless child is a matter of great shocking and repulsion to him:

> Why did my mother say yes to the rape which brought me into the world? Why did she put up with the fruit of this illegitimate intercourse for nine months and nine days and allow me to grow in the foetus? Why did she allow this bitter embryo to grow? How many eyes must have humiliated her because they considered her a whore? Did anyone distribute sweets to celebrate my birth? Did anyone admire me affectionately? Did anyone celebrate my naming ceremony? Which family would claim me as its descendants? Whose son am I, really? (Limbale, 2003:36)

Limbale is aggressive against the power game of upper caste landlords and his voice having a deep cry for justice reveals his *antasphot*:

> After his birth the mansions of the Patil community must have become tense. His first breath must have threatened the morality of the world. With is first cry at birth, milk must have splashed from the breast of every Kunti. (Limbale, 2003:36)

Through the reference of Kunti, he might have hinted the oppressed identity of dalit women and echoes Indian myth of Kunti and her illegitimate son, Karna. Here Limbale shows the hybrid nature of his text combining non-dalit and dalit ethos finding ponderous analogy in perspective of 'forced mother' and 'illegitimate and abandoned child' as Limbale says, "I was growing up fatherless as Karna throughout the Mahabharata."(Dangle, 1994:50) Every iterant expression tells itself the stories of sufferings, deprival and illegitimacy. Concerning his own identity, he re-defines universal predicament of identity crisis and contextualises the women sufferings. His story finds an alternative discourse of narrative even within every mainstream discourse of the text and all stories of marginalisation achieve equal height of significance in term of 'subaltern' perspective. Limbale's micro-narrative penetrates the cultural practises of Mahar community in detail and their authentic lifestyle. The usual food habit of *bhakri* and strong attachment to alcoholic intoxication was granted as regular and common matter for them being considered for their tea. The isolated self of Limbale gives authentic portrayal of dilemmatic identity of a dalit 'bastard' whose oppressed self becomes analogous to the mythical figure Jarasandha, from the epic Mahabharata:

> Am I a caste-Hindu? But my mother is an untouchable. Am I an Untouchable? But my father is a caste-Hindu. I have been tossed apart like Jarasandha – half within society and half outside. Who am I? (Dangle, 1994: 51)

In short, the 'excommunicated' self represents the ghettoisation of the entire Mahar community through alienating the peripheral characters by Brahminic hegemony and two halves of dilemmatic minds are kept in such disharmony that society would not absorb the differences. Whereas 'history from dalit' is concerned as stepping stone, Limbale directs his alternative study by emphasising 'myth from dalit' which not only subverts the mainstream historiography but also the cannon of mythical structure. He creates own myth, breaks traditional myth and unauthenticates '*Puran*' myth challenging the regime of mainstream discourse/ narrative. Inculcating the marginal, oppressed characters like Karna, Jarasandha, Sita, Kunti from Indian mythical tales, Limbale seeks to explore a new narrative structure which is strategic, challenging and convincing to deconstruct the centre; the impurity challenges the pure and established authentic structure falls apart. In this context P. Rajkumar says:

> Re-mythologisation is a domain of specific meaning making for the Dalits. Through this they tactfully contest the hegemonic outlook of the dominant castes. (Rajkumar, 2010:123)

Revealing another level of dalit agonies, P.E. Sonkamble's "This too Shall Pass" is a juggernaut dalit text excerpt from *Athawanitll Pakshi* (Marathi autobiography) exposes an another story of dalit exploitation concerning the domestic violence within the dalit community. The narrator expresses his individual story of traumatic experiences that represent the intra violence and patriarchal domination operated in the society. The narrator's personal relationship with two brothers-in-law, Dhondiba and Kishan are depicted to highlight the male-dominated culture of the society. Dhondiba and Kishan both would torture their wives and become a menacing symbol of patriarchal culture; and their harsh and relentless nature even to the little child (narrator) would prove illiteracy and male jingoism. In fact, dalit exploitation is marked in every sphere of society where many discourses are generated to marginalise dalit identity as the narrator says, "The people there had a bad habit." (Dangle, 65:1994). The character of Kishan is emblematic to suggest the hypocrisy within dalit; the behaviour of Kishan shows his flattery to upper caste and repulsion to poor people. Kishan is metaphorically among those dalits who inflicts torture upon marginal oppressed people and makes a dalit more dalit:

> Brother-in-law only chanted *bharuds* wherever he went. He did not eat meat and he wore the sacred thread round his neck. He was all puffed up with pride about it, and would rarely speak to poor people. He felt he had reached the sky. But he forgot where he had come from. (Dangle, 1994: 65)

Under the veil of personal experiences, Sonkamble expresses his anxiety over dalit sufferings, oppression in macro-level which is often overlooked and ignored. Thus, domestic dalit disgrace is disclosed to convey the actuality of untold truths. As Arjun Dangle writes up that this story is about "the wounded psyche of a young boy from a backward area such as Marathwada" (Dangle, 1994: *Introduction* ix).

Moreover dalit autobiographies representing the voice of protest of dalit culture portray the miserable plight and traumatic experiences of dalit people in wide range of thinking. Though in several aspects those autobiographies are often granted as stories of dalit consciousness in term of pity or sympathetic observation; sometimes dalit confrontation of structural as well as physical violence reflects dalit politics. But the significance of dalit autobiographies lies in authentic portrayal of dalit oppression in their 'own' point of view and unchains oniony layers of violence as 'traumatic narrative' of dalit indigenous confirming the voice of rebellion. These selected autobiographical excerpts reveal sufferings under hidden structure in various contexts – the violence operated by social hierarchy both in caste and gender perspective. While Shankhararo Kharat's "A corpse in the Well" manifests caste conflicts and exploiting social order, Daya Pawar's "We are Kings!" shows the power politics and economic exploitation by burdening the taxes; in other hand "Bastard" by Sharankumar Limbale, discusses the search for dalit identity of an 'Jarasandhaian' self and finally P.E. Sonkamble's "This too Shall Pass" unlocks a new definition of dalit disgrace and humiliation in term of domestic violence and dalit patriarchal practices. Re-defining their 'own' identity all these four excerpts in Dangle's words, being the entire 'saga of dalit social history', "convey the 'differentness' of Dalit literature. How deep a chasm there is between prose of mainstream Marathi literature and that of Dalit literature! We immediately recognise that the language experiences and heroes of Dalit literature are totally different." (Dangle, 1994: *Introduction* viii-ix) In fact, it weaves the cobweb of dalit 'strategic/ alternative narrative' culling thorns of traumatic thoughts and experiences and challenges the empire of mainstream historiography and hegemonic discourse of non-dalit 'Other'. Thus, the essence of the paper is explicit from the following words:

Picking through the Vedas
His top-knot well-oiled with ghee,
My Brahmin teacher tells me,

'You idiot, use the language correctly!'
Now I ask you,
Which language should I speak?

— Arun Lamble; Trans. Priya Adarkar.
(Paswan, Sanjay and Pramanshi Jaideva, 2002: 89)

Work Cited

Anand, S. *Touchable Tales: Publishing and Reading Dalit Literature*. Chennai: Navayana Publishing. 2003. Print.

Dangle, A. *Poisoned Bread: Translations from Modern Marathi Dalit Literature*. Bombay: Orient Longman. 1992. Print.

————. *A Corpse in the Well: Translations from Modern Marathi Dalit Autobiographies*. Hyderabad: Disha Books. 1994. Print.

Limbale, Sharankumar. *Towards an Aesthetics of Dalit Literature: History, Controversies and Considerations*. Tr. and Ed. Alok Mukherjee. New Delhi: Orient Blackswan Private Limited. 2010. Print.

Limbale, Sharan Kumar. *The Outcaste: Akkarmashi*. Tran. Santosh Bhoomkar. New Delhi: Oxford University Press. 2003. Print.

Mukherji, Arun Prabha. Om Prakash Valmiki's *Joothan: A Dalit's Life*. Kolkata: Samya, 2003. Print.

Paswan, Sanjay and Pramanshi Jaideva (eds.). *Encyclopaedia of Dalits in India: Literature*. Vol.11. Delhi: Kalpaz Publication, 2002. Print.

Pawar, Daya. *Baluta*: Tran. Jerry Pinto. New Delhi: Speaking Tiger Publishing. 2015. Print.

Rajkumar, Penial. *Dalit Theology and Dalit Liberation: Problems, Paradigms and Possibilities*. UK & USA: Ashgate Publishing Limited. 2010. E-Text.

Singh, Bijender. *Indian Dalit Autobiographies: Marginalised Voices*. New Delhi: Authorspress. 2015. Print.

9

Problems of Maali Caste in Aravind Malagatti's Autobiography *Government Brahmana*

KUSUM KANGER

Dalits have to undergo all kind of pains, agonies, discriminations, humiliations etc. and many people bear this insult silently but some people raise their voice against it. There are some social activists and writers who don't let their sufferings their own, they publicise them and thus, their problems become the problems of the society. Many Dalit writers have done this work. They have narrated all the problems what they have faced in their homes and at the hands of the society. Aravind Malagatti is one of those talented Dalit writers who have depicted all the pains of his family and community in his autobiography *Government Brahmana*. This autobiography was originally written in Kannada but it was translated into English by Dharani Devi Malagatti, Janet Vucinich and N. Subramanya. This autobiography records Malagatti's experiences of his childhood and youth days. Aravind was born in a *maali* caste which work is generally gardening.

Aravind Malagatti is renowned writer, teacher, researcher and social activist. He is a much familiar name in Kannada literature and he has used his pen to attack on the cruel clutches of casteism. He has worked against caste discrimination in Karnataka. Presently, he is a Professor of Kannada in Kuvempu Institute of Kannada Studies in the University of Mysore. Malagatti has narrated the pains of his community in his autobiography. R. Janani observes about Malagatti's community:

> Malagatti belonged to the Maali community, and he is referred to by the upper caste people only by the name of his community. Wherever he went he couldn't reveal his real identity. To his white-collared friends, if he revealed his identity, they would not understand, but would only be bewildered by him. If he had to go to his old friends as a white-collared gentleman, they would not accept him as before. (Janani, 179)

In this autobiography *Government Brahmana* the writer has worked on the development of the self and identity. A Dalit, in spite of good economic status and good education, remains a Dalit or untouchable in the eyes of the upper caste people. Aravind Malagatti narrates in this autobiography how Indian government is constantly trying to improve the conditions of dalits by reserving them in getting education and job as well. By these crutches, they reach to higher positions. They attain this status due to the help of the government that's why the title of this autobiography *Government Brahmana* suits it aptly. Thus, the term Government Brahmana has been written for those dalits who have the privileges of reservations, scholarships, welfare plans and jobs. S. Johny writes in this context:

> The title *Government Brahmana* might be intriguing to those who are familiar with Indian caste system outwardly. It might look like an irony. In ancient texts of Sanatana Dharma, 'Brahmins' are entitled to occupy the top rung in caste-based hierarchy. The autobiography of a Dalit activist, entitled *Government Brahmana* seems strange as Dalits were branded as untouchables by the same set of texts that celebrate Brahminhood. Thus, the very title of the work provides the reader with a curious connotation. (Johny, 52-53)

Thus, it is clear that dalits belonging to Karnataka states were contemptuously called government brahmanas. To know about the real position, many upper caste people started feeling jealous of them and they tried to humiliate them by calling them government brahmanas.

In the autobiography *Government Brahmanas*, Aravind Malagatti makes it clear that he does not want to present himself as a mahatma. He opens this autobiography with these words, "First let me make it very clear, I do not have any illusions of becoming a mahatma by presenting these few pages of my life story" (1) In this autobiography readers find that his autobiography is much different from Mahatma Gandhi's *My Experiments with Truth* because he has tries to narrate the problems of his caste in this autobiography. Malagatti says:

> You may have seen Aravind Malagatti as a white-clad, thoroughbred gentleman. To those of you who have seen him or would like to see him so, these words may come as surprise. Some of you may raise eye brows; while some others may smirk some may even view the words with suspicion. I am certain that the cause for these reactions is the Aravind Malagatti who stands in front of you as you read. But you have not seen this Maali (the nickname my family and neighbours employ to tease me) as a child. In fact, a few friends who studied with Maali now maintain a distance and address him as 'ri'. No matter how much he attempts to get close, they shy away from him. They no longer talk to Maali or tease him like before. Instead, they move farther and farther away. Reason: they are under the illusion he is a 'big man' now. (1)

The real agony of casteism can be better told only by a Dalit. Dr Jai Prakash Kardam writes in this context, "Only ash knows the experience of burning." Aravind Malagatti also has faced many problems due to his low caste and he narrates the problems of identity crisis of dalits. Dwaipayan Mitra writes in this context, Aravind Malagatti's *Government Brahmana* charts the besmirched identity of a dalit wallowing under the nerve crushing tyranny of caste hegemony. (114)

Dalits, of any caste or community, have to face the bitter forms of casteism. Malagatti narrates in his autobiography that people of their community had to live segregated in his village. Omprakash Valmiki, another Dalit autobiographer, also narrates in his autobiography *Joothan: A Dalit's Life* that they also had to live separately in their village because they belonged to a low caste, Valmiki.

> Our house was adjacent to Chandrabhan Taga's gher or cowshed. Next to it lived the families of Muslim weavers. Right in front of Chandrabhan Taga's gher was a little johri, a pond which was created as a partition of between the Chuhra's dwellings and the Village. (Valmiki, 1)

Like Omprakash Valmiki, Maalis of Malagatti's caste were not the part of creative contribution to society. They were very poor people of the village and they were treated as servants and their requirement was felt only for some rituals of the village. When somebody from the high caste died in the village and his corpse was taken to the graveyard; some coins were thrown on the way and only the lower caste people would grab these coins and the upper caste people did not even touch them. Malagatti asks a question, "If there were no dalits what worth would their coins have?" (1) The upper caste people also wanted dalits to show their supremacy over them.

Education has always been a problem for Dalit children. Malagatti faced many problems in the school. The children of his caste were not allowed to sit on the desks and they had to sit on the floor. It was a very difficult time for him; so he refused to attend the school but somehow he was soothed by his grandmother by providing him a new jute sack to sit in his school. He was badly punished in the school. He had to hang on the walls and the teacher also punished him with a cane. He was beaten black and blue as if he had done some serious crime. Even the language of the teacher was very condemnable. His teacher said to him, "Look at the buttocks of this bastard, bulging like drums after gobbling the school uppit" (12). Thus, the use of such kind of abusive language is really disgusting. The teacher blames him that he is growing fat from the free meals offered by government for the economically backward students of the school. The teacher was feeling jealous at the compassionate attitude of the government for the poor Dalit students. That's why Aravind was punished in the school because upper caste Hindu teachers did not like Dalit children in the school enjoying the free benefits. The teachers would punish Dalit students because they did not sweep the classrooms before morning assembly. Malagatti writes:

> Do you know what the offences were that deserved such severe punishments? Not that we did not do our homework; nor were

> we untidy. The reason was that we skipped sweeping the class room sometimes before the morning prayers at school. It was mandatory that we, friends from the lane, should come early to the school and sweep it fully! (14)

The names of the students were written on the blackboards previous day and then they become the target of double humiliation — one day before sweeping and the day of sweeping. Aravind Malagatti had to face humiliation by other students. His name Aravind Malagatti had resemblances with Hindu names. 'Aravind' means 'lotus' and 'Malagatti' stands for 'a pilgrimage centre' and such names were strictly prohibited for dalits that's why he is called with a different misspelt name 'Mala Katti.' In Kannada the word 'Katti' means 'donkey or ass.' (15) Malagatti had to bear this insult for months. One day he thought to correct the misspelt name written on the board. He reached to correct misspelt word of the blackboard. Malagatti says:

> I do not know where our great teacher was hiding till then. He entered the classroom and pulled out the cane, which was kept on a wooden peg on the wall. I started shivering at the very sight of it. I felt as if all my strength was leaving me. Before I could get down and justify my act, saying, 'They have written "katti"...', he started beating me. (16)

The appalling attitude of the Hindus is clearly depicted in this autobiography. His teacher deforms his name from Gatti to Katti. His teacher was not satisfied with the excuse. He malevolently said, "So what if it is written "Katti" were you trying to make it gatti"? The bastard has just learnt to write and he already wants to correct what is written. A Katti is a Katti any way" (16). Time rolled by and Aravind Malagatti completed his Ph.D. but the caste did not leave him even after it. The people of the high caste did not stop commenting on his caste. He writes, "What else is there? Whatever is the facility given to people below the belt, they won't change." (4) There was other kind of pressure on Aravind. He often wore good dress but upper caste people would suggest him to wear such clothes which suit a Dalit but he refuted it saying:

> You could be like them too, why aren't you? Today you ask me this. Tomorrow you may as well ask, "Why don't you wear a

langta like Gandhiji?" I don't aspire to wear a langta and be called a mahatma. I am an ordinary person. Do understand that I have all the qualities that a normal person ought to have. Please don't preach. (5)

But despite all efforts, Aravind Malagatti could not come out of the issue of casteism. When he was a child, he was beaten and when he got education, maturity and status, he was insulted humiliated and mentally tortured. His autobiography presents the bleak pictures of caste-tormented Dalit society. Dwaipayan Mitra writes about this autobiography:

> Malagatti lays bare the age-old practices of hurling the dalit women to the margin. The Okuli festival was one such tradition. In the name of tradition the dalit women had to wear and *ugachche* (a lower garment worn above the kneecaps) and hold several long branches of the lakky tree. Non-Brahmin men splashed coloured water on the women and the women were expected to duck and hit them with cane. This dehumanizing game offered a sort of ribald entertainment for the audience and the real and yellow shades of colour gave the scene a flavour of a colour movie. (Mitra 116)

Works Cited

Azhagarasan, R. Introduction: "Bama in Context". *Vanmam Vendetta.* By Bama. Trans. Malini Seshadri. New Delhi. Oxford University Press, 2008. xiii-xxviii. Print.

Malagatti, Aravind. *Government Brahmana.* Trans. Dharani Devi Malagatti, Janet Vucinich and N. Subramaniya. Chennai: Orient Longman, 2007. Print

Habib, M.A.R. *A History of Literary Criticism and Theory: From Plato to the Present.* New Delhi: Wiley India, 2014. Print.

Janani, R. "Identity Crisis and Search for 'Self' in Aravind Malagatti's *The Government Brahmana.*" *Language in India.* 14.1. (2014): 175-185. Web.

Johny, S. "Aravind Malagatti's *Government Brahmana*: A Discourse on Suppression and Survival." *Language in India.* www.languageinindia.com 16.08. (2016):50-58. Web.

Mitra, Dwaipayan. *Indian Dalit Autobiographies: Marginalised Voices.* Ed. Singh, Bijender. New Delhi: 2015. pp. 114-120. Print.

10

Alternative Historiography of the Dalits: G. Kalyana Rao's *Untouchable Spring*

DWAIPAYAN MITRA

Autobiography is the act of writing about oneself. The term is said to have coined by Robert Southey in 1809 in connection with his discussion of the works of a Portuguese poet, Fancisco Vieura. The first written autobiography is Augustine's *Confessions* which is full of spiritual elements. It deals with the trials of a man who deems himself as a sinner and beseeches to God to bestow mercy on him. The proliferation of autobiographies emerged in the nineteenth century when individualism was the zeitgeist and the writers imbued with a romantic hue raised their ego to a sublime zenith. In India the wave of autobiographies hit the country in the seventeenth century. Banarasidas's *Ardhakathanaka* is probably the earliest Indian autobiography. Since then a cornucopia of autobiographies has come in course of time. A cursory glance at nearly all such autobiographies reveals that they were flooded by various issues such as nationality, class and gender. However, nowhere do we see the centrality of caste politics which has been plaguing the Indian civilisation from a long time.

The emergence of Dalit autobiographies marks a significant change in the diachronic survey of Indian literature. The hitherto voiceless people who have been marginalised and discriminated against by Brahminical hegemony in recent time have broken down the wall of silence and asserted their own voice. These memoirs registered deep protest against various dictums laid down by the caste-rigid society. It is worthwhile to notice that a survey of Dalit autobiographies reveals to us that they are written in multiple languages existing in India which directs our eyes to the multilingual aspect of the tradition of Indian literature which vehemently inveighs against the notion of 'one nation and one language'. A comparative analysis of Dalit autobiographies across the linguistic barriers evinces the sense of communality and shared fractured entity that resists all such grand narratives regarding the idea of nation, language and culture.

Critics have split upon rocks to come to a unanimous conclusion about the origin of the caste system. According to historians like D.D. Kosambi, the origin of caste can be located in the Aryan invasions. The Aryans were a group of tribes who began invasions of India around 1500 B.C. They domesticated and subordinated the native Dravidians. In order to perpetuate their conquest, the Aryans formulated a caste system. According to J.H. Hutton, a noted anthropologist, the origin of caste was situated in the taboos and divisions of labour. In his book *Caste in India* he observes, 'The origin of the position of the exterior castes is partly racial, partly religious, and partly a matter of social system (1963:207).' Ambedkar does not hold with the division of labour theory and opines this system owes its genesis to the struggle between the 'broken men' and tribes. Whatever may be the origin of caste, the system has unleashed a mechanism that has given birth to fissiparous identities, sowed the seeds of differentiation. Ever since the Dalits have tried to write the wrongs done to them they have attempted an eradication of this abominable system. The life –stories of the untouchable community comprise a narrative that resists the fabricated origin of the caste system and demands remedial actions.

Kalyana Rao's *The Untouchable Spring* is departure from conventional autobiography as it flouts one of the chief parameters of an autobiography – a story of personal achievement. *The Untouchable Spring* is an English translation of the Tamil novel *Anatrani Vasantam*. The author depicts the plight of five generations whose lives have been punctuated by ordinariness. Here the writer conflates the distinction between 'I' and 'We' implying that a Dalit autobiography is not a depiction of an individual life but an ethnographic representation of the community. Although written in the form of a novel, the work has many personal reminiscences which the writer himself admitted. Moreover, this work has epical dimensions with the prolonged depiction of five successive generations. The eighteen chapters of the text are surely reminiscent of the eighteen *parvas* of The Mahabharata. The multiple shades of the work lend it a status that can be termed as 'sui generis' or 'a genre in itself'.

One stigma that is generally attached to the Dalits is their lack of artistic sensibilities. Kalayana Rao tries to debunk the critics by saying that the Dalits do not lack artistic sensibility. Through the story of Yellana, Rao is highlighting the artistic acumen of the subaltern people. The story of Yellana can be called 'kunstlerroman' or the development of an artist. Yellana's life story speaks volumes for the cultural heritage of Dalit culture. Yellana used to weave songs out of whatever he found in his surroundings. Yellana was an illiterate fellow but that did not thwart his artistic genius from coming out:

> Yellana did not write songs. He knew no alphabet to write them in. All he had was a feeling heart, a sharable experience, tear-shedding eyes...(2016:5)

In his salad days Yellana took a keen interest in watching plays and puppet shows. Those performances sowed the seeds of artistic delicacies which germinated in his later life. While growing up, Yellana learnt tune from his aunt Boodevi's song. It is not that the Dalits were devoid of artistic inputs. It is because of the fact that written history has neglected their artistic endeavours and judged them in terms of their rank in caste hierarchy. Rao puts it very beautifully, 'There are no records history has made a note of them in its pages. In this country caste is more important than art (2016: 41).' Rao's celebration of the subaltern life devoid of ostentation recalls one of Gray's eulogy for the common rustic people in his *Elegy Written in a Country Churchyard*:

> 'Full many a gem of purest ray serene,
> The dark unfathomed caves of ocean bear:

> Full many a flower is born to blush unseen,
> And waste its sweetness on the desert air.' (1970:670)

Yellana's act of taking part in dance troupe of Naganna shows his desire to channelize his pent-up feelings. He performed the *Urmula Nrityam* (thunder dance) which is the indigenous art form of the Telegus. The tandava dance was not a means to entertain the audience; but a medium to express the crisis raging in his soul. It was the spontaneous outburst of his agitated soul. The mature Yellana took refuge in the world of music just as the boy Yellana found a shelter in the world of dance. He was a natural song-maker. For his song Yellana drew material out of everyday struggle for existence, bouts of exploitation which fascinated the people:

> In that song figured Narigadu, the flood, the journey of the malas and madigas to the top of the mound, Narigadu's death. (2016: 94)

Keats wrote in a letter that the excellence of every art is its intensity. Yellana's song justified this observation. This invites comparison with K.A. Gunasekaran's autobiographical narrative *The Scar* where the author also delineates the artistic nature of Dalit people.

Rao opines how myth makes the distinction between superior castes and the inferior ones. Myths are cultural constructions that have been circulating among people from ancient time which joins individuals and communities together. According to K. Rao, myths operate as a superstructural unit that legitimise and maintain the distinction between the castes systematically. Kancha Ilaiah opines, 'Hinduism has a socioeconomic and cultural design that manipulates the consciousness of the Dalit bahujans systematically (2012:70).' According to Kancha Ilaiah, this hegemony has been executed by two modes. Firstly, Hinduism has generated an agreement structure which is sustained by manifold images of Gods and Goddesses. Secondly, when such method comes to a naught it relies on relentless violence that has been the bedrock of Hindu ideology. Ilaiah writes, 'That is the reason why many of the Hindu Gods were weapon wielders in distinct contrast to the Gods of all other religions (2012:70).' The story of Kamadhenu which was told to Ruben's grandfather by his grandfather is a typical example of the way how myths are created to keep the subalterns at bay. It authenticates the besmirched origin of malas and madigas. When a young cowboy Channu expressed his desire to drink Kamadhenu's honeyed milk that was used to worship Gods and Goddeses, Parvati suggested him to go to Kamadhenu and ask for it. On hearing the request, Kamadhenu collapsed and died. The rishis asked Jambavanta and Channu to divide the meat of the cow into two equal parts of which only one part would be used for cooking that would restore Kamadhenu back to life. Jambavanta did not divide the meat into two parts and Chennaiah put a defiled piece into the meat which incurred the wrath of the gods and goddesses. Siva cursed Jambavanta and Chennaiah to 'live in Kaliyuga eating the meat of dead cows and sweeping the bazaars (2016: 9).' Jambavanta's children became madigas and Chennaih's children became malas. This obnoxious and spurious myth of origin as a result of curse injected a sense of inferiority complex into the minds of lower caste people that emasculated their inner spirit. Ruth tells rightly, 'Truly, it was the agony of an untouchable. It was a condemnation of his birth that was so cruelly painted, of the crime committed on him in history. A true remonstrance. A rejection, indeed' (2016:6). Rao also fires a salvo at *Manusmriti*, a canonical text that justified and codified the caste hierarchy. It is worth noting that Rao is not critiquing the individuals for the torture and pain but the system which equated them with animals.

Dalits turned to Christianity as means to free themselves from the totalitarian regime of Hinduism. As an epistemology, caste was the by-product of Hindu-Brahmanic hegemony which asserted their supremacy by projecting certain regulatory practices. Such kind of grand narrative involving caste enveloped the Dalits and hurled them into a derogatory position. The notion of *Advaita* (non-twoness), a branch of Hindu Philosophical thought, upheld the virtues of casteist epistemology and de-humanised the Dalit discourse. It was for a search of de-casteist epistemology that the Dalits turned to Christianity However, that step did not prove effective to the Dalits as other caste people also converted themselves to Christianity and concomitantly, same hierarchy was preserved. Martin and Sivaiah were firm believer in Christ and thought conversion to Christianity would put an end to all injustice and sufferings:

> Martins and Sivaiahs believed in Christ to get rid of untouchability. They believed in him to appease their hunger. More than anything else they believed in Christ to save themselves from being hunted by me. (2016:166)

However, they found that Christianity was also tarred with the same brush. Attacks on mala and madiga Christian kept on increasing although reports of attacks on Brahmin Christians were seldom seen:

> Fresh news each day. In every village a story. They kept sixteen mala and madiga Christians in jail in Markapuram. Tortured them. They asked them to forget Christ and pray to Krishna. (2016:169)

Martin was killed by the upper caste people for opposing them. We are reminded of Bama's *Karukku* where we also found instances of the plight of Dalit Christians. This merciless liquidation of the Dalits, an assertion of the statist ideology which divests them of their humanity, can be interpreted in the Agambian theory of 'homo sacer'. In his book *Homo Sacer: Sovereign Power and Bare Life* Giorgio Agamben charts the association between people and the statist power and articulates the notion of 'homo sacer', a hapless figure who is drained of any value both in the divine and human standpoint. This figure, which is derived from Roman legal process, can be killed without any offence but cannot be sacrificed due to impurity. This sacred man is a worthless figure whom the political agency downgrades to a naked 'bare life' that can be ejected from the nation state. This degradation and animalisation of man is the corollary of this process. Dalits in modern India exemplify such figure whose values are zeroed in and then their lives are eliminated without any hiccup.

In the text Rao also raises questions regarding Gandhiji's strategy *vis-à-vis* the Dalit movement. In the novel we find Ramanujan flabbergasted at Gandhi's coinage 'Harijan' as he thought the term was no better than mala and madigas. As he opines:

> This brahminical society had made the malas and madigas untouchables. With the word Harijan, Gandhiji was making them orphans as well. (2016:192)

It was almost a case of justifying the caste system instead of opposing it. When long-cherished hopes and basic needs are deferred day by day the sparks of fire in soul get ignited and take on violent forms. Frantz Fanon in his *The Wretched of the Earth* talks about the 'emancipatory violence' that is needed to uproot the colonial hegemony. In this text we find the likes of Jessie take recourse to armed struggle to wage a battle against the upper caste people. Kalyana Rao agrees with Fanon in this respect to vouch for a violent reaction from the subaltern. One thing worth noticeable in this respect is that the text does not end up becoming a documentation of variegated tortures but also shows vistas for liberation, a path out of the impasse. The clarion call for rebellious violence is a protest against the *dispositifs* of caste-centric society. The way Ruth catalogues the problems corroding at the heart of the society reminds one of Hamlet's cataloguing of the evils in the state of Denmark:

> These governments are completely deteriorating. The leaders' brains have been bought by imperialist governments. In this country every step is targeted to be mortgaged... our government is the pet child of the World Bank. It does not have faith in people. (2016:249)

The mechanism of globalisation has generated an unsavoury culture where conformity rules the roost and all ideology is absorbed by capitalism, laissez faire that engrosses the soul of men. Under such circumstance people forget the mode of rebellion, to carve out a niche for themselves outside the arena of dominant power. In order to assert the submerged self what is need is violent response that can annihilate such flow of power. The collective outburst of pent-up feelings in a radical way seems to be the only hope for Dalit liberation as envisaged by Rao to post a counter-rebellion against the powers that be.

Mainstream historiography operates in a way that often neglects and glosses over marginal and peripheral issues. It often suppresses folk culture and relegates it to the background. As Dalit culture had been in a large degree oral it has been neglected by historiographers. Excavation into the buried and forgotten orature by relying on the power of memory can resurrect and foreground Dalit heritage and culture. Y.T. Vinayaraj opines in his essay 'Envisioning a Postmodern

Method of Doing Dalit Theology', 'The challenge before Dalits is to trace back the history of formation of their subjectivity; how it is constructed and the various modes of power that are played out in the construction of subjectivity (2011:97).' Kalyana Rao in his text banks on the potentials of remembrance to dig up the lost and forgotten stories of five generations of Dalits and offer us an example of 'history from below'. In the course of the text we find sporadic snapshots of such occluded practices. We find Boodevi narrating stories to child Yellana which were aimed at deconstructing the casteist discourse. During the opening of the Buckingham Canal Dalits were left out from doing coolie activities as the higher caste people raised objections to work with lower caste people.

Though *Untouchable Spring* primarily focuses on the quotidian struggle of Dalit men through five generations it is not that the author whittles away at the importance of Dalit women. They also form a part of and took active step in the formation of Dalit struggle. The work ethics, which Dalit culture highly prioritises, compel the Dalit women to come out of entrenched space and assert their existence. The entire narrative is told by the recapitulation of Ruth. In the first part of the story we see such maverick women characters as Boodevi. Boodevi initiated Yellana into the world of art:

> Boodevi brought up her nephew with dance. Brought him up with songs. Laying him down on her legs, she sang Kamamma's story, bathing him. (2016:10)

Subhadra also supported her husband Yellana. She fought with the upper caste men when the malas and madigas were assaulted for fetching water to quench their thirst. Ruby took a part in the armed struggle to register the protest against caste discriminations. Such kind of step was hardly feasible among upper caste women.

The technical *tour de force* of the semi-autobiographical novel deserves special mention. It is this special quality of the text that does not embody it as a discourse on sociology. It goes without saying that there are parts in the text which would help sociology's concern. The resplendence of imaginative insight imbues the text with a hue that covers the rhetoric of anger with an artistic finesse which is the *raison d'etre* of literature. The unique narrative style is a special prerogative of the memory-text. The work unfurls before our eyes through the recollection of Ruth who has heard the story from her husband Ruben. Language employed by the author suits the temper of the text which at times sounds poetic and at times emits venom. Author's use of imagery is apt enough to project the desires, aspirations as well as frustrations of the Dalit people. The village was named 'Yelenna Dini' after an imaginary bird 'Yellanna Pitta'. The image of 'Yellanna Pitta' looms large in the text showing the desire to fly away from the claustrophobic and manacled existence. The dormant search for freedom recurs again and again in the text.

The translation of the text from Tamil into English by Alladi Uma and M. Sridhar is praiseworthy as it has become more accessible to readers across the globe. In this context we need to keep in mind the nuances associated with the act of translation that also entails its own version of politics. L. Venuti in his book *Translator's Invisibility* talks about the invisibility of the translator from the time of Cicero and draws our attention to the fact that the chief quality we attach to translation is its fluency; whether the target text has fidelity to the original. For Venuti, there resides a great amount of politics in such a concept as the text becomes another community to be marketed in a globalised world with its cut-throat competition where not sounding idiomatic or fluent can destroy the life of the target text. In order to come out of this culture Venuti proposes a model of translation he terms as 'foreignisation' that does not aim at fluency but makes a pressure on the values of the target text to register the difference of the source text. In the translation of *Antarani Vasantam* into English the translators have taken recourse to 'foreignisation' model as some culture-specific terms are left intact and a note has been appended in the end to clarify those terms which dismantles the model of easy readability and invites the careful effort of the reader.

Friedrich Douglas comments in the last section of his autobiography that, 'this little book may do something towards throwing light on the American slave system, and hastening the glad day of deliverance to the millions of my brethren in bonds (1995:76).' In Rao's *Untouchable Spring* we also find the note of positivism as the text becomes not only a record of various atrocities meted out to them but a treasure trove that promises the ray of hope and suggests a way to cast off disgrace and psychosis. By challenging the traditional mode of historiography which neglects oral narrative and tracing the forgotten histories, Rao lays bare the hypocrisy latent in our culture and helps inscribe the alternative history of the subaltern community in the idealistic image of India. When our country is repeatedly canvassing the image of glorified India, Rao critically engages with such opulent facades offering us a slice of the seamy side of life and unleashes a praxis marked by the rhetoric of anger to articulate the fissures in the utopian nation.

Works Cited

Agamben, G. *Homo Sacer: Sovereign Power and Bare Life*. University of California: Stanford, CA, USA, 1998. Print.

Douglass, Frederick. *Narrative of the Life of Frederick Douglass*. Quarles. Cambridge: Harvard UP, 1973. Print.

Gray, Thomas. "Elegy Written in a Country Churchyard." *The Norton Anthology of Poetry*. 5th ed. New York: Norton and Company, 1970. Print.

Hutton, J.H. *Caste in India*. Oxford: Oxford University Press, 1963. Print.

Ilaiah, Kancha. *Why I am not a Hind*u. (1996) Kolkata: Samya, 2012. Print.

Rao, G. Kalyana. *Untouchable Spring*. (2000). Trans. Alladi Uma and M. Sridhar. New Delhi: Orient Blackswan, 2016. Print.

Vinayaraj, Y.T. "Envisioning a Postmodern Method of Doing Dalit Theology." *Dalit Theology in the Twenty-first Century*. New Delhi: Oxford, 2011. Print.

11

Documenting the Manifold Contact Zones: An Autoethnographical Study of *Joothan*

ANUSHA A. J.

The psycho-social dimensions of an ethnically vibrant national entity such as India evoke a spectrum of challenges indulged by parallel and junctive variables. Deciphering these visible-cum-veiled templates requires a scrutinised understanding of the formation and reformation of the Self pervaded by anthropological and synthetic factors. The revelational discourse of life writing channelises the conscious and unconscious paradigms to be put into black and white. In the mediatised age saturated with graphics and a penchant for creating breaks in the homogeneous mainstream narrative, there are consistent attempts to bear through the corrupted hegemonic cultural texts.

Explication of the relationship forged between the literary discourse and the socio-cultural productive matrix is symbiotic. While New Historicist critics like Greenblatt have been instrumental in declaring the significance of the deep cut analysis of marginalised literary products as vistas into cultural textures, Clifford Geertz and others vouch that the contested codes and representations of society marked by the structures of language engage in the reinforcement of the politics of identity formation. Therefore the subalterns' chance at self expression in writing ties along the infinite potential of cracking open a highly tight knit semantics of oppression.

The doctrinal episteme of Life writing primarily entails autobiographies, memoirs or biographies. However, the present discourse equation furnishes a broadened scope to testimonies, autoethnographies, diaries, blogs and timelines on social media platforms like Facebook to tweets on Twitter. Bridging the divide, the new media life writing emulates access to the centre and the periphery, creating a semblance of permeation. However, the inked narratives ensign a definitive sanctification of the ethnographic self that, technologically imbibed cultural texts may not be endowed with.

The nineteenth century literary parlance bore witness to the emphatic acknowledgement of pseudo legitimacy and value of autobiography misted by the post-modern crisis of representations. Philip Lejeune's comprehension of autobiography as: "A retrospective prose narrative produced by a real person concerning his own existence, focusing on his individual life, in particular the development of his personality" (193), interrogates it for a chronologically ordered work which methodically charts the metamorphosis of the Self incessantly threatened by fragmentation. Whether it is the self preservatory narcissistic libido in the terminology of Sigmund Freud or that of the subject's obsession with the real in his/ her attempts to transcend the heavy muteness of the desperation of loss, as that in Roland Barthes, the autobiographical memories acts as sites of interventions and interactions amongst the problematic considerations of representation, Self and the fact-fiction engagements. The established myths of the essentialised absolute ideal subject deliberated upon awoke to a realisation as a falsified notion upon the onset of psychoanalysis. Derrida and Barthes gauge the reformed idea of the self as a framework of multiplicities, reinforcements towards which these critics have penned down. Barthes' autobiography remodels the self as the imaginary self, convoluting the nature of the representations. A strategic translation of the epiphanic and non-epiphanic reflections subsumes into the text. The syntax underlying the generic label of autobiography enamors fluidity pertaining to points of conveyance and concealments. The aforementioned facet has been a critical trigger that set off a plethora of discussions.

In the dispersion through these invading complexities, materialised autoethnography's adaptation from the anthropological discursive constructions to its appropriation as a self narrative is positioned in an overlapping matrix of cultural codes and historical ramifications. Coinage of Karl Heider, the anthropologist, the term endured a sustained juggernaut of significations until twentieth century witnessed critics by the likes of Deborah Reed- Danahay, rendering foremost of its definitions in her seminal *Auto/Ethnography: Rewriting the Self and the Social*

> ...a form of self narrative that places the self within a social context. It is both a method and a text done by either an anthropologist who is doing 'home' or native ethnography or by a non-anthropologist/ ethnographer. It can also be done by an autobiographer who places the story of his or her life within a story of the social context in which it occurs (9).

Danahay's evaluation stations autoethnography at the fringes of three disciplines: narrative anthropology, a stem pervaded by the experiences of the informant as an active socio-cultural participant of the ethnic group; the ethnic autobiography reverberates the rebel yell of the minority ethnic self caught in the flux of dominant social structures, the majority shareholders who create, engage and authenticate power, identity and meaning; and autobiographical ethnography featuring the anthropologist as the author of the text, extrapolating the lived experience.

These self reflexive discourses acquired a definitive theoretical standpoint with the inclusive study of Mary Louise Pratt in the critical literary scene. Her discussions of the autoethnographic texts endorse their rendition as a dialogic response to the popular narrative layered fervently with stereotypes of the minorities that permeate the national and post-colonial apparatuses. Ruminations on the dialectics of the genre locate the concept of the contact zone as the locus focii. Pratt proposes and dissects the structures of a contact zone which functions as the psycho-social topography of the narrative. In *Arts of the Contact Zone*, the critic seeks to uncover the paradigms underlying language, representations and culture within these counter-narratives. She describes a contact zone as "social spaces where cultures meet, clash and grapple with each other, often in contexts of highly asymmetric relations of power" (76). The systematised mechanism of language or rather the meticulous depiction of the power in signifiers, here is a conglomeration of the hieroglyphs of both the meaning maker and the ethnic minority entangled in the cobwebs of the dominant culture. The narrative therefore exemplifies a merger enabling it to be subjects of comprehension for both the former and the latter. Vernacular torpedoes the forging of parodying of the consistent set of tenets ruling the theories of representations engraved deep within the systems of societal norms. Marked by transculturation, it unsettles the conventional reception and consumption of literary products.

The analytic-evocative dimension to the realist-impressionist-confessionist approaches, autoethnography, argues critic Carolyn Ellis, envisages a scrupulous interaction of the self with the cultural artifacts. Memoirs, autobiographies and other popular forms of self representation are adjudged autoethnographical provided they have their soul in cultural analysis. These texts are negative to be what New Critics Cleanth Brooks, John Crowe Ransom, William Empson and the like deemed autotelic texts, for they are interpreted with the all-inclusive study of class, gender, race, socio-economic conditions and political orientations. Autoethnography as an enigmatic synthesis of anthropology and literature encompasses an integrated study of culture, an attempt to reveal the shared experiences, belief systems, and the framework of values- ethical, social, religious, economic and political, with the narrator donning the garb of the guide. The expedition into oneself replete with strategies of 'showing' and 'telling' formulates techniques of garnering sympathy and empathy, not only indulging in a revelation of the torturous turbulences that questioned the identity of the Self but also levels as a first hand narrative agency opening up the avenues and commodities of culture. A deliberate effort is visible on behalf of the writer to foreground his experiences as an engrossed member of the community than as an individual. Critic Francoise Lionnet acknowledges the pursuit of balance amidst the "space of resistance" between the axes of the individual (auto), the collective (ethno) and the writing (-graphy) (391). Reliability and validity of these narratives has been engendered from the precise data collection techniques from interviews to document analysis in addition to a diagnostic consideration of the behavioural patterns.

The initiation of the ethnic minority into the dominant circuits of print culture by aligning with autoethnography at the level of transformation of perceptions has been a constructive phenomenon. The naturalised difference of the marginalised, entrapped in the images of the institutions of control, earlier justified ventures a crack in the linear historical account. Within the multiethnic fabric of India, the eccentricities of ideological furnishings force the ethnic minorities to be relegated to the outskirts of the social order, a stigmatised predicament risen from the stubborn adherence to the inhumane Varna system. The repudiation of the inalienable rights of social, political, economic and cultural inclusion of the Dalits involves an interminable acknowledgement of the corrupted conceptual framework of the Dalit discourse. Critic Eleanor Zelliott, based on her extensive research and study, proposes a sociological definition of the term. According to her,

> The term represents those who have been broken and ground down by those above them in a deliberate manner. In the term and concept Dalit itself there is an inherent denial of dignity, a sense of pollution and an acceptance of the Karma theory that justifies caste hierarchy (267).

Understanding the discursive constructions and the literary associations of this term calls for a motivated dissection of the manipulative social systems of alienation and which upon violation outcries of blasphemy echo across the socially reverent hierarchies.

'Dalit' in its modern literary and social parlance caters to the connotations and symbols of oppressed classes and the suppressed subjects, not only the untouchables but also the nomadic communities of Vaidu, Gabal, Laman-Banjara and the like; and even extends to the subaltern subject of women. The origins, development and dissemination of the Dalit movement created a necessity of strengthening in of their ideologies across the literary and social spaces vouching their active existence rather than the effacement from the realms of identity. A medium of rebellion, the recurrent performances within the printed pages of a book, may be what Stephen Greenblatt terms as 'improvisation', the pursuit of the individual to invade the closed system of power relations. Dalit's trials for improvisation can be seen in their dedicated faith in education, making use of structures of oppressive representations to reveal the historiography of humiliations and injustices. Self reflexive narratives are renegades with heart wrenching episodic depictions of attacks and cultural ostracism. A Dalit's life is a tale of potent stagnancy sans mobility outside the imaginary psychological and cultural ghettos. Raising voices in the mainstream are emblematic of a quest for self assertion and a petition for the consideration of the minority as quintessence of the mechanisms of a functionally well build society. The urge to express themselves has grown so intense that most of the Dalit literary products are autobiographical in nature. These autobiographies are trenchant portrayals of a truncated community, encapsulating the historical context of the turmoil as well and the incessant repercussions of trauma. N.S. Suryavanchi's *Things I Never Imagined* (1979), Aravind Malagatti's *Government Brahmana* (1994), Sharankumar Limbale's *The Outcaste* (2003) and Siddalingaiah's *Ooru Keri* (2003) are exemplar pieces of articulation of violation of moral and ethical codes and constructive and reformative possibilities within the liberation movement.

Omprakash Valmiki's *Joothan: A Dalit's Life* (2003) translated by Arun Prabha Mukherjee, is an indictment of the problematic milieu of the Chuhra community, the lowest caste in the destined hierarchy of the Brahminical system of Varna. In this strong emotional testimony, the author paces through a journey of exploitation, misery, poverty, social invisibility and disgusting tendencies of a post-independent India. The fire of embedded hostility and condescension directed towards the Dalits scathed them. The autoethnographic text features consistent narrative transitions between the Self and the community. However, in Valmiki, the self is signified with a single connotation of that of the Dalit. As an autoethnography, the text remains fidel to the emotions generated and experiences relived as a Dalit. The writer's fragmented self engages in a selective recollection of the angst of discrimination through an organic narration of the deep seated conceptions of the caste renders possible the achievement of the perfect balance of auto, ethno and writing. The ethnographic observations in the text are augmented with the retelling of experiences of the vulnerable lower castes. The presence of multiple subjectivities revels in the existence of these sites of data collection.

The onset of the narrative is plagued by the nefarious conditions of the Dalit dwellings. An absurd tormented subject threatened by the poisoned arrows of suppression, the pangs of which the Dalits suffered in silence, foreshadows the perpetual desperation of the Dalit self. Valmiki recollects:

> Untouchability was so rampant that while it was considered all right to touch dogs and cats or cows and buffaloes, if one happen end to touch a Chuhra, one got contaminated or polluted. The Chuhras were not seen as human (2).

The lack of basic amenities, safe drinking water, sanitation facilities, secure shelters, warm clothes, opportunities of education and employment are the consistent items that play in the tormented loop. Valmiki's metamorphosis incorporates a stubborn perseverance to turn down the notions of socially prescribed roles of cleaning roads, working as scavengers and bearing the burden of servitude under the hypocritical upper caste Tagas. In Valmiki, hinged the assured emphatic fortification of an ethnographic impulse, the Self turns the effective vantage point to engage in a comprehensive exploration, understanding and interpretation of the cultural instilments. The deplorable string of instances problematising his thought processes in associations with his identity turns turbid the already murky waters of his psyche. The wandering of a tortured soul ponders over: "Why is my caste my only identity?" (50).

The mechanics of the augmentative institution of education initially seeded optimism of an escape from the invisibility and immobility. The writer's fragmented self acknowledged the body of knowledge as the essential course to power relations. Michael Foucault's theory of knowledge and power initiating a discursive turn in critical thinking deliberates upon the meticulous structures of hegemony—institutions like the schools and colleges, that dictate the cruising of the discourse and thereby contributes to a sustained emphasis of the dominant structures of power. The denial of access to education for the ethnic minorities arises from the disinclination of the social inclusion of these passive forces. Upon seeking access, Valmiki faced stringent oppositions, the resistance on behalf of the power-wielders to prevent its bereavement from their hands. The teachers punish him for this invasion into the prohibited space for the minorities. They relegate him to the margins denying him the mobility to move up the social ladder. The aggressive assaults of the oppressor are incessant to the point of saturation that the lower caste Chuhras most often frustrated, recline to the confines of their shell. The instances of denial of a comforting glass of water, of equality in seating arrangements, active participation in extracurricular activities and the refusal to let the narrator take his lab practical all are punishments for breaking the boundaries that set up to document the linear homogenous narrative. The subject resigns to the desperate conclusion that: "Caste cannot be improved by education. It can only be improved by taking birth in the right caste" (58).

Valmiki's decisiveness of invasions of the institutionalised sites of control returned vigorously as he joined college and upon employment. As a boiling cauldron of humiliations, the Self sought comfort in the writings of Dr B R Ambedkar, Baburao Bagul, Narayan Surve and sharpened his ideological orientations with Marxist books. His life turns full circle as a social critic and an activist for the rights of the Dalits. Despite these consequences and achievements, Valmiki still surmises, "Caste follows one right upto one's death" (78).

The narrative tends to unsettle the myriad preconceived notions of the reader. To broaden the target audience, the text has been subject to translation, featuring a committed interaction between the vernacular and the language of the oppressor in the contact zone. Lucidity in terms of signifiers and corresponding significations ensure an outreach of the representations of the Self. The phraseology of *ghor kalyug*, *Abey Chuhre* etc. in the vernacular, conveys the rawness of the encounters depicted. The title *Joothan,* etymologically, in the vernacular situates the idea of leftovers from someone else's usage. The Chuhras survived on a day to day basis in the pitiable conditions of squalor and malnourishment. They accept leftovers in wedding feasts and other rituals as a means of escape from the declining bodies. However, the generous granting of leftover food, endorses nothing but the narrow-mindedness of the perpetrator. The ardent harbinger of rebellion Dr Ambedkar had called for a denunciation of the *joothan* by the Dalits as a definitive step towards their empowerment. In terms of language, the idealisation of the pastoral is done away with as he comments:

> Their suffering is not just the suffering of individual and there is nothing romantic about it. Their problem is neither ideological

> nor philosophical. They do not seek poetic beauty. Similes, metaphors and symbols are not important. The reality of their life is too hideously shocking, beyond the capacity of fantasy or imagination (67).

The complexities of ethnic identities evinced in the narrative can be seen when placed in alignment with the concrete universal institution of religion. Valmiki's milieus are that of the feudal-Brahminical setup. *Kul devis* or goddesses are fervently worshipped to seek divine intervention in their lives from the source of infinite power. The realisation of the politics of caste dawned on the Self as "Caste has nothing to do with religion; it is harmful to both spirituality and growth" (5). The gross injustices meted out to the Chuhras by the people of the same religious orientation- Hinduism puts the Self in conundrum.

The public space of this rather gripping narrative is marked by the patriarchal hegemonic standpoints. Though the female may breach this space, it remains since time immemorial the monopoly of the male. Women are doubly bound by oppressions owing to the adjunct of caste and the defunct attribution of gendered social roles. Grazing cattle, cooking food, cleaning the house and summing up is inevitably a disciplined subject, passive participant of the contract of marriage to serve the phallus. The female appeases the sources of power be it in her participation of the religious rituals like *vraths* or through the bone-breaking monotony of keeping silence within the four walls of her primary site of oppression. Her historiography is forcefully entrenched in dark depths of discourses.

The narrative destabilises the typified references of the Dalit self, the subject of the Dalit discourse, a voiceless passive victim submissive to the idioms of the majority. Identity is a fluid construction serving the various contextual involvements, in flux. Caste is rigid and stationary and the efforts to denounce the devious system have accounted nothing but failure. Valmiki reiterates:

> Caste is a very important element of Indian society. As soon as a person is born, 'caste' determines his or her destiny. Being born is not in the control of a person. If it were in one's control, then why would I have been born in a Bhangi household? Those who

call themselves the standard– bearers of this country's great cultural heritage, did they decide which homes they would be born into? Albeit they turn to scripture to justify their position, the scripture that establish feudal instead of promoting equality and freedom (134).

The systematic analysis of the components of culture via autoethnography offered an opportunity of expedition to and recognition of the strands of power that initiate, disseminate and authenticate the workings of the social enterprise. The study also laid bare the bloody atrocities committed against the Dalits by institutionalised forces of dominance. *Joothan* is, in conclusion, a literary platform to discern the cultural commodities and an opportunity to attain closure for the ethnographic Self.

Works Cited

Danahay, Deborah Reed. *Auto/Ethnography: Rewriting the Self and the Social*. Michigan: Bloomsbury Academic, 1997. Print.

Lionnet, Francois. "Autoethnography: The an-archaic style of *Dust Tracks on the Road.*" *Reading Black, Reading Feminist: A Critical Anthology*. Ed. Henry Louis Gates. New York: Meridian, 1990. Print.

Lejeune, Philip. "The Autobiographical Pact". *On Autobiography*. Minneapolis: University of Minnesota Press,1988. Print.

Pratt, Mary Louise. "Arts of the Contact Zone". *Professing in the Contact Zone: Bridging Theory and Practice Together*. Ed. Janice. M. Wolff. Urbana: National Council of Teachers of English, 2002. Print.

Valmiki, Omprakash. *Joothan: A Dalit's Life*. Trans., Mukherjee, Arun Prabha. Kolkata: Samya, 2003. Print.

—. "Writing Responsibly". *Journal of Literature and Aesthetics* 8 (2008). 13-16. Print.

Zelliott, Eleanor. *From Untouchable to Dalit: Essays on the Ambedkar Movement*. New Delhi: Manohar Publications, 1992. Print.

12

From Hunger to Thievery: A Study of Laxman Gaikwad's *The Branded*

Suruchi Sharma

Many Dalit men's autobiographies have been translated from Marathi into English and these autobiographies present the very horrifying pictures of the Dalits. Laxman Gaikwad's *The Branded* depicts the horrendous narratives of hunger and thievery of the *'Uchalya'* or *'Pathrut'* community. The people of this tribe had to live from hand to mouth and they had to steal to run their families. The condition of the women was also much debilitated and apathetic. Bijender Singh writes in the preface of his book *Indian Dalit Literature: Marginalised Voices*:

> Dalit personal narratives reveal the collective consciousness of the community which was repressed for a long time. Through individual memoirs, the writers presented before us documentation of a caste-tormented society. (Singh, 14)

Laxman Gaikwad is one of the well-reputed writers whose autobiography *Uchalya: The Branded* has won the Sahitya Akademi Award for 1988. It has been translated as *The Branded* by P.A. Kolharkar. Laxman Gaikwad is a social worker and a Dalit writer who was born in 1956 in the Uchalya community in Dhanegaon, Latur, Maharashtra. He could not complete his matriculation but he has achieved much acclaimed status due to his hard work and dedication. This autobiography presents his struggle to get education, two squares meal and petty job. In this autobiography Gaikwad describes very wretched condition of his community how the people of his tribe were forced to adopt the profession of thievery to feed their family due to deprivation and utter penury. The people of his tribe were considered to be "born criminals" and their livelihood was just "thieving, lifting, pick pocketing" (Gaikwad, vii).

Laxman Gaikwad narrates his nomadic life that he had no native birth place as he was born in such a community which has no permanent habitat. He writes in the beginning of his autobiography, "NO NATIVE PLACE. NO birth-date. No house or farm. No caste, either. That is how I was born. In an Uchalya community, at Dhanegaon in Taluka Latur." (Gaikwad, 1) The autobiography *Uchalya: The Branded* describes the trials and tribulations of dalits who belonged to the *Santmuchchar* community. 'Sant' means 'market' and 'muchchhar' means 'thief'. In this way *santmuchchhars* means those people who steal from weekly bazaars or markets for their livelihood. Sankha Maji observes in this context:

> The book sketches the plight of Pathrut community branded as "criminal tribes" in the All India Criminal Tribes Act first passed in 1871 by the British Raj. The colonisers have left but the stigma has stuck to them permanently. This nomadic "denotified tribe" is subjected to brutal treatment by the state machinery. The light of the so-called civilised world never reaches these people. They have been relegated to the dark world of ignorance, prejudice, poverty and crudity. Thus, the Uchalyas are reduced to outcastes. The stamp of criminal tribe remains with them as inborn identity. This tribal community make livelihood by taking recourse to thieving profession. The people earn totally from pilfering, stealing and pick-pocketing. The Uchalyas are forced to live in the fringes. (Maji, 5186)

Laxman Gaikwad's grandmother, Narasabai was an earning hand in the family while his grandfather, Lingappa was a ruffian and he picked pockets and stole things from the village fairs and markets. He was a notorious thief of that tribe and nobody tried to cross his way. He used Bharat blade to pick the pockets. One day he mistakenly gave a deep cut with his blade in a stranger's body from his buttocks to waist. The man cries in pain and Lingappa was arrested consequently. He was brutally beaten by the police for this act of thievery. The police torture him, "Tell us where you've hidden the stolen money and gold. Show or we'll smash your bones." (Gaikwad, 02) He pleaded, "See Saab, see for yourself, there is nothing in the hut" but the police tortured not only Gaikwad's grandfather but his family members also. The policemen call his wife a whore, "Your whore will know". (Gaikwad, 02) The policemen tortured his grandmother and the other members of the family. They did not spared even the children and the old people of the family, "The police were beating whomsoever they eyes fell upon - women, children. They squeezed grandmother's breasts asking her to show the stolen goods." (Gaikwad, 2) The police rummaged for the stolen articles but it was a futile effort.

Laxman Gaikwad belonged to such a tribe that was not trusted by anybody. Nobody offered any work to the people of this tribe due to their notoriety, "Even if someone desired to do honest work, nobody would employ him. The police would beat us making false allegations of theft; even when, in fact, no theft had been committed." (62) The police took undue advantage of this situation. If there was any incidence of any theft, the people of Gaikwad's tribe would be arrested on suspicion and they were released only after offering exorbitant amounts, "Only then did the police release them without bringing any charge against them in the court. Mother's gold ornaments were kept by the police for themselves. After all, we were thieves by profession; who could we lodge a complaint with?" (15-16)

Laxman Gaikwad's grandfather, Lingappa worked as a state informer of the police and he would provide all the information of his tribe to police and the business of the people of his tribe failed. Consequently, many families of his tribe came on the verge of starvation. Gaikwad's grandfather was considered as a traitor in the tribe. In the meeting, it was decided that he must be killed to save their families from the hunger, "The Uchalya people fell in a big trouble as Laxman's grandfather divulged the names of all people involved in criminal activities to the police and police detained them. His grandfather now became a traitor for the others. They held a meeting and it was resolved that he must be killed" (Gaikwad, 4). They did not only devise a plan for it they murdered him at one day with an axe, "One day they broke into our hut through the thatched roof, gagged our grandfather and hacked him to death with an axe." (Gaikwad, 4) When Gaikwad's grandfather died, there was not much fear of the police now for the people as now traitor had been murdered and the thieves started their usual work of pick pocketing and stealing, "The people resume their usual business of thieving and picking pockets without the fear of being reported (Gaikwad, 4).

Gaikwad narrates how he had to wander from one place to another in the search of food and how the people of his community had to live in the utter unhygienic conditions and their parents would teach them the skills of thievery. The people of this tribal community were so poor that they had to eat cats, rats, leaves and roots or they had to remain hungry.

Gaikwad's father, Martand had a soft corner for his children. He inspires and motivates Laxman to get education so that he may be able to acquire a good status. He does not give him a Bharat blade to pick the pockets but he gives him a slate and pencil so that he may get education. Martand works as a guard the farm of a rich farmer whose name was Chamle. He got inspired from there and that's why he wanted that "a child must learn to read and write" (Gaikwad, 16). Martand did not let his son go for picking the pockets of people but he sent his son to school. He took some money in advance for his salary and spent it for Laxman's education. He got hostile response both from the upper caste people and the people of his community. Martand had a different mentality. He was an honest, truthful and hard-working man and he did not allow Laxman to go on hunting with his brothers. Whenever a family member would eat roasted cat, rat or fish he would punish him.

When Laxman Gaikwad started getting education, the children of his community suffered from cholera coincidentally but the people of Laxman's village held Laxman's father responsible for it as they thought that their children have loose motions due to Laxman's going to school. The people of his community wanted to ostracize Gaikwad's father, Martand from their community but Martand got his defense with the help of the Panchayat and Kulkarni Guruji. Guruji told and convinced the upper caste people that it is cholera due to which their children were suffering and they needed to consult a doctor for the treatment.

> Because you have admitted your son to school, our children are suffering from loose motion and vomiting. Never had our lane suffered from cholera before. No illness or epidemic had touched our lane. Look, Martanda, since your bastard of a son has started going to school, diseases are visiting us. We are not merchants and Brahmins to admit our children to school. Has anybody from the thieves community ever gone to school? Oh Martand! Schooling was never good for us. Has anybody from among our forefathers ever gone to school? If our children started going to school, our race would be doomed. Goddess Yellamma will be furious. Look Martanda, if your son continues to go to school, we shall call the Panchayat and ostracize you. (16-17)

Gaikwad's mother, Dhondabai also was a different woman like her husband, Martand. She also does not like the dirty ways of stealing. She gets beaten and tyrannised by the police because her sons were involved in the dirty profession of thievery. She runs her family by selling milk and even gets iron sheets for her hut due to her business. She had to sell out her sheep for the bail of her son but she never involved in the heinous act of thievery.

Laxman Gaikwad depicts a touching incidence of his life when he and his sister-in-law were sleeping in the yard. Somebody comes suddenly on his sister-in-law at midnight and he forcibly sexually assaulted her. She tried to resist and cry but that man held her mouth tightly. He disappeared in the darkness until she cried brashly. When the members of the family asked her what had happened, she just told them that the man had tried to lie on her. She did not tell the reality to anyone because if she had divulged everything, her husband could divorce her. But it was Laxman who knew everything.

Laxman Gaikwad had to see very bad days in his life. He lived in very unhygienic conditions. He had to sleep in one coverlet with his brothers and this coverlet was washed only once in a year at the occasion of Dusserah. This coverlet had lice.

> On getting up in the morning we never washed the coverlet but spread it on the roof to dry. The piss smell filled out nostrils with a strong odour, yet we used the same sodden coverlet. Our senses were dead and we were beyond tellings. The coverlet teemed

> with lice. When we killed them Harchanda and I kept the count mostly up to hundred or two hundred and then gave up.... I did not take a bath for months, nobody from the house hold ever told me to take a bath washing clothes was not even thought of. (Gaikwad, 11-12)

The women of the village used the empty space near their hut as a shitting spot. Pigs were also killed at this place. Gaikwad also lived there without having bath in dirty clothes. Not only this, starvation was rampant in the family, that's why Gaikwad had to skip his school on Tuesdays and Fridays so that he may get some food at the temple. He had to eat coconut and food from the cremation yards. He had to eat the roasted mango-stones and tamarind seeds which were collected from rubbish. He had to eat *Joothan* many times and he had to go at distant places on foot through mud and thorns to collect food for him. Sometimes he would carry bowl with him so that he may get food for the members of his family. He searched beehives so that he might get honey, pigeon nests so that he may get eggs from them and he was beaten by his guru when he was noticed doing it.

He starts working in the spinning mill at Latur, Maharashtra and this job elevates his social and economic status. He starts to take care of his ailing father and in order to give proper attention; he starts working in the double shifts. He starts selling fruit and bread also so that he may get some extra income from his part-time job. But he does not get a good response from his supervisors at the sinning mill who were corrupt and favoured nepotism. There were unhygienic working conditions at the mill. The workers of the mills worked for eight hours and they were allowed lunch only for fifteen minutes. The workers were beaten for being late and they were dismissed from their job for fifteen days for this trivial fault. In the beginning, he remained silent but ultimately he raised his voice against it. He delivers a speech on the Labour Day and creates awareness about the working conditions of the mill, the deafening noises of the machines, jeopardy of the cotton particles and the excessive use of saccharine which may impact the health of the workers and many workers suffered from tuberculosis and they had to borrow money from others at high rate so that they may spend this money in dispensaries outside as there was no dispensary in the mill.

Laxman makes his union and he is elevated as a leader of the workers. At the occasion of the Independence Day he delivers another speech and throws light on the injustice, irregularities and nepotism prevalent in the spinning mill. He is penalised and even expelled from the mill for his trivial mistakes. The workers had to see the very bad phase without wages but their families support them and ultimately, the management had to increase their wages. Laxman had to sell tea, fired fish, chili powder and ground nuts when he is expelled from his job but he never does the work of thievery and pick-pocketing like his brothers or in-laws. His wife had to run a grocery shop to help him financially. He starts working as a secretary in Aurangabad in a dairy cooperative which was run by his sister-in-law. He works there for three months but he does not get satisfied there and he returned Latur without his pay for three months.

Gaikwad sees the grim pictures of poverty to the extent that he could not afford a cup of milk for his daughter. He starts a cycle repair shop and later starts working as a sweeper in a school in Latur. He starts working as a peon in the Municipal Corporation and he notices the anomalies there. He finds the Municipality officials dishonest and then he is forced to think why these people are not given the brand of a thief. He considers it injustice that the poor people of his community are called thieves who steal to fill their stomach.

As a conclusion it can be stated that Laxman Gaikwad has a revolutionary mind and his struggle opened some new avenues for the poor dalits and labourers. He becomes an inspiration for his community that a person of his tribal can live his life with respect without picking the pockets. He ignites the spark of education and job among the uneducated people of his tribe. His autobiography *The Branded* is a heart-touching autobiography which narrates the utter penury of his tribe which makes them the branded thieves while the upper caste people and officials do the same things but are never given this brand.

Works Cited

Maji, Sankha. "Voice from the Fringes: A Postcolonial Reading of Laxman Gaikwad's The Branded." *European Academic Research*. 3.4. (2015): 5185-93.

Gaikwad, Laxman. *Uchalya: The Branded* (1998) Trans. P.A. Kolharkar. Delhi: Sahitya Academy, 2009. Print.

Singh, Bijender. Dalit Resurrection in Laxman Gaikwad's *The Branded. Indian Scholar: An International Multidisciplinary Research E-Journal.* 1.1. (2014): 49-55.

————. Ed. *Indian Dalit Literature: Marginalised Voices*. New Delhi, Authorspress, 2015. Print.

Limbale, Sharankumar. *Towards an Aesthetic of Dalit Literature: History, Controversies and Considerations.* Trans. Alok Mukherjee. New Delhi: Orient Longman, 2007. Print.

Bhattacharjee, Archana. "Poignant Narratives of Tribal People in Laxman Gaikwad's *Uchalaya: The Branded.*" *Indian Dalit Literature: Critical Ruminations*. Ed. Singh, Bijender. New Delhi, Authorspress, 2014. Print.

13

Analysing Hegemony, Ideology and Ideological Apparatus in Gunasekaran's *The Scar*

Guni Vats

> Wounds made of fire might heal but wounds made of untouchability would continue to give trouble. — (Ravikumar xvi)

In the vast ocean of Indian literature, historians left behind the saga of a section of society deliberately pushed to the periphery. K.A. Gunasekaran's *Vadu* is a humble attempt to portray what was left unsaid. He weaves together his experiences of the amalgamation of religions and its diminishing boundaries with the scars inflicted on the young boy by the people of his own religion and village. The tone of his writing is not evocative of any anger but the consequence of every experience leaves the Dalit questioning his existence and the non-Dalit ashamed of his action. The dissatisfaction does not demand a violent revolution but an insistence of his fellows to learn from the pain and educate their way towards a respectable tomorrow. *Scar* is not any depiction of wound that might inflict pain but the continuous humiliation of a scar marked for a lifetime, a label of caste that does not fade away with time and every time that the Dalit attempts to flutter his wings he is reminded of his place in the society, a place that no human deserves. Gunasekaran does not beg for mercy or waits for a savior to protect him but earns a respectable place through his music, an art that breaks the barriers of caste and is accepted by all. The subjective pain of Gunasekaran's *The Scar* only shows the wound through his experience but the pain inflicted is indeed the cry of all, the community which is seldom heard. As P. Dayanandan said in a talk at the book release of the *Anthology of Tamil Dalit Writing*:

> It is a story of many people, knit together in overflowing concern for each other, transcending caste and pouring affection to affirm life...Scar is not a story of a sobbing Dalit but of a triumphant Dalit, a symbol of dignity and humanity, telling the world that it is possible to bury caste.

Gunasekaran begins his novel with a historical conflict, a blur in the history of religions and the monuments constructed for their worships. The Rettaimalai Srinivasan and Ayodhidasa Pandithar's accouts that the Siva temple of Elayankudi, one which the author had never entered, was constructed by the Saivities putting at stake the thousands of Jains to whom the site actually belonged. The historical glitch shakes the very foundation of all the evidences that the upper caste boasts of in order to create a natural condition of eternal sanctity. It questions the power position that snatches from the Dalit his very right of any identity and humanity. It questions the base of a State Apparatus that skillfully dominates nearly one-fifth of the population in the name of a history. The prejudices of a society that believes and make believe that being a Dalit is a curse, a punishment of the sins of the previous birth and forces them to slave for the upper caste as redemption of their sin of being born a Dalit!

Caste is an unarguable mark of identity in India. It affects each individual born under the wing of Hinduism and allots them a position in the caste hierarchy irrespective of their intellectual evolution or economic position. The same tag that elevates a section to the zenith pushes down another to the abysm of inhumanity. The oppressed loses a sense of true identity and is tricked into a lifetime of slavery. The declaration of Gunasekaran's caste is accompanied with the instance of his relatives being ashamed of their existence and shying away from the co-bearers of the tag. Every Dalit struggles with the authenticity of his existence; he doesn't wake from the grave of oppression and question the so-called superiors but accepts his fate and dexterously work towards improving his condition. In seeking an identity he stumbles through multiple identities none of which is respectable enough that he could pass onto his generations. He toils slavishly, accepts the leftover, respects his superior, and plays by the rule of hierarchy but after every attempt he is thrown to the dungeons. The only solution that remains is a migration, a cultural migration, an artistic migration, an occupational migration, a migration from his reality, from his existence, in the words of P. Dayanandan:

> So we look for Buddhist or Naga lineages, link to Pallava, Pandiya or Sakya royal families, connect with Devendran whether he is the Vedic Indra or the Buddhist Aindriran. And we all want to be Adi Dravida, ex-untouchable, older brother of a Brahmin, and my original religion was Buddhism!

Gunasekaran's experience, his struggle for an identity and his toil towards acceptance sketches a portrait of a hegemonic society where the dominating caste ensures its status by exhausting every hegemonic tool. From coercion to forced acceptance, every form of power is used to ensure that the hierarchy of the oppressor and oppressed is maintained. Foucault's analysis of power suggests that "power is everywhere" and that these power relations are embedded in the very iota of social life that then governs the actions of an individual from birth to death. Where Foucauldian power points at an oppressor, Gramsci believes that the power is operated at the level of a mutual interaction in the "hegemonic" discourse. Gramsci deduces that power is exerted through ideology, through constantly working on the mentality of the mass via institutions of a civil society. According to Marx, ideology is a system of ideas that dominate the mind of a social group. Althusser on the other hand understands ideology with the help of Freudian concept of consciousness and believes that 'ideology is external, exactly like the unconscious.' (Althusser, 47) It is this ideology then that forms a "collective will" which is the operative awareness of historical necessity, a 'protagonist of a real and effective historical drama' (Gramsci, 130). A drama that always has a dominant and a dominated, a binary relation of power that complies with the dominant will of the time. This will is a strategic manipulation of the ruling class so that they continue to dominate by winning the 'active consent' (Carnoy, 65) of those over whom they rule. The main function of a State is then to create 'conformist' citizens who 'internalise the most restrictive aspects of the civil life, and accept them as their natural duties without having any resentment.' (Gramsci,

242) Gunasekaran's village that is bound together on the very basis of caste acts as the ideal setup of a Gramsciam State and it becomes essential to unfold every layer of the State apparatus to diagnose the very foundation of the scar that never heals.

The hegemonic State functions through the synchronised working of a superstructure that includes the civil society and the political society or the Ideological State Apparatus and Repressive State Apparatus respectively. Where the political society (RSA) operates through coercion and ensures the final formal domination may that be through violence, the civil society (ISA) works towards consensus and spontaneous submission of the mass through creating and proclaiming an ideology. Althusser enumerates eight categories of Ideological State Apparatus which include the religious, educational, family, legal, political, trade-union, communications and cultural. The educational ISA proves the most effective as it kneads the mind of young and ensures a future of dominance hence ensuring a generation that reproduces the relations of production. *The Scar* enumerates such instances where the alienation of the caste begins at the very vulnerable years when not many are aware of their role in the State Apparatus. While talking about the formative years of his life, Gunasekaran talks about his school and college in detail which unfolds the working of the educational ISA, he remembers:

> 'How many in this class are Parayars?' he would ask.
>
> Even now it hurts to think about those times when we had to stand up in front of the others in the class, shrinking and cringing. They would reinforce caste identities by labeling us Pallars, Parayars and Chakiliyars in front of our friends who never knew what caste was. (Gunasekaran, 5)

The school that is supposed to build the foundation of tomorrow and break the fetters of today reinforces the ideology of the dominant class so that the young minds are carved with the same tool and shaped in accordance with the collective will. In the discussion of State power and State Apparatus, Gramsci talks about a very important participant, the intellectual. He talks about the two types of intellectuals, organic and traditional, where the organic intellectual works within a class towards strengthening its position the traditional intellectual is merely the residue of the previous class formation. The organic intellectual works towards providing its class with intellects and ensures domination through ideological consent which prevails among the masses through different institutions. Gramsci believes that these intellectuals perform a specific social function and work as the functionaries towards any revolution. It would not be wrong to understand through the Gramscian notion that Ambedkar's rigorous attempt at educating every Dalit of the society was to create a force of organic intellectuals who possess the revolutionary possibility of subverting the existing dominant order and establish the hegemony of the oppressed. Every Dalit autobiography thus reserves a special place in the functioning of the ideology of organic intellectuals.

The hegemony of the State not only ensures that the Apparatuses work in accordance to the dominant ideology but engages its decentralised separation of powers (legislature, judiciary, executive) to ensure the same. This conception could be understood at the micro level, where ideological nurture failed ideologies were enforced through force. The enforcement would not stop at the school level but would continue at every walk of their lives, every minute they would be reminded of their place in the hegemonic superstructure. The lower castes had a separate hostel to themselves but the facilities at the Harijan Hostel reminded them that they were the oppressed and were required to submit to the "will" for their mere survival. They were not given enough to eat and majority of the times they would have to stay hungry. The functioning of the intellectuals gets defeated out of mere starvation and so fails the revolution to subvert the dominant ideology. The Apparatus ensures that the oppressed is caught up in the vicious circle of the materialistic existence and all that is expected from the institution that forms the foundation is that

> Nothing will ever change
> Neither rasam nor sundal. (6)

Althusser believes that ideology plays a crucial role in reproduction of relations of production and that 'if a certain regime fails to reproduce its conditions of production, it itself will cease to exist' (Althusser 22). It thus becomes important for the dominant to make available condition of reproduction of relations of production for the oppressed because although they do not want to threaten the ideological apparatus but for the working of the State they require the oppressed to live. The oppressor thus provides the oppressed with wages, though not enough for them to live comfortably but a meager amount so that they continue to live and be a passive subject to the hegemony. Gunasekaran talks about the slavish jobs he would be asked to perform for their "master". He remembers the time when he would have to stand outside his master's home with old tin boxes and would be given some rice and dry fruits in lieu of mats as if it were a favor from the master and not the deserved price of the mats. The upper castes would employ the lower castes to deliver news of the dead to neighboring villages, where although the sender would not pay the messenger but the receiver might give a measure or two of paddy and it was unarguably accepted as the wages. In the season for reaping, the Dalit would be busy with rat-hunting and the rainy season would bring the occupation of rabbit-hunting. When an ideology is accepted and the State functions around the collective will it clearly refers that the oppressed confirm their status and the hegemony operates through the consensus of majority. The mass that refuses to confirm are left but with the only option of migrating and thus escaping from the clutches of the State Power, whereas those who abide by the power relations accept any intellectual claiming his dominance with some historical evidence and the precise use of his intellect. The Dalit agrees to the slavishness he is subjected to and does not require a Brahmin to order him around, he unquestionably accepts any master that claims the upper ladder of hegemony. The lower castes that did not get respect from the upper castes would direct their hatred towards the lowest order of the Apparatus and thus hegemony grew like venom in the veins of State.

The day would break every morning in the cheri with their arrogant voices calling the lower castes to work in their fields. The lower castes on the other hand were happy to accept these Konars as their masters and would proudly refer to 'my master's house' and 'your master's house' in their conversations. This is a type of slavery. (36)

In my mother's birthplace, Keeranoor, Maravars would act like Brahmins. In my Periamma's village, the Konars were the Brahmins.

The Konars were not treated well by the Brahmins, and they in turn appropriated the caste arrogance of the Brahmins and showed it to the people of the Cheri. (36)

Foucault talks about the objectification of human that ultimately makes him a subject and the struggle against this subjection then churns power and thus the force of the society. It is this process that demands not only the mere wages but an interaction of punishment and praise. According to Foucault, the law does not only repress and restrict but also produces the rewards. It helps in binding the oppressed to the ideology that ultimately makes him slavish. The punishment urges him to perform better and imprints the lesson in his mind whereas the rewards justify the punishment and encourage the subject to increase his praiseworthy activities. The subject thus is reduced to the infant who is taught the very first lessons of his life through the futile praises and encouragement. The praise letter given to Gunasekaran in the college after he sang might have encouraged him to participate in the cultural activities but it also seemed like a consolation to the pet animal that is insulted in the public but only after he proves himself worthy of his master's affection does he deserve a consolatory pat. The punishments would be instantaneous and harsher. The one time when Gunasekaran had set up a shop with a gift sheet in front of a school, he was wronged by an upper caste boy and though Gunasekaran did not bulge and followed him right through the upper caste street and hit him he was only punished with threats that subjected him to leave the premises of the village with immediate effect. The rights and wrongs narrowed when it came to the segregation of caste and the only concern that lingered was 'how can a fellow from your (paraya) caste enter the upper caste street? And worse, how did he enter our house.' (26) The premises were rigid and any defiance would be greeted with punishment. The dalits would be advised to keep a distance of at least eight feet when an upper caste passes by and any deviation would result in slaps that would get imprinted. The roads were for the sole use of oppressors and whatever may the condition be the lower castes would always have to tread in the mud. If a Dalit requires a mere signature in the school scholarship form he would be subjected to menial jobs. The subjection constructs a power relationship where not only the ideology but the identity including the name is fabricated and allotted, a name that reminds the oppressed of his place in the hierarchy.

> Do you know whom you have addressed as "Dei"? We will cut your tongue. Are you aware of the difference between your caste and ours…be careful and know your caste before you speak. (51)

Louis Dumont sees hierarchy as the opposition between pure and impure, the relationship of encompassing and being encompassed. He states that in the caste system, the principle of purity encompasses the impure. It is this segregation of purity and impurity that the lower castes are subjected to most ruthlessly. They are considered impure and the regime of purity is exercised through untouchability, a demon that engulfs the humanity. Gunasekaran remembers the separate bowls he was made to eat in at his 'master's' home and the separate tea cups that would demarcate their status or the exclusion from the temples. They still console themselves with what little affection is thrown at them, 'unless our people play the drums first, the drum inside the temple will not be played. It is our people who will lead the procession of the deity by playing the parai.' (90) The instruments would be played by Dalit and they would lead the processions but the politics of purity would not let them enter the temple beyond a certain point as if the impurity would corrupt the deity and still the conformist mass felt rewarded, 'they have allowed us to enter at least till here even after knowing who we are.' (90) Dumont studies the division of Indian society and the disintegration of groups under three characteristics, the first of which separates the caste in matters of marriage and contact, direct or indirect. Gunasekaran in his novella explicitly talks about the glitches of love marriage in his village where intercaste marriages are forbidden and any action otherwise would only result in honour killing. The reality of love marriages is only a cinematic dream, a dividing line from where the real and reel lives tear apart.

> The idea that the village exists because of caste must change, only then will intercaste marriages be possible…the village high caste people, wanting to safeguard caste, would round up the couple…and finish them off quietly…the love they depict in the movies simply vanish into thin air in reality. (Gunasekaran, 39)

A State Apparatus cannot function without the ideology of the mass confirming to the collective will and in the case of caste exploitation the situation worsened because illiteracy and poverty forced the lower castes to become the intellectual slaves of their counterparts. They not only accepted the ideology but internalised the hegemonic system of classification so much so that even when not under supervision their actions would confirm to the ideology of the oppressors. They would not disturb water in fear of it turning muddy and smelly and thus unfit for the upper castes and the fear of being beaten. The tag of caste went with them wherever they went; it was like the scarlet letter tied to their bosom. The condition of a Dalit in the State Apparatus was like that of the Kasukkati bird which had entered the class by mistake and was subjected with chalks and dusters, her fate bringing her down dead and ending up as an appetite of the teacher. Gramsci believes that the mere control of political society would not change anything; the hegemonic institutions within the civil society must also be done away with. Foucault claims, 'nothing will be changed if the mechanisms of power that function outside, below and alongside the State apparatuses, on a much more minute and everyday level are not changed' (Foucault, 60). Any change at the micro level would only be expected if the Dalit stop and think if he is a mere object or a subjugated subject in the hegemonic structure. The question that Gunasekaran indeed raises at the end of his novel, in a song;

What is this, O deity Jakamma? The world,
Is hanging upside down – is it right? (95)
Human Being! We are human beings,
Like you, like him.
We too are human beings,
Our bones and flesh bake in the fire lit by you,
Your government and court,
Pouring oil on it.
You keep declaring this and that as allowance-
When we were all burning down,
Whose hair,
Did you go to pluck? (95)

Works Cited

Althusser, Louis. "Ideology and Ideological State Apparatuses". *Literary Theory: An Introductory Reader*. Eds. Saugata Bhaduri and Simi Malhotra. Delhi: Anthem, 2010. 21-67. Print.

Carlyle, Thomas. *Historical Essays*. Ed. Chris Vanden Bossche. California: University of California Press, 2002. Print.

Carnoy, Martin. *The State and Political Theory*. Cambridge University Press. 1986. Print.

Daldal, Asli. "Power and Ideology in Michel Foucault and Antonio Gramsci: A Comparative Analysis". *Review of History and Political Science* 2. No. 2 (2014). 149-167. Web.

Foucault, Michel. *Discipline and Punish, 2nd* ed. New York: Vintage. 1995. Print.

Gramsci, Antonio. *History, Philosophy and Culture in the Young Gramsci*. Eds. Pedro Cavalcanti and Paul Piccone: Telos. 1975. Print.

Gramsci, Antonio. *Selections from the Prison Notebooks.* 6th ed. London: Wishart Publications, 1980. Print.

Gramsci, Antonio. "The Formation of the Intellectual". *Literary Theory: An Introductory Reader*. Eds. Saugata Bhaduri and Simi Malhotra. Delhi: Anthem, 2010. 9-20. Print.

Gunasekaran, K.A. *The Scar*. Trans. V. Kadambari. Chennai: Orient Blackswan, 2009. Print.

Kavitha, K. "Dalit Literature in India". *Paripex-Indian Journal of Research* 3. (2014). 239-241. Print.

P. Dayanandan. *Personal Interview.* 10 April 2012.

Roy, Pascal. *Design and Truth in Autobiography*. London: Routledge and Kegan, 1960. Print.

Rege, Sharmila. *Writing Caste / Writing Gender, Narrating Dalit Women's Testimonios*. New Delhi: Zuban, 2006. Print.

14

Casteism, Discrimination and Hindutva Philosophy in Kancha Ilaiah's *Why I am Not a Hindu*

Ashok Kumar

Kancha Ilaiah is also known as Kancha Ilaiah Shepherd. He was born on 5th October, 1952 in the village of Papaiahpet in Warangal district. His belongs to a sheep-grazing Kuruma Golla caste. He has earned his M. Phil. and Ph.D. in Political Science. He has taught Political Science at Osmania University, Hyderabad. Presently, he is working as a director of the Centre for Social Exclusion and Inclusive Policy in Maulana Azad National Urdu University, Hyderabad. He has been awarded the Mahatma Jyotirao Phule Award and he was a Nehru Fellow from 1994 to 1997. He has appended "Shepherd" with his name in May 2016 to show his roots. He has written many books and articles. His main books include *Why I am not a Hindu*; *God as Political Philosopher: Buddha's Challenge to Brahminism*; *Post-Hindu India: A Discourse in Dalit-Bahujan; Socio-Spiritual and Scientific Revolution*; *Untouchable God: A Novel on Caste and Race, The State and Repressive Culture*, *God As Political Philosopher: Buddha's challenge to Brahminism*; *Buffalo Nationalism: A Critique of Spiritual Fascism* etc.

Ilaiah's autobiography *Why I am not a Hindu* is a ground-breaking text in the history of Dalit literature. This book has seven chapters. The first chapter "Childhood Formations" tells about his childhood experiences. The second chapter "Marriage, Market and Social

Relations" deals with issues on marriage, market and relationships and it offers a comparative analysis of his caste and Hindus. The third chapter is "The Emergence of Neo-Kshatriyas and the Reorganisation of Power Relations". The fourth chapter "Contemporary Hinduism" tells about present concept of Hinduism. In the fifth chapter "Hindu Gods and Us; Our Goddesses and Hindus" Kancha Ilaiah narrates how Dalitbhujans' gods and goddesses are far better than the Hindu gods and goddesses. The second last chapter "Hindu Death and Our Death" also deals with the rituals and philosophy about life and death between Hindus and Dalitbahujans. "Dalitisation Not Hinduisation" is a concluding chapter and in this chapter Kancha Ilaiah gives many reasons why he prefers to be a Dalit and not a Hindu. Kancha Ilaiah writes in the Preface of his book:

> This book is an outcome of my constant interaction with the Dalitbahujans in the Dalit and civil rights movements, who kept telling me, in a variety of ways, about their culture, economy and politics. What I have done is to put their ideas down in a systematic way. Apart from my personal experiences all the ideas in this book are picked up from illiterate and semi-literate Dalitbahujans and also from a few formally educated Dalitbahujan organic intellectuals (Preface, vi).

Present paper is an attempt to analyse some aspects of Kancha Ilaiah's autobiography *Why I am Not a Hindu*. He has frankly narrated every aspect of his Dalit community. Kancha Ilaiah writes in the Introduction of his book:

> I was born in a small South Indian Telangana village in the early fifties and grew up in the sixties. Our villages had undergone all the turbulence of the freedom movement as they were part of a historical struggle known as the Telangana Armed Struggle. Perhaps as part of the first generation that was born and brought up in post-colonial India, an account of my childhood experiences would also be a narrative of the cultural contradictions that we are undergoing. Village India has not changed radically from my childhood days to the present. If there are any changes, the changes are marginal. Urban India is only an extension of village

India. There is a cultural continuum between village India and urban India. (x)

Kancha Ilaiah's *Why I am Not a Hindu* is an interesting book to explore many issues on the Hindutva ideology. Such books should be prescribed in the syllabus for the UG and PG students so that the students may be acquainted with the Dalit literature. This book describes the bad experiences of people belonging to the shepherd community and their skills how they were capable to breed and look after the sheep. The book attacks on the Brahministic system and how the upper caste people have deprived them even from their rights on gods.

Kancha Ilaiah has not seen Brahmin children in the fields because they were always busy in eating food or chanting some *mantras* or hymns. They were completely adhered to the religion and there was no any negotiation of sex in their homes. Only lower caste children were seen in the fields. Ilaiah tells that Dalit children knew about sex because it was taught at their homes while Brahmin children knew nothing about it and it seemed as if sex does not exist on the earth.

Kancha Ilaiah narrates some points in this autobiography due to which he has become the centre of controversy among Hindus. He narrates that Hindus treated their children untouchables and mothers did not touch their children. The married women and widows were treated very inhumanly.

Kancha Ilaiah attacks on the Hindu mythological gods Lord Rama and Krishna. He tells that Hindu gods are violent and big cheaters. In an indirect way, he wants to tell that Hindus are the followers of the Lord Krishna who has always done the *ras leela* and he has always won the wars by dint of cheating. Pandavas kill the Kauravas because they belonged to a lower caste and Pandavas were the children of gods. Likewise Lord Rama also had killed the king of the monkey, Bali by cheating by hiding behind a tree. So Ilaiah does not believe on such Hindus whose gods are like this. Kancha Ilaiah openly attacks on such hypocrisies of the mythological epics of the Hindus. Hindu scriptures have also become the cause of mass destructions also. The invention of atom bomb was inspired from the Bhagavad Gita and such kinds of books should be banned. Even people who discovered atom bomb were influenced by Bhagwad Gita. Later these bombs took lives of numerous people in Hiroshima and Nagasaki —two main cities of Japan.

Kancha Ilaiah is not sure that he was born in a Hindu family as their parents were not the part of the Hindu society and they had a different world of their own. They just knew that they were born in Kurumaa caste.

> I was not born a Hindu for the simple reason that my parents did not know that they were Hindus. This does not mean that I was born as a Muslim, a Christian, a Buddhist, a Sikh or a Parsee. My illiterate parents, who lived in a remote South Indian village, did not know that they belonged to any religion at all. People belong to a religion only when they know that they are part of the people who worship that God, when they go to those temples and take part in the rituals and festivals of that religion. My parents had only one identity and that was their caste: they were Kurumaas. (1)

Kancha Ilaiah's family was not excluded from the social system of the village as his ancestors have been caste heads for two generations. He narrates it in his autobiography:

> This does not mean that my family alone was excluded from the religious process because it was a family that could be ignored or neglected. Not so. For two generations my ancestors had been the caste heads. My mother and her mother-in-law (that is, my grandmother) were members of a leading family of the Kurumaa caste. In the village economy, Kurumaas, Gollaas, Goudaas, Kapuus, Shalaas, Chakaalies, Mangalies and Maadigaas, formed the majority in terms of numbers. The entire village economy was governed by the daily operations of these castes. (02)

Not only this, there were different eating habits in the Hindu and Dalit families. The people of Kancha's caste enjoyed non-vegetarian food while Hindus disliked this kind of food. They even never discussed about meat:

> For all Dalitbahujans good food means meat and fish. We enjoy it, we relish it. For Brahmin-Baniya boys and girls even a discussion about meat and fish makes them feel like vomiting.

> For Maadigaas and Muslims beef is an item to be relished; though for us it was prohibited, we never hated it as the Brahmin-Baniyas did. (12)

There were different terminologies of knowledge in the Hindu and Dalit families. Hindus just considered knowledge only through religious books and learning them but the people of Kancha's caste were practical in their attitude towards life. Kancha offers a comparative analysis of the Hindus and Dalits:

> In the *Ramayana* and the *Mahabharatha*, knowledge and courage were defined in these terms. But in our real life a knowledgeable person is one who has knowledge of social functions—one who knows about sheep-breeding, agriculture, rope making; one who can diagnose the nature of the diseases of animals and human beings. A courageous person is one who can fight tigers, lions, snakes, wild bulls; who can travel deep into forests, swim the rivers and find the missing goats and sheep. (17)

Kancha Ilaiah tells that the people of their caste are hard-working men but the Hindus just eat and learn the mantras to perform rituals. They don't have fellow feelings and when they perform the rituals they ask the money without keeping in view the economic condition of the man. They are selfish also. Kancha Ilaiah tells the real pain of his heart in these words:

> The Brahmin-Baniyas walked over the corpses of our culture. They were the gluttons while our parents were the poor starving people—producing everything for the Other's comfort. Their children were the most unskilled gluttons, whereas our children were the contributors to the national economy itself. Their notion of life was unworthy of life itself, but they repeatedly told our parents that we were the most useless people. Having gone through all these stages of life, having acquired the education that enabled us to see a wider world, when we reflect upon our childhood and its processes it is nothing but anger and anguish which keep burning in our hearts. (19)

To sum up it can be stated that Kancha Ilaiah has narrated the pains and sufferings of his caste silently but somehow he gives many reasons why he is not a Hindu. His caste has its own rituals and many of them are much better than the rituals and traditions of the Hindus. Dr Raj Kumar observes, "When the Dalits endeavour to rise up in the social scale, they are too often brutally crushed by the upper castes and sometimes by the state machinery." (Kumar, 116) If this book is read with a concentrated mind then the readers get an ample idea of the evils prevailing in the Indian Hindu society. This book is a critique on the Hindu social order. Dr Abid Kotta remarks about this book:

> The book *Why I am not a Hindu* is a classic and a critique that serves as a blue print for the later dalit sensitisation. With a sincere academic honesty, Kancha Ilaiah diagnoses pathologically the malevolent diseases that India suffers. Along with a beautiful preface and introduction, the text has seven wonderful chapters. Those chapters are the real life pictures of India. The text discusses childhood formations, marriage, market and social relations, emergence of Neo-Kshatriyas and the reorganisation of power relations, contemporary Hinduism, Hindu Gods and Us; Our Goddesses and Hindus, Hindu death and our Death and finally Dalitisation Not Hinduisation. (Kotta, 51)

Works Cited

Abid, Kotta. "Identity Blueprint: The Dalitisation Efforts in Kancha Ilaiah's *Why I am Not a Hindu*." *Indian Dalit Autobiographies: Marginalised Voices*. Ed. Singh, Bijender. New Delhi, Authorspress, 2015. pp. 49-57. Print. Dalit Nation–The Only Authentic Voice of Dalits. Kancha Ilaiah–Why I am not a Hindu. December 14, 2007. Retrieved on 15/07/2016.

https://dalitnation.wordpress.com/2007/12/14/kancha-ilaiah-why-i-am-not-a-hindu/

Ilaiah, Kancha. *Why I Am Not a Hindu: A Sudra Critique of Hindutva Philosophy, Culture and Political Economy*. (1996) Calcutta: Samya, 2002. Print.

Raj, Kumar. *Dalit Personal Narratives: Reading Caste, Nation and Identity*. Hyderabad: Orient Blackswan, 2012. Print.

15

Transformation of Dalits from 'Being' to 'Becoming': A Study of Narendra Jadhav's *Outcaste: A Memoir* and Omprakash Valmiki's *Joothan*

DIPAK GIRI

Dalit Autobiography is a distinctive literary form in the sense that it shifts from personal 'I' to universal 'We'. This shifting from individualism to universalism differentiates such autobiographies from mainstream autobiographies where the autobiography only centres round personal experiences of the autobiographer concerned. On the other hand, Dalit Autobiographies deal with double aspects– both the individual writer and the community he or she belonged to. Transformation of individualistic 'I' into universalistic 'We' makes such autobiographies completely distinctive literary form. Dalit Autobiography as a completely distinctive literary form came into existence in the 1960s when a group of Dalit writers took their pen inspired by the message of Mahatma Jyotirao Phule and Dr Ambedkar, *"Don't let your pen be restricted to your own questions"* (Nimabalkar, 32-33). The first phase of such autobiographies mainly covered the Dalit writers of Maharashtra who wrote their autobiographies in Marathi between the periods of 1960s and 1970s. From 1980s to 1990s Dalit autobiographies spread out from the regional level to the national level. During this period many Dalit writers made their appearance in the literary arena of Dalit Autobiography and then such autobiographies were written in various regional languages.

Later Dalit autobiographies earned great popularity among public and the growing interest of public took this literary form from national to global level when many Dalit Autobiographies were translated into English. Among such autobiographies, Narendra Jadhav's *'Outcaste: A Memoir'* translated into English from Marathi *'Amcha Baap aan Amhi'* and Omprakash Valmiki's *'Joothan'* are worth-mentioning. The origin of former is Maharashtra, one of the important states of Southern India, whereas the later is written in Uttar Pradesh which comes under the territory of Northern India. Though they are written in different regions, languages and cultures, they serve same object and purpose reflecting the plight and struggle of Dalits.

Although, the term *'Dalit'* was first used by Ambedkar in 1928 in his journal *'Bahishkrit Bharat'* (Outcaste India), yet the origin and history of Dalits was not as new and modern as Ambedkerian time, rather its origin was as old and ancient as Rig Vedic time. The mythical figure of *'Purusa-Sukta'* mentioned in the *'Rig Veda'* was the origin of the Indian Caste System. Purusa is *"the man...with thousand heads, a thousand eyes, a thousand feet...the ruler of immortality"* (Doniger o' Flaherty, Wendy, 2000:30). All creatures were believed to be parts of Purusa and it was believed that human beings also came from his mighty body. *"His mouth became the Brahmin; his arms were made into the warrior, his thighs the business people and from his feet the servants were born"* (Ibid). This formed the very basis of Vedic Caste System – *Brahmins, Kshatriyas, Vaisyas* and *Shudras* which fell into many sub-divisions and among those sub-divisions, the lowliest of all which is presently identified as *'Dalit'*, was considered as the most despicable class which stood apart the value structure of contemporary caste and social system. This class of people was considered as untouchable, the stigma of which they had to bear throughout their life. History says that they have been being exploited, tortured and abused by the upper classes since the very origin of Caste System. Presently they are called by many names in different parts of India like *dasa, dasya, raksasa, asura, avarna, nisoda, panchama* etc. After India got freedom, they were given constitutional rights and they all came to be identified as *'Scheduled Caste'*. Though the Article 17 of our constitution is against the practice of untouchability, untouchabiliy is still seen in some form or other in our present social system. Narendra Jadhav's *'Outcaste: A Memoir'* and Omprakash Valmiki's *'Joothan'* awaken Dalits with voice of protest against the existing social system which divides man to man creating two classes of people – *'haves'* and *'have-nots'*.

Narendra Jadhav's *Outcaste: A Memoir* is the story of struggle and success of a Dalit family in Maharashtra spanning three generations of the family concerned. The autobiography can be read "*in two levels- it's the story of a family on the one hand; it's also about the social metamorphosis that has taken place over the past 80 years*" (Anand, 32). The book falls into four divisions entitled 'Up Against Bondage', 'Towards Freedom', 'The Struggle' and 'Making of the Second Generation'. The Epilogue has been attached by the youngest member of the fourth generation of Jadhav family, Apoorva, seventeen year old daughter of Narendra Jadhav. The narrative is written from Damu's point of view. Damu Runjaji Jadhav, father of Narendra Jadhav belongs to the first generation of the family and is the central figure of all the incidents described in the narrative. Narrated from the perspectives of father, mother, himself and his teenage daughter, the memoir traces the journey of Damu, the author's father, from a small village in Maharashtra to Mumbai. This journey proves the most crucial event in Damu's life giving his and his family a true identifiable life from their past anonymousness. The journey is a transition of Damu's family from poverty-stricken life to a life of dignity and recognition.

The image of Damu in Narendra Jadhav's *Outcaste: A Memoir* is an image of a rebel who is in against of present society which treats people born in low classes worse than animals. In his Author's note, Narendra Jadhav describes Damu as, "*Damu was not a leader...but he refused to define himself by circumstances and aimed at shaping his own destiny*" or, "*Damu had no formal education...yet he steered his children to educational heights and inculcated in them the spirit of excellence*", or "*Damu was not a guru...but he taught his children to believe in themselves and retain human dignity*", or "*Damu was often humbled. Yet he maintained, goats are special offerings, not lions*" or "*Damu was an ordinary man, they said.....but he did an extraordinary thing; he stood up against the tyranny of the caste system*" (Jadhav, XI-XII). The portrayal of Damu goes beyond the ordinary portrayal as it has given force and energy to Dalit movement. When the narrative starts, we find Damu as a member of Mahar caste living at Ozar village of Nashik District in Maharashtra. Mahar caste comes under the category of untouchable caste. The people of Mahar caste perform menial works which include dragging the dead animals, conveying the message of death along with guarding and protecting dead bodies. In return they get the stale food from the houses of Savarna people. Inspired by Ambedkarite Movement, Damu stands against the tasks assigned to the Mahars. He protests the duty of *'Yeskar Mahar'*. *'Yeskar Mahar'* is the privileged Mahar whose duty is to beg for *'Baluta'*, a special right bestowed on a fortunate Mahar to collect the stale food from every Savarna household by begging. He also refuses to obey the order of a Fauzdar even after being beaten severely to get the corpse of the Savarna woman out of the well. When his eldest cousin tries to remind him the conventional duty of Mahars, he came in rage and replied him haughtily: *"What kind of a tradition is this that treats Mahars worse than cats and dogs?...I spit on these inhuman traditions. I am not going to abide by such traditions. I am a man of dignity and I will not go from house to house begging for Baluta. What are all of you going to do? Kill me?" (Ibid,* 10).

After being humiliated from Fauzdar and Mamledar, Damu decides to leave the village that very night. He flees away with his wife Sonu to Mumbai for new prospect of life: *"together, they started walking towards freedom" (Ibid,* 26). Struggling there hard Damu gives his family and his next generations a dignified life. He has to work at various places to run his family- in the Railways, the Port Trust and some textile mills. He never compromises with hardships and difficulties and his continuous labour finally gives him everything he has desired in life. He responds to the call of Ambedkar and joins the Ambedkarite Movement for the emancipation of Dalits involving himself actively in the Mahad Satyagrah (1927), the Nasik Temple Entry Movement (1930), the conversion movement (1956) and other Dalit movements. His participations in these Dalit movements give him the sense of dignity as a human being, the sense which he later teaches to his family members. His philosophies become the life-guiding principle to his next generations. His visions of life have a far-reaching influence upon all the members of the family. Inspired by his father's vision of life, Narendra Jadhav affirms, *"If others look down on me in their belief that my caste is low. It is their problem, not mine. I certainly don't need to torment myself over it. I pity them, for they are the victims of their own obsolete prejudice....Dignity, after all rests in the mind and heart and soul. I have to reclaim it not from outside, but from within. And for that I must cut off the albatross of the caste system from my soul, once and for all"* (*Ibid,* 214). Following the footprints of his grandfather and identifying herself among Dalits Apoorva, Jadhav's daughter forgets her past identity as Mahars. Dalit identity gives her confidence and pride to reject her ascribed status as a low caste Mahars. She feels: *"Now I think, I know who I am. I am Apoorva, not tied down by race, religion, or caste"* (*Ibid,* 263). Frank confession of Sonu to her husband Damu shows clearly how Damu's decision in being identifiable with Dalits has added a new happy chapter in their life: *"Truly, we sensed a change in the way we carried ourselves. We proudly proclaimed ourselves Dalits, with our chin up, and we looked everyone in the eye. We began to lose our former servility, associated with being born in a low caste"* (*Ibid,* 178).Thus, Damu, in spite of having low birth, sets the minds of his family members free from the stigma of caste teaching them the value of humanity.

Inspired by Ambedkar's message, Damu takes the weapon of education to fight against the prevalent caste system and this weapon proves very effective. His sons get fame and recognition becoming educated. Education has earned for them a distinctive place in the society. Jayavant is an IAS officer who is striving for upliftment of Dalits. Dinesh who is an administrative officer at the Mumbai Municipal Corporation is working for the welfare of Dalits. Last but not the least, Narendra, the youngest son of the family is the Vice Chancellor of University of Pune who is trying to keep contributions on the development of Dalit community. Damu even tries to educate his wife Sonu, something that was very rare in those days. His efforts bring colour as his sons rise to high positions in their professional fields.

Omprakash Valmiki's *'Joothan',* though written in different region, language and culture, conforms to the same tone and temper of Narendra Jadhav's *'Outcaste: A Memoir'*. The very title of Omprakash Valmiki's *'Joothan'* reminds us the custom of begging '*Baluta*' from Savarna household in Mahar community in Nashik as the very word "*Joothan*" in Hindi means scraps of food left on a plate, intended either for feeding animals or throwing into the garbage. Both *'Baluta'* and *'Joothan'* are excess of food left by the eaters. Again, education which is the solution of every problem becomes the main motto in both. Just as Damu works hard to educate his children to fight against unjust and irrationality, likewise Valmiki's parents never gave up their struggling life in their noble mission of educating Valmiki. Both these memoirs are inspired by the message of Ambedkar for the empowerment of Dalits in India. Both these writing reveal the reality of Dalits in the present social set up. Both aim to reform the conditions of Dalits. Both inculcate in Dalits the spirit of dignity and fill in them the true passion for freedom and equality from foot to the crown.

Omprakash Valmiki's *'Joothan'* narrates the story of a Dalit boy confined into the four walls of a village school which proved for him the caste stigmatized walls of torture and inhumanity and his escape from those walls. Valmiki belonged to Chuhra caste which was known as the lowest caste at the village of Barla which was the birth place of Valmiki situated in the Muzzafarnagar district of Uttar Pradesh. Those who belonged to this caste during Valmiki's time had to do menial works like sweeping the roads, cleaning the cattle barns, mopping the floor, getting involved into disposal of dead animals, working in the fields during harvests and performing other physical labour for upper caste people, including the Tyagi Brahmins. People of Chuhra community were of low birth and they often became the victims of inhuman treatment. People of upper caste, including the Tyagi's abused them and instead of calling them by name, they called them out, "*Oye Chuhre*" or "*Abey Chuhre*" in insulting way. During his boyhood, Valmiki's entire family worked hard, yet they, "*didn't manage to get two decent meals a day, not the least because they often didn't get paid for their labour and instead got sworn at and abused*" (*Valmiki,* 24).

Valmiki's "Joothan" is penned with the tears of pain and anguish of a little Dalit boy experienced during his childhood at school.

Valmiki suffered ill-treatment both from his fellow students and teachers when he was attending school. "*The Tyagi children would torment me by calling the son of Chuhra. Sometimes, they'd beat me up for no reason. It was a strange painful life that had made me an introvert, irritable and short-tempered. If I got thirsty in school, then I had to stand near the hand-pump. The boys would beat me in any case, but the teachers also punished me. All sorts of stratagems were tried so that I would run away from the school and take up the kind of work for which I was born*" (*Ibid,* 13). He was not allowed to take part in school activities: "*I was kept out of extracurricular activities. On such occasions, I stood on the margins like a spectator. During the annual functions of the school, when rehearsals were on for the play, I too wished for a role. But I always had to stand outside the door. The so-called descendants of the gods cannot understand the anguish of standing outside the door*" (*Ibid,* 16). He did not get permission of entry to experiment in chemistry lab and when he complained the principal against the chemistry teacher, no action was taken. As a result he performed poor in chemistry examination. "*Not only did I do very poorly in the lab tests in the board exam, I also got low marks in the oral, even though I had answered the examiner's questions quite correctly*" (*Ibid,* 65). He was not allowed to sit with the children of upper class: "*I had to sit away from the others in the class, and that too on the floor. The mat ran out before door*" (*Ibid,* 02). Not only had the students and the teachers but other officials of the school also treated him worst than animals: "*During the examinations we could not drink water from the glass when thirsty. To drink water, we had to cup our hands. The peon would pour water from way high up, lest our hands touch the glass*" (*Ibid,* 16).

The most important side of the book is the educational support of Valmiki's father which needs to be mentioned. Just as Jadhav in 'Outcaste: A Memoir' is indebted to his father Damu who adopted every means to give him proper education, likewise Valmiki's father showed great interest in making Valmiki well-educated. He was ready to fight against all odds hindering on the way of Valmiki's education. At one occasion, when Valmiki was made to sweep the playground of the school by the head master without the knowledge of his father, his father was passing by the school and seeing his son sweeping the playground he asked him the reason and knowing that Valmiki had been being made sweep for the last three days he faced the teacher and walked away holding Valmiki's hand saying loudly enough for the head master to hear, "*You are a teacher...So I am leaving you. But remember this much, Master....This Chuhre ka will study right here.....in this school. And not just him, but there will be more coming after him*" (*Ibid,* 06). Valmiki's father was highly ambitious about educating his son. Valmiki had many debts to his father who took every possible means to bring him on the road of success through education. It was only for his father that Valmiki could pursue his higher education after completing his school education. But stigma of caste left him nowhere. Education added fuel to his smouldering heart but the fire smouldering within his heart found no outlet: "*I too have felt inside me the flame of Ashwatthama's revenge. They keep on burning inside me to this day. I have struggled for years end to come out of the dark vaults of my life*" (*Ibid,* 27).

During his stay at DAV College in Dehradun, Valmiki came under reading of Ambedkar which opened a new chapter in his life:

> *I felt as though a new chapter about life was being unfurled before me. A chapter about which I had known nothing I felt. Dr Ambedkar's life-long struggle had shaken me up. I spend many days and nights in turmoil. The restlessness inside me had increased. My stone-like silence had suddenly began to melt. I proceeded to read all of Ambedkar's books that I found in the library* (*Ibid,* 72).

He was forced to leave college for poverty but his interest in reading never stopped. He considered books as his best companions: "*Books were my greatest friends. They kept up my morale*" (*Ibid,* 79). When he was posted to the city of Jabalpur and came into his own, he did extensive study on Chekov, Turgenev, Dostoevsky, Hemmingway, Zola and other Western writers. He appeared first as a poet and a columnist, next as playwright and short story writer. His present autobiography "Joothan" was published when he was at his age of maturity as a writer. Towards the close of his autobiography he brought the present social set up under question:

> *Times have changed. But there is something somewhere that continues to irk. I have asked many scholars to tell me why*

> *Savarnas hate Dalits and Shudras so much? The Hindus who worship trees and plants, beasts and birds, why are they so intolerant of Dalits? Today caste remains a pre-eminent factor in social life. As long as people don't know that you are a Dalit, things are fine. The moment they find out your caste, everything changes. The whispers slash your veins like knives. Poverty, illiteracy, broken lives, the pain of standing outside the door, how would the civilised Savarna Hindu know it?* (*Ibid,* 134).

In the conclusive lines, Valmiki talks about the demoralising side of caste system:

> *'Caste' is a very important element of Indian society. As soon as a person is born, 'caste' determines his or her destiny. Being born is not in the control of a person. If it were in one's control, then why would I have been born in a Bhangi household? Those who call themselves the standard – bearers of this country's great cultural heritage, did they decide which homes they would be born into? Albeit they turn to scriptures to justify their position, the scriptures that establish feudal instead of promoting equality and freedom* (*Ibid,* 134).

Thus, both Damu in Jadhav's *Outcaste: A Memoir* and Valmiki in *Joothan* are not mere individuals, rather they represent their community. Their autobiographies turn into the voice of millions. They give voice to those who are unheard; they give action to those who are inactive and they give identity to those who are identity less. They successfully explore those questions which remained unexplored for ages. The age-old concept that the caste stigmatizes one's life from which one cannot be completely free is challenged by them. They believe if one cannot completely free from the stigma of caste, one can certainly weaken the effect of this stigma if one educates oneself properly as education is the solution of all kinds of problems. Both autobiographies turn the silence of Dalits into revolution truly conforming to the message , "Educate, Unite and Agitate", once given by Ambedkar, the Messiah of Dalits as a summoning message for all Dalits to come in action. Transforming Dalits from a mere 'being' to a powerful 'becoming', both Narendra Jadhav's *'Outcaste: A Memoir'* and Omprakash Valmiki's *'Joothan'* prove more a voice of a class than an autobiography of an individual.

Works Cited

Nimabalkar, Waman. *Dalit Literature: Nature and Role.* Trans. Vandana Pathak and Dr P.D. Nimsarkar. Nagpur: Probodhan Prakashan. 2006. Print.

The Rigveda: An Anthology. Trans & ann. Wendy Doniger O' Flaherty. New Delhi: Penguin. 2000. Print.

Anand, S. *Touchable Tales: Publishing and Reading Dalit Literature*. Pondicherry: Navayana. 2003. Print.

Jadhav, Narendra. *Outcaste: A Memoir*. New Delhi: Viking. 2003. Print.

Valmiki, Omprakash. *Joothan: A Dalit's Life*. Trans. Arun Prabha Mukherjee. Kolkata: Samya. 2003. Print.

16

Daya Pawar's *Baluta*: An Autobiography of a Male as a Mouthpiece of Conditions of Female

Dr Deepika Rani

An autobiography is a record of one's life, the record of exchange between self and society. While writing about its own life, an autobiographer involves people around its life. Sometimes it becomes biography of others. Narrating incidents of its life including socio-political upheavals the autobiographers becomes a source of evidence of its surroundings and life of others. Likewise it, Daya Pawar; an autobiographer in his book *Baluta* became a mouthpiece of oppression and marginalisation of women of his community as well as other women. In his autobiography, Pawar records his life and sufferings. At the same time he records the exploitation, tormentation, dalitaisation, and discrimination, subaltern meted out to women and provides an insight to the living conditions of females. Narrating various soul numbing anecdotes he provides voice to unvoiced. Thus, the present paper seeks to study condition of female through an autobiography of a male.

Hunger makes an individual disgraceful and disrespectful. An empty stomach stresses a person to do anything on morality sake. It is the starvation that makes a woman to forget all of her self-respect to assuage her hunger of food. The motive of a hungry person is to fill the stomach by hook or crook. An empty stomach becomes cause to select wrong way to get food. A dalit woman does all the odd jobs to earn livelihood. But when she fails in doing so she sells her body to fill her stomach. She becomes a whore. Morality dooms when a woman has to sell her body. It is the tragedy of a woman that to fill her belly, she has to fill her womb. Due to unavoidable circumstances dalit women had to offer their bodies in exchange of food.

> Masterji was also a womanizer….Masterji had some kind of arrangement with those women. The school keys were in his keeping. One morning when I went to school early, I found paper, string and crumbs of laddoos all over the floor. .. some leftover bhakri was enough to buy the favours of a destitute woman. (49)

Rape was considered as a right of males. It was not taken as a crime. It was a sign of masculinity to assault women. Women were considered a tool to satiate the animal lust of man. Crushed body, crushed heart, crushed honour of a woman by man in the form of rape was a matter of pride. Many anecdotes in the autobiography depict the cruel behaviour of men towards women. To satisfy his lust, man can go beyond any limit. In the autobiography, *Baluta* writer Daya Pawar wrote this bitter truth. Even the labourers were not spared. They were blackmailed by hiding their instrument. "Women would come to cut the grass. He would hide scythe a woman using and say to her, if you let me have sex with you, I'll return your scythe'." (37) Shame on such males who could go to any extent to satisfy their animal hunger. Regarding rape Dr Sigma G.R. writes in her paper, "Women in the Adiya community are exploited sexually by party members and people from other castes. Outer world used young tribal girls to quench the sexual thirst. Sexual exploitation happens in its worst forms and they give birth to fatherless babies and no one is questioned". (G.R., 257) It is the pitiable plight of women that neither she was safe before independence nor after independence. What does male think of female? She is mere a source to satisfy his desires. Females were raped to take revenge. A novel on partition *Pinjar* by Amrita Pritam records the crisis of people during partition times but at the same times it explores the worst condition of women when they were used as a weapon to take revenge from enemy. It brings out the bitter reality of condition of women. Whosoever was in power either Hindus or Muslims, they abducted women of their opposition and raped them. Dr Deepika Rani writes about rape, "They did not abduct mere women but annihilated her dreams, wishes, heart, self, body as well as their spirit. It was not a rape of mere body but psyche, wishes and soul were also crushed. The novel works as an eye opener to those who still have cheap mentality of considering a woman as a thing for their animal satisfaction". (Rani, 52) In this autobiography *Baluta* the males of own caste were abducting the women of their own caste. Housemaids, labourers and relatives none was spared. They became victims of such males who hid themselves and waited for their pray.

> Dada was a womanizer too….I tell Aai everything. She smiles sadly. Perhaps she knows already. To womanize is a badge of honour, a sign of masculinity, or so it is believed around here. People look at such a man with admiration. Dada's women were very ordinary. Some were housemaids; others carried loads on their heads to the lorries. How many came and went? There was no counting. (25-26)

Above quoted stanza not only shows the lust of male but the stamina of having patience of a wife. A wife couldn't do anything even after knowing the physical relations of her husband. What a pity! What to call it: destiny or bad fate that a woman is considered a thing. She is not taken as a human being. She can be used sexually she can be sold she can be a weapon to take revenge. Where is her own existence? Where is her identity? There is no limit for males as they have freedom to go to any extent. Even a wife can be property of her father-in-law also. Here is an example of this cruel and bitter reality.

> Her husband was working in Mumbai. He had not found suitable accommodation there and so had not taken her with him. His father was a widower, an ordinary man. But one night he had made his way to where his daughter-in-law was sleeping. When she found her father-in-law at her side, his intent amorous, she raised a stink….(109)

This was not enough to torture a woman. Not only father-in-law but her husband had also the right to assault her physically or sexually. As woman was a common property of all the males of a family.

She belonged to all. One can't imagine the reply of the husband of a wife who had been assaulted by her father-in-law.

> While resolving the matter the bridegroom announced. 'When I married this woman, she was meant to be the common property between my father and me. Thus, she belongs to my father as much as to me. I'm not going to hurt my father's feelings. If this is unacceptable, her family may take her back.' (110)

This was the reply of her husband who was considered her fate-writer. Shame on such type of society and also on the husband who instead of favouring his wife; morally crushes her completely by telling that she belongs to him and his father. Who can be the saviour of a woman? A father finds the best match for his daughter but what he can do if the defender becomes an offender. A well known proverb, Run with the hare hunt with the hound is apt here. Some incidents in the book give goose pimples while reading it. It shows that the lust for female body is limitless. "In Kawakhana, it was no big deal for a man to bring a sex worker from Golpitha to live with him. One young man threw his ripe young bride out on the streets while he cootchie-cooed in his home with a prostitute." (150). On one hand brides were left to have sex with prostitute. On the other hand females of Parayas (in Novel *Karukku*) had to bear torture of police who used vulgar language. Once there was a serious fight between two caste people-the Chaaliyars and Parayas. When police came to arrest Parayas, they ran away from their houses and their females had to pay for them. Police announced the females to entertain them until their males come. "They used obscene language and swore at them; told them that since their husbands were away they should be ready to entertain the police at night winked at them and shoved their guns against their bodies." (Bama, 40) It shows that every man is eager to satisfy his lust and woman is taken as a source to satiate their lust.

Beating a woman can be taken as a sign of masculinity but in reality it is a sign of brutality. Beating of a wife could be a common scene. It was so because a woman was taken as a property. She was a commodity. It was up to the husband to beat his wife or not to. No one could object on that. Even he could beat her, torture her and sold her. In the autobiography a woman named Jamuna was sold.

"Jamuna's husband would beat her often. It was he who had brought her here and sold her. Found it difficult to believe that a man could sell his own wife."(152) The same incident of beating had been recorded by Bama in *Karukku* in which a man Uudan who dragged his wife and beat her up with his belt and the viewers could never try to stop him. Males used to beat their wives to vent out their frustration. It was total disgusting. Condition of female has been very pathetic in some of Indian societies. Why woman has to bear all the tortures? Why she becomes a property? Before marriage she has to follow her brother and father's orders and after getting married her commander changes. Now for the whole life, she becomes the property of her husband. It is up to him to keep her under his shoes, beat her, assault her or sell her. The incident in the autobiography rolls out tears of every female when she read about Gaoo. Gaoo was an uneducated girl. She had done a lot of physical labour. Due to hard work her hands become rough and dry. She was very beautiful. Everyone had eye on her. Not because of her beauty but due to not wearing a choli. Different rules had been made for her caste. She was denied to wear choli. Can anyone imagine that there were such rules that denied a woman to wear full clothes? Anything could happen in the male dominated society as they were the rule makers. Daya Pawar recorded: I remember asking her once, "Why don't you wear a choli?" in truth, she would have liked to. But the rules of her caste panchayat were strict. She would be ostracized if she were to put one on. Why they didn't wear cholis is another story." (187). Rules of wearing clothes had been imposed upon Gaoo then how could she had the right of selecting her better half. Thus, unwillingly she was married to her brother-in-law.

Dalit women had to please the upper caste people to survive. Their lives were not better than the slaves. Living life as a slave is worse than an animal. The women were exploited physically as well as sexually. Beating of wife by her husband was a common scene. Wife was considered as a property of her husband. He could do whatever he wanted. He could beat her as much as he wanted. Once a man Tatya beat his abandoned wife; for the reason that she came on his way. "A cart full of sugarcane was standing there. He took a sturdy stick from it and began to beat the woman, as if she were an animal.

The other pilgrims got in the way and freed the woman."(137) Such type of incidents shows the marginalised status of women. If dalit male should be shown pity then a dalit woman deserved double pity as she was living on the mercy of dalit males. A dalit male had to face the upper caste society but a dalit woman; she had to live under the upper caste as well as her own caste.

> None of the women observed purdah. How could they? They worked harder than the men. They scavenged scraps of paper, rags broken glass and iron from the streets, sorted them out and then sold them each morning. And how much their drunkard husbands beat them they continued to served them, hand and foot, and indulged their addictions. (7)

Women do harder work than their males. Most women did work of scavenging. They gathered discarded paper from the cloth shops of Mangaldas market. It was not all done after collection. They had to sell that in order to get money. Selling the collected material was not an easy task. They had to bribe the shopkeepers' servants to be allowed to take their waste paper away. They did all the jobs to get money to serve their families. After doing all the hard labour what they got, nothing. They were assaulted, they were beaten. This was not at all. When a woman gets married; she applies vermillion and wears a necklace of black beads called mangalsutra; a symbol of her husband. But when her husband dies; these signs of her marriage are taken off. She is called a widow. This very woman becomes a matter of pity for all. She is not allowed to take part in ceremonies of a marriage function. Already torn from heart after losing her husband, she is realised many times that she is a widow now. "The women of the area broke the thread of black beads that Aai had around her neck, the symbol of her status as a married woman. The one gold bead left on it was placed in dada's mouth in a roll of betel leaf. The koonkoo on her forehead was wiped off; her glass bangles broken." (53) The colourful world bounds in one colour i.e. White. Even she is considered as a person to whom anyone can order anything. In the autobiography people expected a widow to help clear away dead cattle. If someone died in the village whatever the weather, off the widow would have to go announcing it to all and sundry. The autobiography is full of many anecdotes that records the brutal treatment met to widows. The sinners' roam free whereas an innocent gets punishment. In the autobiography *Baluta;* an anecdote records this statement. When an old widow goes to pay the tax and after paying that she forgets to take the receipt. The next day she goes to take the receipt but what she gets. Oh! God.

> She is accused of stealing the money. She begs and pleads. She swears her innocence at the feet of the goddess. But no one has any pity on her. All the villagers spit their scorn at her. She is handcuffed and taken to the taluka headquarters, deemed guilty of theft. The clerk walks out scot free. The old lady serves a jail sentence of two or three months and returns. (67)

It shows how a widow was subordinated and marginalised by society. Society never spares a woman. Either it is a girl child, a young, wife, widow or a woman unable to produce child. People find reason to criticize them. A woman knows her pain when she is unable to give birth to a child. She is called by many names. Already in pain woman is tormented by the society. Once a woman named Vithabai tried to get rid of taunts of people. "Vithabai did not have any children. So she made much of me. Generally, childless women have a streak of restlessness. So Vithabai decided to pretend to be pregnant. She tied on a 'bulge' made of cloth. When the truth got out, all the women mocked her."(51) Instead of saving herself from various comments, she became a source of mockery. Then what should a woman do? Where should a woman go? Society had problem from Vithabai for not having child but at the same time society had problem from another woman for having a girl child. Can someone hope when this so called traditional society will leave a woman to live her life at own? A girl child is always unwelcomed.

> When Aai was born her father died. Hardly had her father been shoved into the earth, when the family began to torment my grandmother. That she had not produced a son was counted against her. They starved the young mother. They made her work like an animal. They fed her bhakri made of chaff and husk. Finally, she tired of this persecution and returned to her father's house. My mother was at the breast but she was snatched from her mother. Aai would say: 'Once your grandmother went home, she never returned. She married again.' (54)

These incidents clearly indicated the pitiable condition of woman in male-dominated society. Here goes one more incident that arise goose pimples to all. However, committing such shameful moral crime may give happiness to the accuser but it fills the heart with hate to the accused.

> One night, a woman was bathing at a tap, under cover of darkness. Suddenly a stream of hot water began to rain down on her. The woman was puzzled; she had been bathing in cold water. Where had this hot stream come from? She looked up and found that one of the goons was pissing on her. (224)

Totally disgusting incident it was. Male-dominated society wants to show their masculinity by such ways. If they have power then they must show it in right way. But such types of incidents are condemnable. Why these males consider woman as a commodity, as a right to use her in any way. Why she is not taken as a human being who has heart and flesh. The autobiographer Daya Pawar admits his mistake when he couldn't bear his wife talking to any other male. He abandoned his wife. This was the same girl to whom he loved very much. This was the girl to whom he wanted to marry at any cost. But alas! Where did the love disappear when he took the initiative to leave this girl Saee. He did not tell her that he was going to leave her. "Saee had no idea she was to be abandoned there. When I was leaving, I told her family I had tuberculosis: 'Keep her here for a while'."(275) Condition of Saee was becoming bitter day by day. Her husband did not go back to take her. Thus, truth was revealed. When her parents realised that Daya will not come to take her back then she was remarried.

> Saee got married to an old man; he could have been my father. They say he had children of my age. Why had she commited hara kiri in this way? Once or twice, I saw her in passing at the Sangamner market. She was dressed in rags. On her head, a bundle of fodder. On her back, a young child strapped to her with a dhotar. I did not dare to catch her eye. I felt responsible for her condition. (295)

Merely due to talking with another male; a husband abandoned his wife and left her. Although he realised his mistake but there was no use crying over spilt milk. Thus, these anecdotes realize us the ground reality of condition of woman. Although this is the story of 1940's and 1950's but in the year 2016 we are not sure that woman is enjoying a free life. The scenes and news of acid attacks, rapes, sexual assaults, bride burning, demand of dowry and female foeticide are still there. We are living in a free democratic country India. But can we witness the freedom of woman in the same country. Government has made rules of reservation of seats for women and constitution announces right of equality. But still there is a need to look upon the real condition and to let her live with dignity and let her define her own 'self'. She has equal right to live and she needs not any imposed identity of woman as a timid. She wants to fly in open sky and let her to do what she wants. Let her consider as an individual instead of a commodity to assuage the physical hunger of male as she is a person with heart and flesh.

Works Cited

Bama. *Karukku*. Trans. Lakshmi Holmstrom. New Delhi: Oxford, 2012. Print.

G.R., Sigma. Dalit Tribal Women: A Study of Silence in C.K. Janu's *Mother Forest*. *Indian Dalit Autobiographies: Marginalised Voices*. Ed. Bijender Singh. New Delhi: Authorspress. 2015. Print.

Pawar, Daya. *Baluta*. Trans. Jerry Pinto. New Delhi: Speaking Tiger Publishers, 2015. Print.

Pritam, Amrita. *The Skeleton and That Man*. Trans. Khushwant Singh. New Delhi: Sterling Publishers, 1987. Print.

Rani, Deepika. "Women as Skeleton in Amrita Pritam's *Pinjar*." *Indian Women Novelists: Feminist Reverberations*. Ed. Bijender Singh. Maharashtra: Thematic Publications. 2015. Print.

17

Dalits and Social Structure: A Study of Shankarrao Kharat's *A Corpse in the Well*

DR DELER SINGH

The term Dalit literature is used for the literature written by the Dalit and it mainly focuses on their oppression by the rich and the influential classes of the Indian society under the Indian caste system. It is a voice of the resistance and the protest of these writers who refuse to be the victims of an age-old insensitive classification of individuals on the basis of the caste they were born into. At present, Dalit literature forms an important part of Indian writings as literature written in the regional languages. The roots of Dalit writings prevalent today may be traced back to Marathi literature of the 1960s. A similar kind of literature was seen in many other languages such as Hindi, Tamil, and Kannada in the form of short stories and autobiographies. Dalit portrayals are peculiar in terms of their rendering of their real life experiences in a realistic manner. It focuses mainly on the mechanism of oppression and the psychological and social impacts of this oppression. Many of these works are available to a wider readership as English translations. Dalit literature has often been compared to African-American literature dealing with racial issues.

Some scholars trace the origin of Dalit literature back to Bhakti tradition during the medieval times. The reason for this association is rooted in the fact that most of Bhakti tradition poets were lower caste singers and preachers. They sang against the practices that denied equal rights to the lower castes. Famous poets Kabir and

Namdev are considered to be the exponents of this tradition. The other names associated with this tradition are Ravidas,Tukaram, Eknath, and Chokhamela. Among the poets of the eleventh century Madara Chennaiah is considered to be one of the important Dalit writers. He was a cobbler saint and regarded as the father of Vachana poetry. Dohara Kakkaiah is another name that survives in the genre.

The term Dalit literature was first used by eminent personalities such as Jyotiba Phule and Bhimrao Ambedkar in 1958 in the first conference of Dalit Sahitya Sangha in Mumbai. Dalit literature was however renamed as Ambedkari Sahitya/literature in 1993 during Akhil Bharatiya Ambedkari Sahitya Sammelan, mainly to acknowledge the efforts and contribution of Dr B.R. Ambedkar in fighting caste discrimination and inequality in the society. Baburao Bagul's collection of Marathi short stories, 'Jeyha Mi Jat Chorali' (When I had Concealed My Caste) published in 1963 is one of the landmarks in the history of Dalit literature. It has been made into a film and it is considered to be an epic of Dalit literature. In the year 1992, English translations of some prominent works of literature brought a major revolution in the field of Dalit literature. *An Anthology of Dalit Literature* which was edited by Mulk Raj Anand and Eleanor Zelliot and *Poisoned Bread: Translations from Modern Marathi Dalit Literature*, edited by Arjun Dangle made this genre very famous.

The word Dalit has been derived from the Sanskrit word *dalit* which means divided, split, broken or scattered. This etymology itself implies at the condition of the people who have suffered age old oppression. According to Hindu mythology, there are four *varnas* or categories into which all the people fall. We find a reference to this classification in a hymn in the Purusukta of *Rig Veda* in its reference to the caste system. It says

Brahmnoasaya mukamasti
Bahu rajanayah kruta
Uru tadasay yadvaishya
Padabhayam Sudro ajayat

This hymn ascribes the origins of various clans/castes in Indian society where *Brahmanas* are born from the mouth of Brahma, the *Kshatriyas* from the shoulders, the *Vaishyas* from his thighs and

Shudras from his feet. This classification makes Shudras inferior to the other clans owing to their origin which later on took an ugly form in the form of discrimination that they had to face in the society. Because of this code's existence in Rig Veda and other Hindu texts such as *Manu Smriti*, upper class clans have propagated this belief that God himself has made this code and thus decided the destiny of all the people and thus humans should follow it. Dalits are however excluded from even this four *varna* system and form the fifth unmentioned lower *varna*, also known as *Panchama*. The present usage of the word Dalit includes *shudras* and any other oppressed class falling in its ambit. Commenting upon the usage of the term, Sharan Kumar Limbale, a prominent Dalit writer, says that, "Harijans and Neo-Buddhists are not the only Dalits, the term describes all the untouchable communities living outside the boundary of the village, as well as Adivasis, landless farm labourers, workers, the suffering masses and nomadic and criminal tribes" (Limbale, 30).

In Dalit writing, we observe a rendition of the mechanism of mental conditioning and internalisation going on in the psyche of the victims which affirms and establishes their belief that their sufferings and the dejected conditions which they live in are their destined lot. It is something that has been fated for them by God himself and it is for this reason that they were born in a specific clan. The belief gradually becomes a part of their existence. Illiteracy and poverty add to this belief when combined with oppression and mistreatment by the rich and upper class society. There are scholars who compare this condition and mechanism of oppression to racism. In such a comparison, John Arthur rightly observes that, "Racism is usually a form of prejudice in just that sense: it is an attitude that is grounded in the beliefs formed on insufficient evidence, or beliefs that are held too firmly without adequate regard for other information that may call these beliefs into question (Arthur, 12). We see a similar adherence to the age old traditions in the unjust treatment meted out to Dalits, both in the real as well as literary world of the writers.

The present work deals with the autobiographical story 'A Corpse in the Well' by Shankarrao Kharat which has been translated from Marathi into English by Priya Adarkar. Shankarrao Kharat was a Marathi writer born at Aatpaadi in Sangli district, Maharashtra on

July 11, 1921. He is famous as one of the most prominent Dalit writers, though he wrote on a much larger canvas. Being a Dalit himself, he had seen and experienced the hardships and social segregation of Dalits. In his writings, we see realistic and autobiographical accounts of Dalit life but in a very sensible way. He never seems to be polemical or outrageous. He was greatly influenced by the teaching of Dr BR Ambedkar which made him convert to Buddhism. He has written several short stories and many of them have been translated into English. He has written several novels also. His autobiography *Taraal Antaraal* is considered to be a great work in Marathi literature.

Shankarrao Kharat was son of a village Mahar and had personally endured the hardships that he describes in his works. He had seen his father, family and the entire Mahar society experience the discrimination that they had to face because of their Dalit status. They "did the work delicately described in British records as that of the "inferior village servant"-cutting wood, carrying messages, bringing fuel to the burning ground, working on others' lands, dragging out dead cattle" (Maloney, 84). The experiences had a great impact on the psyche of his young mind and scarred him for life. "His childhood experience and the life he saw in the slums are the subjects of his fictional writing" (Paswan and Jaideva, 21), and we can find the echoes of these experiences along with resistance against this treatment in the short story 'A Corpse in the Well'. This resilience is not peculiar to Kharat only. It is in fact considered to be the characteristic of Dalit literature. "The Dalit writings by the Dalit writers have their resilient motivation for agency, not to accept silently but to give voice to resistance and challenge the dominant oppressive discourses" (Singh, 47). In the story, Kharat not only describes the oppression that Mahars face at the hands of influential and upper caste clans, he also records the protest through the resistance shown by the narrator when he asks his father to have his food or later to refuse going down the well to take out the corpse.

In the beginning of the story itself, we see the nature of the duty and the condition of the people involved in it when the narrator says that he "knew clearly the dangers of village duty" (*A Corpse in the Well,* 1). He further adds that "It was a perpetual noose around the neck of a Mahar! My father was crushed flat by this duty" (*ACW,* 1). As the story unfolds, the hypocrisy of people who crush Mahars in the name of duty is exposed. It also reveals the helplessness which leaves no option for these Mahars but to follow the dictates of the society. The protest seems to worsen their situation only. We see that father of the narrator has not eaten for more than a day because he is on his duty of guarding an unclaimed corpse. When the narrator asks him to eat, he tells him that, "the chief constable and the constable are yet to arrive! They will carry out the inquest; only then can the Mahar rest" (*ACW,* 2). Ironically, "the head constable has arrived in the village. But he is dining. He'll come only when he has finished eating and drinking" (*ACW,* 2).

The helplessness of the young narrator is expressed when he is unable to understand this dichotomy. He is yet to understand that a Mahar is considered a lesser human being and he is not supposed to expect or demand equal rights for himself. However, he registers his protest and angst in his questions when he asks that, "Anna! The constable will come after his meal. The village chief has also filled his belly. Then why can't you too eat your bread? Why must you remain hungry" (*ACW* 2)? His father is not able to give him any satisfactory answer. He just repeats an old age explanation that they are different from him and can't work on empty stomach. He also adds that, "Who cares if a Mahar lives or dies" (*ACW,* 2)? The comment not only shows his acceptance of his fate in the society but also shows how these values are passed on from generation to generation by the victims themselves who consider their lot as their destiny.

The Mahar on the guarding duty is not supposed to touch the corpse as doing so will pollute the corpse and such an action by a Mahar may have serious consequences. But when the constables find it dangerous to take out the corpse from the well themselves, they order Mahar do so. In spite of Mahar's repeated protests, they make him do so. They threaten him and the narrator who also joins his father in the protest. They call the narrator a bastard and his father "lump of dirt!" (*ACW,* 3).The narrator acknowledges that "in those days, the oppressive power and prestige of the head constable were tremendous. Against this power, a Mahar was a mere wisp of straw"

(*ACW,* 2). In spite of his awareness of these conditions, the narrator keeps on trying to look for an answer for his predicament regarding this injustice:

> Seeing and hearing all this was a shock to my young mind. I heard their curses, their threats, their shouting. I thought, whose dead body is this anyway? Whose well? Why should my father have to be cursed and threatened because of them? This was rank injustice to my father; I was old enough to understand that and also had some education to my credit. So I could see clearly the injustice being done to my father. He had not done anything wrong. His only crime was being the Mahar of the village. (*ACW,* 3-4)

His father has given in to the demands of the society he lives in. He has learnt how to survive in the society which needs him for its menial jobs but at the same time forbids him a humane status. He knows that even if tries hard, he can neither change his life nor others' behaviour towards him and his people. That is why he asks his son to keep quite when he questions the constables and village chief. He tells him, "Shut up son. You are not old enough to understand. Don't say a word. I'll have to bear whatever happens" (*ACW,* 4). This shows his helplessness and his acceptance of his fate. But we see that he does not want the same fate for his son. He makes him go to school and refuses to take his help in guarding the corpse when he asks for it. His helplessness makes him go down the well and perform the duties which were not even meant for him. He is forced to descend into the well to take out the body even after a snake is spotted in the well. They say, "It's not a snake, it's a reptile! It won't bite" (*ACW,* 4)! Though the snake does not bite his father and he successfully brings the corpse out, the incident leaves the narrator with a storm of questions about whatever happens on that day. It is not a stray incident, rather a very normal event that happens in the lives of Mahars every day. The events of the day terrorize the narrator.

Though education helped shattering the beliefs and unquestioned domination, yet education is a luxury not available to many Dalits. The awareness generated by education among the lucky few makes them misfits in a society by inciting protest and anger against a social system that they are powerless to change. As Omprakash Valmiki observes in his autobiography *Joothan: A Dalit's Life*:

> Times have changed. But there is something somewhere that continues to irk. I have asked many scholars to tell me why Savarnas hate Dalits and Shudras so much? The Hindus who worship trees and plants, beasts and birds, why are they so intolerant of Dalits? Today caste remains a pre-eminent factor in social life. (Kuortti, 134)

In a similar manner the narrator finds himself disillusioned with the discovery that the Mahars had moved the High Court fighting for the Mahar vatan share, a quarter of the share. As he states, "Only after I myself had become an advocate did I learn that for the sake of this hereditary right — this worthless right — the Mahars had played the game of litigation right up to the High Court" (*ACW,* 6). The frustration of the writer is evident in this anti-climax and echoes the sentiment of the oppressed Dalits who pay the price for being born into the wrong caste.

Works Cited

Dangle, Arjun. ed. *A Corpse in the Well: Translations from Modern Marathi Dalit Autobiographies*. Hyderabad: Disha Books, 1992. Print.

John, Arthur. *Race, Equality and the Burdens of History*. New York: Cambridge University Press, 2007. Print.

Kuortti, Joel. *Joothan: A Dalit's Life*. Surat: Popular Prakashan, 2003. Print.

Limbale, Sharan Kumar. *Towards an Aesthetic of Dalit Literature*. New Delhi: Orient Longman Private Limited, 2004. Print.

Maloney, Clarence. ed. *Language and Civilisation Change in South Asia*. Netherlands: Brill Academic Publishers, 1978. Print.

Paswan, Sanjay. Jaideva, Pramanshi. eds. *Encyclopedia of Dalits in India: Literature*. New Delhi: Gyan Publishing House, 2002. Print.

Singh, Prabhat K. *The Indian English Novel of the New Millennium*. UK: Cambridge Scholars Publishing, 2013. Print.

18

A Critique of Casteism in Omprakash Valmiki's *Joothan: A Dalit's Life*

Dr Dipali Sharma Bhandari

For a country riddled by the caste system, the talk about the people from marginalised communities is certainly a fresh draught of air. However, for a society which has fed on this system and nurtured it for ages, change is not too easy to come by. The *Purush Sukta*, said to be the source of the original *varna* system, divided the community into four section based on the kind of work each section performed, attributing their origin from the respective organ of the *aadi purush* which corresponded to that work. The idea behind the division was that a nation required people to perform all kinds of work to strengthen it. It needed scholars and philosophers, warriors and businessmen and people to put in their share of labour and for a smooth functioning of the society and the nation. However, in the later ages these four sections got divided into various categories and sub-categories. With the passage of time the fluidity of the caste system which was earlier based on work dissolved and the caste structure became rigid, based on birth. Today, as Ramanathan puts it, "The four castes are subdivided into multitudinous sub-castes and there is a final stratum of this ethnic division known as the untouchables, the lowliest of all, so impure and despicable that they stood outside the caste and social structure of the Indian people altogether. This final stratum is known as 'Dalits' in modern linguistic terminology." (Ramanathan, 327)

It is really sad that untouchability prevails even in the twenty-first century modern Indian society in a country where practice of untouchability is banned through Article 17 of the Constitution. Dalit literature is the expression of the anguish and protest of the Dalit writers against the caste system. It highlights their sufferings and candidly speaks of the exploitation, humiliation and suffering brought down upon them by their Dalit status which any amount of education does not change. Many writers from the upper classes have championed the cause of Dalits in their literary works. Munshi Premchand, Mahashweta Devi, Amrita Nagar, Salman Rushdie, Mannu Bhandari, Mulk Raj Anand, Arundhati Roy and many other writers brought out social purpose and criticism in their writings rather than mere adherence to the purpose of literature as means of pleasure. However, it has been variously argued that without truly experiencing the hardships of the Dalits; the writers cannot understand the deep angst that the Dalits have to suffer daily. Therefore, only the works by Dalit writers are included in the genre and the works on these themes by other writers, even though they deal with similar subjects, do not fall into the ambit of Dalit Literature. In its contemporary context Dalit Literature advocates the rights of the Dalit community and inspires the people from the social peripheries to rise against oppression and exploitation. The prominent notes of the Dalit literature defy the prevalent social notions and literary traditions.

Dalit literature has been around for centuries but it got recognition and identity only around 1958. The fact can be attributed to the societal hegemony in all fields of life whereby the equations of power and caste decide everything. The emergence of Dalit literature came almost at the same time as their recognition as a political class. Despite universal adult franchise being instituted in the country the Dalits were never conscious of the power that it carried or of the equal status conferred on them by the Constitution of India. Wherever they were; they were denied even the basic dignity due to a fellow human. As Omprakash Valmiki comments in his Autobiography:

> Untouchability was so rampant that while it was considered all right to touch dogs and cats or cows and buffaloes, if one happened to touch a Chuhra, one got contaminated or polluted. (Valmiki, 2)

The term 'Dalit literature' – 'Dalit' meaning oppressed, broken and downtrodden – came into use officially in 1958 at the first conference on Dalit literature in Mumbai. Dalit literature for a long time was disregarded and not taken seriously in the literary circles. The emergence of the Dalit Panthers in 1972 in Maharashtra is a significant moment in the history of Dalit literature which was furthered by various literary movements across India. The publication of translations from modern Marathi literature entitled *Poisoned Bread* edited by Arjun Dangle had already sparked debates in the literary circles. However, the awareness and the output of Dalit writings has been more voluminous in the southern part of India. In the northern part of India, caste equations are much more rigid and works in this genre are fewer. Also, there has been considerable reluctance to accept Dalit literature as a literary genre.

Under the aegis of academics as Arun Prabha Mukherjee, who translated Omprakash Valmiki's *Joothan* (1997) into English in 2003 and wrote an introduction to it, the reluctance to accept new literary genres by the dominant literary structures, has resulted in wider acceptance and circulation of Dalit literature in India and abroad. However, the acceptance of Dalit literature has not done much to better the conditions of Dalit community. For most of the people, it makes a good reading and a topic of discussion but it does not evoke fellow-feeling for the marginalised people in them. These autobiographies have inspired the Dalit population to a large extent despite the fact that the number of educated people in this community is significantly low (if we exclude the creamy layer) due to extreme poverty.

Omprakash Valmiki's autobiography *Joothan: A Dalit's Life* is a rendering of the first-hand experiences of his trials and tribulations. His struggle against poverty and the caste system and his aspiration to educate himself are central to his story. Like most other Dalit writers Valmiki too writes of the social and legal injustice he and members of his community suffered at the hands of the people of the higher castes. Through a series of reminisces, he describes the exploitation he had to suffer. He reflects:

> ...if I were really a Hindu, would the Hindus hate me so much? Or discriminate against me? Or try to fill me up with caste inferiority over the smallest things? I also wondered why one have to be a Hindu in order to be a good human being... I have

> seen and suffered the cruelty of Hindus since childhood. Why does the caste superiority and caste pride attack only the weak? Why are Hindus so cruel, so heartless against Dalits? (Valmiki, 41)

Dalit literature captures the living conditions and records the Dalit experience as it exists in the society. The authors of this genre truthfully and realistically portray what they have experienced. It offers a critique on the behaviour of typical high caste people and their domination and exploitative actions. Dalit literature is a weapon to raise voice for a positive transformation in the social and political status of the marginalised community. In this quest they use autobiography as their tool.

However, the autobiography also questions the effort of the constitution to provide equality to all irrespective of their caste. For, in a caste-ridden society, nearly 70 years after the constitution came into effect, Dalits are even now not allowed to enter temples or fetch water from the community taps or wells in certain areas. Even today, the average Indian first asks the caste of any person he meets for the first time and only then opens up to the next level of friendship. In marriages and love, a lot of importance is attached to the caste. Sometimes people from the Dalit clans resort to masking their identities by changing surnames to be accepted in the society. Sometimes they convert to other religions which provide them an equal status. They may have braved the odds and emerged successful in their attempt to educate themselves and earn a decent living but they still remain the people standing out the door; for as soon as their caste is revealed, people quickly withdraw from them. Valmiki says:

> Dalits want to join the mainstream of society after getting an education but the Savarna prevents them from doing so. Discriminates against Dalits. Thinks of them as inferior beings. Doubts are cast on their intelligence, their ability, their performance. (Valmiki, 127)

His father constantly exhorted him to study to be able to defeat the caste system. But he realised through bitter experience that "...'caste' cannot be improved by education. It can only be improved by taking birth in the right caste". (Valmiki, 58)

Om Prakash Valmiki belongs to the Chuhra community. They worked for the higher caste people tending their animals, fields and cleaning their *baithaks* and *ghers* throughout the year or all the work they do they got some grain and one *roti* 'specially made by mixing husk with the flour for the chuhra' (Valmiki, 9). At noon from every house along with the *joothan*, food which is left on the plates, after the people of the household have eaten which is either disposed as garbage or given to animals. At the wedding and other celebrations they collected the *pattals* on which the guests had eaten. This *joothan* sticking to the *pattal* was dried and used to tide over the rainy season. Sheer poverty made people consume and even relish the food which someone else had left on the plate after having his fill. Valmiki remembers the elders delightfully reminiscing about the weddings where the *baratis* had left behind months of *joothan*. The mere memory of standing guard over the drying *joothan* subjects him to utter humiliation, agony and shame now that he is more aware. The oppressive power-system keeps the Dalits in a perpetually poor state with little hope of betterment as their children are denied any opportunity to study due to the unpaid labour and other menial jobs they are made to do as well.

For Valmiki it was a big achievement to actually pass high school from his village, as the Tyagi families who were the elite of the area did not take kindly to the fact that a boy from the *chuhra* caste was trying to raise himself at par with their children. Valmiki's father called him *munshiji* which indicates his yearning to educate his son. He realised the value of improving their lot through education. Valmiki became the first boy from his caste to pass high school despite all odds. When he was admitted to school, his teacher made him sweep the school for the first three days. All kinds of stratagems were devised so that he would leave the school and take up the work intended for the Chuhra community. He was not allowed to get water for himself. The situation worsened as he advanced to the higher classes. He remembers how his Chemistry teacher Brajpal Singh purposefully kept him out of the laboratory and he failed class XII as he did not get the passing marks in chemistry practical because of the biased attitude of his teacher. He also remembers how his Maths teacher whom he approached for help with some questions told him to come over to his home. When he reached there, he was sent to get the wheat ground and by the time he went back, the teacher left his home to avoid helping him. A third incident happened when he went to his teacher Brajpal Singh's village to pick up a sack of wheat since he could ride a bicycle. As long as the family did not know their caste, they treated them well and even served them food in their own utensils. They even made them sit on their cots. But as soon as they came to know their caste, they insulted and beat them. His commentary on the entire episode sums it all in just a few words, "The hollowness of their hospitality had been exposed. It is the guest's caste which entitles him to respect." (Valmiki, 51-52)

He also mentions how he was taunted at school alike for wearing even slightly good clothes and if he wore dirty clothes he was made fun of. He also recalls how the dhobi refused to iron his NCC uniform for him as he was afraid of its social repercussions for himself. Regarding this incident, he says, "I had lost faith in God. One can somehow get past poverty and deprivation, but it is impossible to get past caste." (Valmiki, 18) He also remembers how he had to skin the carcass of a bullock when no other elder was home and how he furtively walked around in the streets to avoid being seen carrying the hide because his family could not afford to lose the money the hide would get at the leather market. The instance where he had to go with his friend Hiram Singh to perform *Salaam* to the patrons of his in-laws after his wedding and the similar custom for a bride disgusted him.

After finding a decent opportunity to work at the ordnance factory and go for a training to Maharashtra, his life changed somewhat. While living at the hostel, he gradually started mingling with people. But here too, the oppressive caste system was rampant. The Kulkarni family he got close to thought he was a Brahmin due to his surname and treated him like one, even inviting him for the ritual chaturdashi bath before Deepawali. He felt very uncomfortable and kept thinking, "what would happen if these people found out that I was born in the untouchable Chuhra caste?"(Valmiki, 95) Once he saw the Kulkarni family serving tea to Professor Kamble, a Mahar by caste, in a different type of cup while he was served in the family's own cups because they assumed him to be a Brahmin. Sudama Patil, his Brahmin friend told him that Maharashtrian Brahmins don't allow Mahars to touch their dishes and their dishes are kept separate. (Valmiki, 97) This incident made him realise that untouchability was as pervasive in the seeming liberal Maharashtra as in the caste ridden society of Muzaffarnagar. Savita, their daughter, unaware of his caste, started getting attracted to him. When he told her he was an SC, she did not believe it. When he pressed the truth upon him, she retraced her steps. Despite the fact that he had never loved her, Valmiki felt agitated. He felt that the distance between them had increased. "The hatred of thousands of years had entered our hearts. What a lie culture and civilisation are", says he. (Valmiki, 98) Same happened when the new commandant of the DSC from Barla was transferred to Chandrapur. The first thing he assumed on meeting him was that Om Prakash must belong to the Tyagi community since Barla was a Tyagi village. When he came to know his surname he was visibly uneasy. The visit was abruptly cut short. He also remembers how a family in the train got friendly to his own while travelling and as soon as the question of caste arose, there was an uneasy silence for the rest of the journey. He reflects, "As long as people don't know that you are a Dalit, things are fine. The moment they find out your caste, everything changes. The whispers slash your veins like knives." (Valmiki, 134)

Valmiki does mention how some friends from the higher castes never bothered about his caste and treated him like an equal human being; although such cases were few and far-between. The autobiography loudly echoes the notes of rebellion against the oppression of people in the name of caste.

He also expresses his deep anguish at the efforts of untouchables to hide their castes in order to become one with the mainstream. He remembers how a family in Barla named their children in the fashion of Sikhs to be identified as Sikhs. He tells us how his niece Seema denied knowing him in front of the class to avoid being identified as a Valmiki among her friends. To justify her action she said, "What is the point of going around with the drum of caste tied around your neck?" (Valmiki, 128) He also remembers how his relatives did not include his name on the wedding card of his sister-in-law because they did not want to reveal their Dalit status. Same happened at another wedding where the wedding invitation included the names of all relative except him. According to Om Prakash Valmiki:

> The Dalits who have become educated face a terrible crisis – the crisis of identity – and they are trying to find an easy and instantaneous way to get out of this crisis. They have started to use their family *gotra* as their surname after just a little bit of fine-tuning.....They find that the easy way out. Behind all such acts is the anguish of identity crisis, which has come about as a reaction to the blatant inhumanity of casteism. (Valmiki, 126-127)

He adds, "When someone like me comes around with his caste marker surname, all those people who want to hide their caste become wary. They feel that someone is letting out their secret. They find it easier to run away from the problem. But the truth is that change won't come about through running away. It will come about through struggle and engagement." (Valmiki, 127)

He raises valid questions and yet the answer is elusive. He asks, "If it was in my control, why would I have been born in a Bhangi household?" (Valmiki, 133) "Why Savarnas hate Dalits and Shudras so?" (Valmiki, 134) "The Hindus who worship trees and plants, beasts and birds, why are they so intolerant of Dalits?" (Valmiki, 134) "Why is my caste my only identity? (Valmiki, 134) Valmiki is no more among us. But his reflections on the caste system and the various questions he raises shake us to the core. Even today the country has not been able to shake off the shackles of casteism despite loud proclamations of equality and justice. The poorest of the poor continue to stand outside the door. A social revolution raises its head now and then. Then the storm blows over and things go back to the state they were in. As Valmiki says in the preface to his autobiography:

> Dalit life is excruciatingly painful, charred by experiences....We have grown up in a social order that is extremely cruel and inhuman. And compassionless towards Dalits. (Valmiki, vii)

Dalit literature captures the rhythm of society. In this autobiography emerges as a powerful tool because it situates itself in real life and authentic experiences. By portraying the bitter reality in a realistic manner, which sometimes borders on the repugnant; the authors are trying to create empathy for these classes in the society.

True empowerment cannot take place without emancipation. This is what the Dalit autobiography has set out to achieve.

Works Cited

Ramanathan, S. "Situating Dalit literature in Indian Writing in English". *Language in India*. Vol. 14:12 December 2014. 327-338. Print.

Valmiki, Omprakash. *Joothan: A Dalit's Life*. Trans. Arun Prabha Mukherjee. Kolkata: Bhatkal and Sen. 2003. Print.

19

A Reading of Dalit Autobiography as a Literature of Protest

Dr Prachi Priyanka

Derived from three Greek words meaning 'self', 'life' and 'write'; autobiography is a style of writing that has been around for ages. However, as a form of literary writing it appeared first in eighteenth century. Robert Southey coined the term in 1809 to describe the work of a Portuguese poet. As a literary genre, it signifies a retrospective narrative that undertakes to tell the author's own life and it generally aims to represent more about private, social, public, political and moral life of a writer. Some scholars have defined autobiography as a "retrospective prose narrative produced by a real person concerning his own existence, focusing on his individual life, in particular on the development of his personality." Despite disagreements how inclusive the category of autobiography should be; there are characteristics that are common to most of the autobiographical works. These features are the grammatical perspective of the work, identity of the self, and self-reflection and introspection. Individual achievements, personal experiences, oppression, imprisonment and struggles of the author form the core part in autobiography.

However, unlike autobiographies written by mainstream writers, dalit autobiography is not confined strictly to the author's life and struggles or the happy moments and accomplishments. Though narrated in first person, it is not just an account of one's own life, but a reflection of the traumas and hardships faced by the dalits as a community. Moreover, Dalit autobiographies tend to focus on the period before Ambedkar and so adequately represent history of agony and anguish.

The literary corpus of dalit literature has been written in various literary genres, however, there is a marked tendency to equate all dalit literature with dalit autobiographies. While recognising the diversity we come across in dalit literature, Sarah Beth argues that: "Within this larger trend of literary assertion, autobiography in particular has been one of the most important genres since many dalit writers of Hindi have launched their literary careers by first narrating their life story, making autobiography an institutional space through which dalit writers can first enter the literary public sphere."

Valmiki argues that dalit literature as autobiography does not capture the diversity of articulations of dalit literature for it does not dwell on discussions on the literary trends. This kind of revaluation is important for "literature, society and politics are complementary to each other. One of the central concerns of the Dalit consciousness is to oppose and rebel against the hollow ideals entrenched in the prejudices, to rebel against society based on the ideals of inequality and to rebel against anti-human values. It becomes essential to re-evaluate the preceding literature, for the roots of a social system are often hidden under the deep layers of life." (2001: 102)

Though not dismissive about the importance of Dalit autobiographies in shaping Dalit literature, D.R. Nagaraj feels "uncomfortable with the genre of Dalit autobiographies", for "within one tale, ten sagas are miniaturised." His observation in this regard is symptomatic: "Dalit autobiographies have become important not because of the vast expanse of experience but by its violent bonsaisation....Bonsai trees are cute, true, but they can never be a substitute for giant woods."

But it can be argued that the significance of such writings lie precisely in deconstructing the individualistic self as the locus of autobiographical writing. The presence of 'Dalit' in dalit autobiography' gives us a perspective that cannot be reduced to the idea of self, embedded in the general assumptions about autobiography. Dalit autobiographies therefore, are not simply accounts of one individual's life history. They are also representative of the life lived in the stigmatized community and reflects upon the shared nature of life lived.

Before we move further, it is important to understand the term 'dalit' and its gradual evolution with advances in dalit literature. The term dalit is used today as a thoroughly radical grouping of that segment of Indian society that is socially, culturally and physically subjugated – its subjugation a result of a state of ritual pollution commonly called 'untouchability'. Many dalit social thinkers and writers like Limbale strategically chose to broaden the reach of the term to include various other subaltern sections of the society like women, religious minorities and the working class. In a seminar paper on 'Dalit Literature in the Eyes of Dalits', Omprakash Valmiki asserts that the term dalit had a "more inclusive meaning'. The term encompasses everybody everywhere who is oppressed and exploited. As Savyasaachi writes "a prostitute is as much a dalit as is the spouse of an upper caste patriarch who is ill-treated, as are the victims of ethnocide and communalism irrespective of whether they are Hindus, Christians, Muslims or Sikhs. (Savyasaachi, 2004: 1659) The Delhi Panthers, in their manifesto, defined Dalits as:

> Members of SC and ST, neo-Buddhist, working people, landless and poor peasants, women and all those who are exploited politically, economically and in the name of religion.

However, this argument was found less sustainable and thought to be improper to include those whose centres of power and privilege is due to other forces of oppression and exclusion like modernity, gender and economics. The words dalit today applies more accurately to those sections of the Indian society whose liminality is a result of a caste-based hierarchical order that inscribes them as perennially polluted and therefore untouchable. It is for similar reasons that upper caste writers who give vivid accounts of the lives of dalits and empathise with their situations – do not fall under the category of Dalit writers because they don't represent the true dalit consciousness.

While dalit literature or in Marathi, dalit sahitya, as a school, was a self-conscious movement and a product of 1960s; individual writers among the untouchables appeared in the fourteenth century and again in the Mahar movement which began in the late nineteenth century. Dalit literature is not a new concept of the modern era but has a long history that dates back to the period of Buddha in sixth century BC, writings of Vachana in the eleventth and twelfth century AD, Chokhamela in fourteenth century AD, and Mahatma Phule (1828-90) and Professor S. M. Mat (1886-1957) who all are considered to be originators of dalit literature. These great men understood the pain and plight of the dalits and protested against such kind of discrimination on the basis of caste and unjust division of society. A huge mass of literature is created in the light of the teachings and vision of these men. The dalit literature was also inspired by the writings of the Bhakti movement and the works of Afro-American writers; from where they derived ideas and energy to fight against the age-old social prejudices and practice of caste.

Dalit is a term more recently popularised and these communities were called by different names. One of the first categories used was 'ati-shudra', a term coined by Jyotirao Phule in the nineteenth century and fittingly evoking the marginality of this section of the population. It has generally come to mean down-trodden, subjugated community and it was used in the 1930s as a Hindi and Marathi translation of 'depressed classes'. Gandhi called them Harijanas, the children of God, with the aim to restore humanity and self-confidence in those who had been oppressed for several centuries. However, many dalit intellectuals found the term patronising and humiliatingly pacifist, and discarded it quickly.

Dr B.R. Ambedkar, the most significant Dalit leader called them 'bahishkrit' to indicate their ostracism from the Hindu social and religious order, and also used the designation of 'Depressed Classes' given by the imperial government for official settings. Soon Schedule Castes became the official category of political and social affirmative action taken by the Indian state and its agencies for the uplift of the former 'untouchables'.

Every Dalit writer feels indebted to Dr Ambedkar for the way he was instrumental in arising in dalits the revolutionary spirit necessary to uproot the suppressing system. It was he who made dalits aware of their slavery and instigated them to fight against this evil system. Oppressed under the Brahminical rule of hate and humiliation; Dalits therefore felt the need to voice their pain and sufferings. They chose to protest against the inhuman behaviour that they were subjected to and let the world know what they had to go through under the Brahminical rule of hate and humiliation. Dalit literature was a medium to express the agony and summon truth from the past about abject poverty, helplessness and the conflicts of submission and resistance to the societal norms.

Dalit writers had been expressing their thoughts and experiences about their lives in the casteist society through their writings. Initially they chose to express their pain in poems, but later they moved to other genres as well. Autobiography became a very influential form of writing through which dalit writers presented realistic picture of their world. The objective was simple: to work towards the cause of dalit liberation and to provide authentic accounts of the drudgery and struggle of the dalits. The dalit autobiographies were first written in 1930s. Dr Gangadhar Pantavane, Marathi dalit writer, says that "Only Babasaheb Ambedkar is the first dalit autobiographer."

It was Dr Ambedkar who had awakened them from the deep slumber and instigated them to wage against the pernicious and exploitative Hindu caste system. Ambedkar led conversion of the Mahars from Hinduism to Buddhism and his charismatic personality and vision galvanised the dalit community into seeking a transformation in their religious and socio-political situations. The conversion acted as a force of transformation on both the individual and collective identity and self-perception of the dalits. On the collective level it facilitated the unification of dalits and on the individual level, it released the converts from a self-perception of pollution and inferiority that they were subjected to in the hands of authoritative Hindus. The resulting changes in the mental attitude and social practices were a welcome break from the years of oppression. Most of the converts described their experience as a rebirth, and for many, life began anew after the conversion – bringing in new hope of a better life.

It is said that Dalit autobiographies often dwell on the process of "digging out stench from hateful waste bins of the past." Historically, they were outside the hierarchical Hindu system, more specifically treated as outcaste. They were excluded from participation in the social, economical, cultural, intellectual and political life. This caused the dalits to live in miserable conditions, life full of superstitions and at the mercy of the upper caste. They did not have their own identity, nor did they possess any self-esteem. They were denied education and were forbidden from participation in the process of development.

In the initial dalit literature, we find an exploration of the exploitation that the dalits had been subjected to for generations. They were not given a place in the mainstream literature and their first task was to create a place for themselves in the regional literature. It is noted that the distinctiveness of dalit literature lies in its authentic unity of language and content. The disillusionment and disgust, accompanied by a desire for revenge comes alive in the writings of young dalits. Gail Omvedt and describes the life of dalits amongst hunger, pollution and cruelty.

It can be observed therefore, that most of the dalit writings are autobiographical in nature, expressing anger against long drawn injustice and can be read as a literature of protest. Priyanka Shrivastava in her study observes that Dalit literature poses a major challenge to the dominant episteme by its insistence on not only a presentation but also a representation of its own – and by extension, of others' – socio-cultural and political reality. It also seeks to revise traditional aesthetics and Indian literary theories by introducing into the mainstream literary culture the creativity and the inventiveness of a hitherto marginalised subculture and literature.

With such enormous task of being the representative voice of an entire community, dalit autobiography holds a crucial place in dalit literature. And it is because of this collective responsibility that dalit autobiographies, though written in first person narration, is more about the events witnessed and the socio-cultural framework of the times.

The first and foremost thing that these autobiographies dwell upon is the caste oppression and abject poverty in which the dalit community had to survive. Poverty is a paralyzing condition for all, but in case of dalits it became a curse. Laxman Gaikwad's *The Branded* contains instances of extreme poverty that the author had experienced. He used to eat gruel in which worms would float. Sharankumar Limbale's *Outcaste*, originally written in Marathi entitled Akkarmashi, is a brutal description of poverty. Though his father belongs to upper caste, his mother was from Mahar community. Sharan, thus puts in words the life he lived as an untouchable, as a half-caste and as an impoverished man. The book depicts his struggle against poverty, deprivation, discrimination and caste violence. Limbale portrays the pathetic and unenviable life of a poor, oppressed community and raises some pertinent and thought provoking questions like how is a man born with his caste and how can he become untouchable as soon as he is born. The condition of the untouchables is such that they steal, beg, fetch dead animals and eat them in order to appease their hunger. Their stomachs are like a passage to the graveyard that continuously swallows the dead.

M.G.K. Nair compares Sharan's story with Jean Genet's "The Thief Journal". Genet was born illegitimate in Paris in 1910. He never knew his parents. Being an orphan he became a thief at the age of ten and was sent to a reformatory. He spent thirty years of his life wandering in the European underworld. In *The Thief's Journal* he has stated that the simplest reason that made him a thief was the need to eat. He resolutely rejected a world that rejected him. Limbale has also unveiled a bizarre world of poverty, untouchability and the pathetic human condition prevailing all over the world. But unlike Genet, in Sharan's case there is hope and light at the end of the tunnel.

Treated as untouchables, these dalits suffered under tremendous pressure from the 'upper' castes to stay aloof and not 'pollute' their social system. The ideology of purity and pollution that renders dalits as untouchable marks them out as distinct from the caste Hindus. This was evident from the way they were treated in the physical, occupational, residential and ritual segregation. And interestingly, while the dalits were marked by ritual pollution, their labour was essential to maintain the purity of the caste Hindus. They used to be commonly involved in menial tasks like cleaning the lavatories and removing dead animals.

In dalit autobiographies, we meet these outcastes who are living in seclusion outside village bounds, on pavements, village outskirts as well as forests and hills and they would often compete with animals around them for survival. In his autobiography *Ooru Keri*,

Siddalingaiah describes how he used to stay in the graveyard. In Omprakash Valmiki's Joothan (2003), we are told how his family members dry left-over poories for the rainy season. Dalit life and left-over food almost become inseparable. On another instance, we learn that Omprakash was allowed to sit in the classroom only after sweeping the classroom. Dalit autobiographies are not only a quest for true self, but depict violation of social and moral code.

Illiteracy was one reason why the dalit community was exploited by the upper castes and had to live in humiliation and utter misery. Shankarrao Kharat in his autobiography *Taral-Antaral* narrates how his father was exploited by a non-dalit because no one in the community knew how to read and he needed assistance to read a letter that he later comes to know, carried the sad news of his daughter's death. While this instance shows the illiteracy that prevailed in the dalit community; *Ooru Keri* brings out how a dalit educated boy who would read and write letters for them, was regarded with respect and loved like God. He was even offered gifts and food in return for the good work that he did. We thus see how education forms the basis of human life and how it was the biggest obstacle in improving their living standards.

The policy of reservation that facilitated dalits to educate their children and help them enter the mainstream society was also something that was won on mass agitation. It aimed at bringing about change in social, economic and political conditions in the lives of the community. The several success stories of the dalits in various professions that have found place in some autobiographies is to a large extent, result of the reservation policy of the government. Limbale comments:

> "whenever I heard that reservation facilities for dalits were about to be cancelled it used to scare me. If these facilities are cancelled, give us our own Dalitsthan. We are educated only because these facilities exist; they were like a father to us. If there were no facilities we would have had no such education, would have been at home grazing cattle and helping our parents."

Limbale's words demonstrate the centrality of the reservation policy for the purpose of socially empowering the dalits and helping them to be part of the mainstream society, failing which could result in a new land that they claimed for in adverse conditions.

Self-recognition and search for identity in a world that treated them as non-existent was the main motto of dalit autobiographies. Writers made query regarding the dominance of the upper caste and trace out the evolution of an 'individual self' as well as depict the collective suffering of the community. Priyanka Shrivastava makes an apt observation in this regard.

> The proliferation of evocative terminologies to describe this particular experience of sublaternity testifies to the significance of giving appellation/naming for individuals and social groups, as well as the right to choose it for self. The rejection of an imposed appellation in favour of a self-bestowed one is an act of rebellion and redefinition of the self and its destiny. Dalit literature, which seeks its proliferation in the twentieth century, offers this space to the Dalits for defining their individuality and cultural identity.

We can see the conflict in defining the dalit identity as revealed in the work 'Joothan' where Valmiki tells the reader that most of the 'upper' caste people called them 'Oye Chuhre' or 'Abe Chuhre' and did not bother to address them by their names. This designation of the dalits by their caste titles instead of their names by upper class people was an act of negation of their human identity by the latter. It is this kind of injustice and humiliation that the dalit literature stood out to protest. Valmiki tells how everyone calls him Chuhre and even at the end of the autobiography, he informs the reader that several of his friends and colleagues are upset by his persistence in using Valmiki as it brands him with his caste of origin. His insistence to use the surname for it has become his badge of identity is in itself a metaphor for dalit literature which engages in bringing out the complexities of self-definition, cultural identity and the right to represent the self by the Dalits, in life and art.

It is important to note here that the fidelity to community over self is evident even in the titles of some of the autobiographies like *Outcaste: A Memoir, Joothan: A Dalit's Life, Taral Antaral* and *Growing up Untouchable in India.* None of these titles employ the name of the narrator or gesture towards his individuality as a subject. They all powerfully evoke the collective experience of dalits as a community.

However, as Sipra Mukherjee raises her concern – "Dalit literature has often been criticised or questioned for being, among other things, self-pitying, monotonous, overtly ideological, narrow and propagandistic." It has also been viewed as 'infused more with passion than with concern for literary effect' (Mendelson and Vicziany, 1998: 215). Similar argument has been raised by Gros and Kannan when they write that "early Marathi literature is closer to 'testimonies' than to works of art, chronicles rather than artistically conceived texts, lived experience rather than poetic experimentation, and material more suited to the study of anthropology rather than that of literature. (Kannan and Gros, 2002: 24)

Though there is some truth in it and we find dalit literature predominantly marked by revolt and negativism, it is also closely associated with the hopes of freedom from the shackles of caste discrimination and an equal stand in the mainstream society. The sincere efforts of their writings bring to our focus the fact that it is essentially the literature of suppressed class of society who don't require sympathy or empathy but demand the right to live with dignity and be treated as equals. Written mostly in the autobiographical mode, dalit literature thus maps the dalit spirit – the human spirit of endurance and courage at its core. And the assertion of dalit consciousness through literature is, in the words of Dasari. Praveen and Dr B. Raju, "a fight more to make the society aware of its hidden, dark truths that need to be confronted in order to change and transform into a better and equalitarian tomorrow and will perhaps lead to the conviction that –

'In the end there will be no margin,
In the end there will be no centre,
In the end there will be no play,
In the end there will a free play of playfulness
Without margin...
Without centre...'

Works Cited

Abraham, Joshil, K. Barak, Judith Misrahi (ed). *Dalit Literatures in India.* Routledge, New Delhi, 2016. Print.

Limbale, Sharan Kumar. *Outcaste.* Trans. Santosh Bhoomkar. New Delhi: Oxford University Press, 2003, Print.

Moon, Vasant. *Growing Up Untouchable in India: A Dalit Autobiography*, Trans. Gail Omvedt. New Delhi: Vistar Publication, 2002. Print.

Moon, Vasant, and Omvedt, Gail. *Growing up Untouchable in India.* Rowman & Littlefield Publishers. 2002. Print.

Prasad, A. N. and Gaijan, M.B. (ed). *Dalit literature: A Critical Exploration.* Sarup & Sons, New Delhi, 2007. Print.

Siddalingaiah. *Ooru Keri.* New Delhi: Sahitya Akademi, 2003. Print.

Valmiki, Omprakash. *Joothan: A Dalit's Life.* Trans. Arun Prabha Mukherjee. Kolkata: Samya, 2003. Print.

http://samyukta.info/archives/vol_4_1/book%20review/sharankumarlimbale/the%20story%20of%20an%20outsider-the%20outcaste.htm

http://www.researchfront.in/07%20APRIL-JUNE%202014/1.pdf

https://www.academia.edu/1615543/_Dalit_Autobiographies_The_Artists_Representations_of_Self_and_Community_

http://worldlitonline.net/breaking-tenets-a-study.pdf

20

Hollowness and Shadow in Siddalingaiah's *Ooru Keri*

DR SUMITRA SINGH

Ooru Keri is an autobiography of Siddalingaiah where he talks about the slum life of Dalits and the ill treatment metted out to them who even tried to change their religion for a better treatment. In some cases, the conditions improved while in others, it did not. This marvelous piece of writing depicts the story of self empowerment from the socio-economic hassles and hardships and all protests against all injustice at the hands of upper castes. Through his writings, Siddalingaiah has reinstated and reassured self-respect for the entire Dalit community through his prolific writing style.

Siddalingaiah's *Ooru Keri* presents a dismal picture of the Dalits in the Karnataka state. He tries to bring forth his long struggles as a Dalit, the atrocities that he has seen and witnessed and also how agony took over him and the others alike being a Dalit.

Days back in the past, there was a water tight compartmentalisation of caste. Caste barriers were represented through various lanes distinguishing each other as a superior and an inferior caste. Siddalingaiah said, 'Ours was the last house in the colony.' (Siddalingaiah, 1) His house being last in the village with a collapsed roof, showed the hollowness of people's mindsets truly showcasing as a Dalit being. Many a time, the Dalits had to migrate and the graveyard settlement was one of the destinations. As they did not have any permanent address, the Dalits had to keep on moving.

This is only one aspect represented by Siddalingaiah. In *Ooru Keri*, there are also various unexplored elements of poverty, humiliation and also the kind of oppression, they suffered at the hands of the upper castes people. The writer seems to have a fresh memory as he walks down the memory lane with utmost depression, pathos and a different type of passion that truly denotes his Dalit sentiments. He portrays the real social life of the people who lived with him and how himself was strangled in the clutches of indifference and indignation. Although voiceless people dominate the area but his voice somewhere overtook the depression of many and he himself rose amidst all deprivations. He describes the pitiable conditions of the deprived Dalits of Karnataka who even slogged for their daily morsel:

> That was a time of drought everywhere. People had to struggle even for a morsel of food. Some threw ceremonial fests to appease the rain gods. During fests, the Holeyas were made to sit in a corner. We were noticed only after people of the upper castes had been served. I felt contented with whatever little food came my way, and wouldn't think too much about the discrimination. (OKA, 7)

Although logical thinking and critical thinking and analysis are considered to be a behavioural trait of humans, yet for Dalits in *Ooru Keri*, the story was different. Sense of dignity and honour come with the fulfilling the basic requirements of food, shelter and clothing, which was denied to the Dalits. Rather, they could hardly seem to provide themselves with those basic requisites. They wore torn and ragged clothes and held a life of very low esteem. Siddalingaiah narrates, 'Occasionally, Ainoru also give me some old, tattered shirts and pants that his son had discarded. I was younger than his son, and the clothes fitted me very loosely. Yet I wore them folded up, looking odd among my companions.' (*Ibid*: 3) Dalits, thus, lives like animal which has no logical power.

Actually the name Ooru means the so-called civil and lavish settlement of the upper castes that had all the basic necessities to live a dignified life like a school, hospital good homes, roads, shops and also free movement although it was separated by wall and bushes. Keri represented a geographically separated area which was off the mainstream as if "an abuse" or "ataboo". It was very natural that the children of Dalits did not go to good schools but the lowly ones where also they were not allowed to sit with the upper caste people. The author himself had faced such oppressions and negligence. His father faced a lot of humiliation in Magadi where he worked as a labourer and had to finally relocate to Bangalore for a job. This was the time when Siddalingaiah decided to introspect into Dalit lives and culture and decided to stand up to emancipate them. The author remembers a well from where the Dalits could not take water although, it was in the vicinity. They had to go to far off places to fetch only a little amount of water. Such was the humiliation! Extreme poverty, harassment, discrimination, Siddalingaiah's a child had lost all hope in god! If they went to someone's house, they were offered the leftover food only. In total, the Dalits were treated in an animalistic way which was very tough for the author to bear as a growing child.

The author's mother worked as a sweeper in Srirampura where again she had to undergo all the ill treatment at the hands of so called upper caste authorities. She used to carry the leftover food which was offered to the workers after it had been served to the menfolk. Famines and droughts were also common in those areas, but as luck would have it, the Dalits were the last beneficiaries, if at all. Otherwise, death rate was normally high too.

Siddalingaiah had seen all that. He decides to attend the night schools and learns through his teachers. Although there was abject poverty and rejection, he gets inspired by Dr Ambedkar, in the manner he became self-empowered through education. He started feeling the same spark in him and took up the tool of education to enlighten himself and others and at the same time work for the true emancipation of the Dalits on ground. Once Siddalingaiah remembered, "That was a time of drought everywhere. People had to struggle even for a morsel of food. Some threw ceremonial fests to appease the rain gods. During fests, the Holeyas were made to sit in a corner. We were noticed only after people of the upper castes had been served. I felt contented with whatever little food came my way, and wouldn't think too much about the discrimination." (OKA, 7) Such emotional turmoil existed in the minds of Dalits that time. And Siddalingaiah made it a point that he has to come out of all this and also make his kinmen come out of that. There was a time of famine when his family had to move to

Bangalore and his father worked hard in the nearby firewood depots to support the family. Their main food included tuber, yams and greens. Not just his father, but many more became huge debtors on the Marwadi shop eventually. Siddalingaiah remembers when one day his father was deliberately beaten by someone, torn his clothes and left him wailing on the streets. This was not just one occasion. There were many such occasions when the Dalits were treated mercilessly as if they have done a crime. Siddalingaiah became an educated boy and would help others write and read their letters! Siddalingaiah remembers, "People felt very happy because I not only read the letters but explained their meanings also. Some would make me write letters to their relatives. I would then get, besides a generous amount of eats, some money as well. For the handful who got love letters, I was equal to god." (*Ooru Keri*: 33-34).

Once, in Government of Arts College, Bangalore, a non-dalit lecturer mistook Siddalingaiah to be a Lingayat and asked him to fetch water. But later when he came to know about his caste, he refuses him to do so, "Why he still chose me to fetch water became a subject of discussion in class. He had mistaken me for a Lingayat. I was liberated from the task of fetching water after he came to know my caste." (76)

As Siddalingaiah was growing up, he joined the Goplaswamy Iyaer hostel, nearby which Kannadigas and Tamils lived in Srirampura. The growing Siddalingaiah studied day and night and gained knowledge. He started giving lectures on Caste system and orthodoxy. This won him many prizes which he sold to bear the expenses of his own education and support his family. Eventually and slowly, he became a rationalist and started opposing many Hindu beliefs. He as such, had already lost faith in god. Once he said, "God does not exist." He put off the light which was pointed out as evidence to the existence of God. He challenged, "If God does exist, will it stop me speaking." (81)

Siddalingaiah had to face many manmade calamities that mean obstruction in any work that he did by his fellow non-dalit people. He faced a hard time to come out of all that. Of course, education was his successful tool. Siddalingaiah remarked that the Dalits were god fearing people, many a time, they had blind faith in god. He had heard of gods and goddesses ever possessing a Dalit? Siddalingaiah came to know that he has a separate God and *gurus*. Once, his mother said 'our guru had arrived; our entire family went to the mulberry tree up the street. They fell at his feet and presented their offerings. He was in the lineage of Mentaswamy's disciple.' (*Ibid:* 8)

Apart from all this, Siddalingaiah also remembers many ghost stories. He said: 'One evening, when I was returning home all by myself, I heard a clapping sound. I was aghast, and fled, stumbling and falling along the way. I caught my breath only after I reached home.' (Siddalingaiah. 2003: 2)

Siddalingaiah was influenced by Dr B.R Ambedkar and stared teaching and preaching his doctrines to the masses. Soon, he joined the Karnataka association and was made the Joint Secretary. He then associated himself with great leaders of that time like Dejagow, Maryappa, Ventatashbhaiah. Later, he founded the Vicharavadi Parishat, a society had a community consciousness of the Dalits. He took all the problems related with the Dalits to the Government of Karnataka which humbly tried to improve the conditions of Dalits by increasing the scholarship amount, renovating dalit hostels, providing food etc. Slowly, his political affairs improved with the rationalists of that time. He started writing in the magazine titled Shudra and started a night school for the slum children of Bangalore. This brought empowerment and enlightenment to many dalit lives. They shout, "....Do something to get us to attend you classes..." (OKA, 101). He started the Dalit Sangharsh Samiti and later became the Member of Karnataka Legislative Council. He received his M.A. in Kannada language and also a position of research Assistant at Kannada Research Centre. S. Bhartiraja said:

> Siddalingaiah grew up like any Dalit wanton boys- humiliated and unable to comprehend why his family was made to suffer. His early memories, he said, were of how his father was unable to find work in Magadi, causing the family to move finally to Bangalore. All through his growing up, hungry, suffering, and humiliation at odd jobs while studying are his chief memories; they made him lose faith in God, and also mark the beginning of his Dalit introspection. He first emerged on the public scene as a

> student leader in the 1970s, a period when Dalit rights issues had begun triggering conflict with upper classes. However, Siddalingaiah did not join active politics then because he had too much work on hand. Although he was both a teacher and an activist, it was his autobiography that would be most influential, shaping the literary thinking of the time. (Opp. Cite., Bhartiraja: 2012: 76)

Over four decades, Siddalingaiah has been inspiring the lives of many Dalits and also many non-Dalits. Many believe that he has been a messiah for the Dalits. But fact remains that, he himself has evolved as a phonenix from his life struggles, education empowered him and his belonging to his community enlightened him. Siddalingaiah has been a source of inspiration to millions in India.

Works Cited

Siddalingaiah. *Ooru Keri: An Autobiography*. Trans. S.R. Ramakrishna, New Delhi: Sahitya Akademi, 2003. Print.

Bhartiraja, S. "Siddalingaiah's Self Sprung Achievement in *Ooru Keri- An Autobiography*: A Study" in *Development of Scheduled Castes in India* edited by Rao P. D., New Delhi: Serials Publication, 2012. Print.

21

Solitude as Metaphor in Y.B. Satyanarayana's *My Father Baliah*

Dr Zainul Abid Kotta

Solitude and loneliness are the two perennial concerns faced by the Dalits in India. The major theme of Y.B. Satyanarayana's *My Father Baliah* is moving around these notions of solitude and loneliness. Satyanarayana's biography named *My Father Baliah* is a vivid portrayal of an exodus of a family that belongs to the Dalit Madiga community of Telengana in India. It is a family saga of a family named Yelukati, a village wandering between modernity and orthodoxy. The family mentioned here strives hard to make both ends meet. As S. R. Sankaran rightly comments in the foreword of the book, My Father Baliah is a detailed delineation of the different facets of the unique world of untouchables- the inviolable societal boundaries and attitudes, the social, economic, and cultural land-scapes, the norms and patterns of intercommunity and interpersonal relationships, the ways of life and means of living, the negotiations and compromises and the aspirations and shortcomings as well (xi). The unromantic picturisation of solitude and alienation in the memoir is heartbreaking and really mirroring the existential dilemma of a class whom the majority of the Caste Hindus considers as filthy and ugly. It was a paradox that they are the food suppliers. Their energy and women were used extensively. Almost all characters in the novel are facing the acute curtailment of freedom and mobility. Even their mobility is chained and were terribly left alone. The left alones contribute much for maturing the anatomy of the memoir. It is Octavio Paz, who had beautifully tried to explain the relationship between solitude and human condition. Paz takes it quite romantically and defines the same in an acceptable format. But Indian Dalit sensibility cannot be studied under the Pazian observation.

> Solitude is the profoundest fact of the human condition. Man is the only being who knows he is alone, and the only one who seeks out another. His nature – if that word can be used in reference to man, who has 'invented' himself by saying 'no' to nature – consists in his longing to realise himself in another. Man is nostalgia and a search for communion. Therefore, when he is aware of himself he is aware of his lack of another, that is, of his solitude. (Paz, 195)

Satyanarayana's memoir deals with the emancipatory dreams of three generations. It has an epic grandeur and sensibility, which is being shared by many Dalit authors and activists. As SR Sankaran comments in his Foreword, this memoir depicts continuity as well as change over a period of almost two centuries and three generations. But it is not merely a family chronicle. Rather, it is the depiction of the lived experiences of members of the Madiga community over several decades in different places, settings and situations, making it a unique social history of the times. (*My Father,* xi) The novel is a search, the true search for the roots in an apparently rootless system. It is a quest for memory and history. The history, the memory and the writings come closer here.

Pierre Nora's idea that "the quest for memory is the search for one's history" (289) provides a new angle to look at the interrelationship between history and memory, the dichotomy on which Satyanarayana works with. On reconstructing the communal history of the Madigas, Satyanarayana relies heavily on the use of memory as a means to rewrite the history of those oppressed because of caste, race, class and/or gender in a world where historiography has been controlled by the upper casteist Hindu coloniser. Memory is closely related to the reclamation of identity and history — both personal and collective. Memory and history dominate in *My Father Baliah* from the very beginning. Like other Dalit writers, Satyanarayana firmly believes that memory and imagination are essential parts of the narrative art, especially in a Dalit perspective. The use of memory and imagination reaches the realm of myth and fantasy in him. The author has a personal historical past marked by the oppression (internal as well as external), violence, and exploitation developed either by caste system, racial marginalisation and the consequences of technological progress and industrialisation. Satyanarayana's narrative is the recreations of his own and his community's history recorded. As other Dalit emancipatory artistic memoir, *My Father Baliah* too, plunges to memory. The memoir he prepared after his continual oral communication with his grandmother and other relatives. Most of the Dalits in India had oral transmission of knowledge, since language is alien to them. The memoir is dedicated to his unlettered mother Narasamma. "This is the story of three generations of my family, and I have woven it together from the memories I have of conversations with my grandfather Narsiah, my father Baliah, my aunt Pentamma and my elder sister Bachamma" (*My Father,* ix).

Every character in the memoir- both living and dead- voyages through the labyrinth of solitude. All aspects of human life experience the extreme form of solitude. The situation became worst when one feels totally out of existence. A classic example of solitude and alienation is visible in the following lines:

> A tall man [Narsiah, a Madiga, a chamar (untouchable)], walking away from his village with a heavy heart, his wife's body tied to his back, and almost dragging a little boy, his son, in a chilly evening drizzle, towards a distant stream that flowed from west to east. It was a small village that he was walking helplessly away from; his three years old son weeping aloud as he, half naked, followed his father in the gloomy evening…The man with the dead body on his back came from the Harijanwada, the untouchable dwellings in the village. He walked fast so that he could reach the banks of the stream before dark. He was powered by the thought that he had to dig a grave to bury his wife and that he had to do it all by himself. Despite the drizzle, the man was sweating under the weight of his wife's body. (*My Father,* 03)

This typical passage from the text provides a cinematographic description of the Dalit life in India. If we list the adjectives used in the passage we will get a connecting thread to make a narration of all the episodes. The hero of the passage is not explained by his profession, instead he was described by his social status: a chamar, an untouchable. He was all alone. He was totally helpless. Nobody follows him to the graveyard. His son was not well clad, he was half naked, instead. A stomach full of food, decent dress, a safe abode for night shelter, a decent burial, a good company etc. are the distant dreams of many Dalits. They don't have fertile land to cultivate for them. It was believed that Dalits are not entitled to occupy land. The caste Hindus and their Gods would be angry if a Dalit had occupied land. The basic amenities, they were depraved of. The amenities like water, land, shelter etc. were believed to be destined to the high class. Once the family was given some land, but the village lord, who represents the upper caste sensibility snatched it from them.

> Narsiah's father was given fifty acres of cultivable land with two wells by Nawab Mir Tahaniat Ali Khan Afsal. But the land was later snatched away from him by caste Hindus. Satyanarayana says that the village has a typical nature of any Indian village. A village has the perfect Hindu caste set-up with all the characteristic features codified by Manu. It has two types of dwellings, varna houses and avarna houses, separated by either a boundary or a well=maintained distance. (*My Father,* 4).

Junior Narsiah's life was more pathetic and pitiful than other characters in the memoir. He was only fifteen. He was exposed to all forms of human cruelty, the type of which ordinary human beings cannot tolerate. His was the perfect solitude and total alienation. He was compelled to do bone shattering hard work. He was a bonded labourer, and was compelled to work in the field without any wage.

> His son, about fifteen years old, worked as a jeetagadu-a labourer who worked for the landlord day and night without being paid any wage-and often slept in the cattle shed in order to be accessible to the landlord and his family at all times. He was also confidant of his Dora, and received some grain and paddy when his master felt generous (*My Father,* 6).

The sleep in the cattle shed perfectly embodies the loneliness and solitude of a man, who develops a sense of communication among animals. It is one of the sterling images used in the memoir by Satyanarayana. As we said above, even minor characters are also facing the problem of solitude in their strenuous attempt of existence. There is an interesting toddy tapper there in the memoir. The toddy tapper too faces certain amount of solitariness when he was alone at the top of the palm tree.

> As they walked, they saw men and women hurrying towards the toddy shop to retire after working hard through the day. Tapped and sold by men from the Idiga caste, a sub-caste of Sudràs, palm wine was a favourite drink among the villagers. Toddy tappers, also known as goundlollu, would risk their life and limb to procure toddy from tall palm trees. (*My Father,* 07)

When the whole village was devastatingly suffocated with cholera, the untouchables really tasted the pain of solitude together. Nobody dared to touch the living as well as the dead. The individual solitude became the loneliness of a community. In those days, infectious diseases were widespread. Every house experienced two or more deaths due to these contagious diseases. It became an everyday affair.

> People called this dreadful disease gattara and were even afraid of touching the dead body of a person who had died of this disease. Only the inmates of the house could carry the dead body for cremation (*My Father,* 12)

There are myriads of instances in the text that clearly illustrates the perennial question of Dalit identity cosmetized with the extreme form of solitariness. Here we can see a deviation from what Octavio Paz talked about solitude. In a typical Dalit perspective, this solitude is nothing voluntarily clad, but is forcefully thrust upon them. The European rational mind cannot easily understand it. All the basic necessities of life like water, land, shelter etc. were depraved for them, hence plunging them into desperate solitude.

Ramaswamy alias Baliah, the third generation representative of the genealogy is different on many aspects from other characters. His solitude is not stereotypical with other characters. He not only falls prey to his own thoughts and aspirations but also with societal interventions. His urge for education makes him a better and different human being. He experiences the wrath and comforts of solitude at the time of his teens. When he was ten he had an important role to play; to take care of his younger brother Yelliah and his three years old sister Pentamma while their mother was busy. He was forced to do all types of jobs at his home. When his father was away, the step mother Ramakka abused him. He went to sleep with empty stomach for most of the days. He received food after the children ate, and many a time it was only the leftovers.

> Ramakka was envious of the handsome child that Ramaswamy was. She even beat him increasingly frequently, but he bore everything patiently and in silence. (*My Father*, 22).

Patience and silence is the phrase that unequivocally speaks about the depth of alienation the Dalits in India exposed. Centuries old regression made them think that they were destined to suffer all caste aggressions. They were the outcastes and untouchables. Ramaswamy wanted to learn and master knowledge. His young mind was unable to decipher that untouchables were not permitted to read and write in India. With childish curiosity and enthusiasm, he approached his father one day. But Narsiah discouraged his son adding that reading and writing were the business of the higher castes not the lower castes. Their conversation is beautifully picturised by the writer.

> "Father I wanted to go to school". Narsiah looked at his son's innocent face, and drawing him close, said, "Dear child, we are Harijans, they won't teach us" (*My Father*, 22).

That is the reason. Harijans were not supposed to learn reading and writing. Going to school and mingling with other students must be natural way to do away with solitude. But that was not possible in such societal framework. Ramaswamy began to quarrel with his father, because he was not able to understand the logic and rationale of this behaviour. He even suggested his father that he would sit away from others and learn things. Narsiah made him understand that the position in the class room was not the major issue but the teachers were strictly following the codes of *Manusmriti.* That will not allow an untouchable to enter the school. At this point of time, Satyanarayana intervenes directly to the narration and pinpoints two important blockades to which Dalit community fell susceptible to the concept of sin and punishment. *Manusmriti* argues that learning by a Dalit itself is a sin and will be forced to punishment. The notion of sin and punishment is a labyrinthine metaphor from which Dalits could not escape.

Many Dalit writers like Satyanarayana and others moved their pens with the Dalit labyrinths of experiences. Labyrinth is a term applicable here to explore the Dalit sensibility. In Latin American perspective George Luis Borges' *Fictions* (1944) popularised the concept of Labyrinth. Borges patented the concept in elaborating his own conception of what reading, writing, thinking or culture are. This labyrinth may be natural or manmade above or below ground, designed as a puzzle, entertainment, trap or prison. This labyrinth may sometimes be real or imaginary, metaphoric, symbolic or mythic. Labyrinths may be essentially symmetrical or spiral. It may be centrally or severally focused. It was Sigmund Freud who tried to define the labyrinth as the archetypal uterine symbolising simultaneous longing to the maternal origin and fear of regression to the preconscious world of chaos, and historically a journey from darkness, enveloping matriarchal consciousness in the light of knowledge and patriarchal civilisation. Though his theories are essentially Eurocentric and limited in its scope, his psychological insights have universal appeal. The Latin American expert Gerald Martin's thesis about the labyrinth is highly usable in this regard. According to him, there are fields and paths for this labyrinth. Fields include language, culture, memory and text whereas paths comprise of utterances, discourses, images and themes. (Journeys, 26) So Dalit identity in India is essentially labyrinthine. The following quotation from the text clearly illustrates the argument.

Narsiah unsuccessfully tries to convince his son about the problem of reading and prescribing a way out of the labyrinth of existence.

> Narsiah had no answer to his son's argument; he was unable to explain to his son the laws of Manusmiriti, that sage Manu had codified everything about the Hindu way of life, and untouchables had, for centuries together, been segregated. Sin and punishment—*papamu* and *dandana*—are infallible tenets of Hindu laws regarding Sudras and untouchables. This ideology conditioned the minds of untouchables to believe that they would be committing a grave sin if they went against this law. According

> to Manu's laws, touching Caste Hindus amounted to a sin, so did standing or sitting in front of them, and wearing a turban or footwear in front of them. (*My Father,* 22).

Ramaswamy, though very young, identifies a way out of this labyrinth. He identifies the power of education, the only means by which the Dalits could assert their rights and privileges. Quite accidentally a mullah comes to his life. The mullah is a Muslim who follows Islam, the religion which staunchly argues that all men are equal before God and the superiority of an individual over others is solely depended on righteousness and rectitude. The mullah so passionately offered all helps to Ramaswamy to learn to read and write. There were two concerns in the mind of Ramaswamy. The first he being an untouchable, the second is of about the sin of learning to read and write. The mullah replied that he would take care of the two concerns and asked Ramaswamy to go to the nearby mosque, where he stays. The boy was so overwhelmed by the offer, and his father told him to keep it as a secret. Satyanarayana wonderfully narrates:

> The next day, after finishing his work, he bathed, and having dressed as neatly as he could, he went to the mosque. The mullah was surprised by Ramaswamy's promptness and the interest he showed in learning. He made the boy sit beside him. Ramaswamy, conditioned as he was, moved away slowly, fearing the pollution of his touch! The mullah wrote the first few Telugu letters on a slate and asked the boy to learn by writing over them. Thus, it came about that, against all social and religious odds, after many centuries of being denied learning by caste Hindus, a Muslim teacher sowed the seeds of learning in the Yelukati family-something for which the coming generation would be forever indebted to this first teacher of the family (*My Father,* 23)

Solitude again haunts the family when they were transferred to another station by the Railways. The metaphor solitude is so rampant and dormant throughout the memoir, especially in the first part. The Dalits in India still fight to conquer the solitude and they make efforts for merging with mainstream. But in many parts of India, Dalits are still committing suicides for this drive. Satyanarayana's memoir is a land mark in this regard. He puts a full stop to this work by the following lines:

> I know my father to have been a great man in his own way, and it is in his memory that I write this book. It is my tribute to him (*My Father,* 211)

Works Cited

Borges, Luis Jorge. *Fictions*. Trans. Anthony Kerrigan, Alstair Reid et al., New York: Grove, 1962.

—, *Doctor Brodies Report*. Trans. Norman Thomas de Giovanni London: Allen Lane, 1974 Martin, Gerald. "On 'Magical' and Social Realism in Garcia Marquez". Gabriel Garcia Marquez: New Readings. Eds. Mc Guirk Bernard and Richard Cardwell. Cambridge: Cambridge University Press, 1987: 95-116.

Nora, Pierre. "Between Memory and History: Les Lieux de Mémoire." History and Memory in African-American Culture. Ed. Geneviève Fabre and Robert O Meally. New York: Oxford UP, 1994.

Paz, Octavio. *The Labyrinth of Solitude*. N.Y.: Grove Press, 1961.

Satyanarayana, Y.B. *My Father Baliah*. New Delhi: Harper Collins India, 2011. Print.

22

Omprakash Valmiki's *Joothan-A Dalit's Life*: Interpretations from Different Perspectives

Dr M.B. Gaijan

> "Those who keep singing the glories of democracy use the government machinery to quell the blood flowing in our veins. As though we are not citizens of this country. They have suppressed the weak and the helpless for thousands of years, just in this manner. No one will ever know how many talents their deception and treachery have wiped out." (*Joothan*: 46)

Every nation has her culture; this culture remains sources to cultivate future generations of the concerned nation. Culture also remains the powerful factor to shape the nation as the "Powered Nation" too. Political governing systems, social structure of the society, faith of the people, and general character of people are the essential aspects of culture. Culture is variously defined. Clifford Geertz has cited Clyde Kluckhohn's *Mirror for Man* in his work *The Interpretation of Cultures*. Clyde Kluckhohn has interpreted culture by considering the key points;

(1) "the total way of life of a people";
(2) "the social legacy the individual acquires from his group";
(3) "a way of thinking, feeling, and believing";
(4) "an abstraction from behaviour";
(5) "a theory on the part of the anthropologist about the way in which a group of people in fact behave";

(6) a " house of pooled learning";

(7) "a set of standardised orientations to recurrent problems";

(8) "learned behaviour";

(9) a mechanism for then formative regulation of behaviour;

(10) "a set of techniques for adjusting both to the external environment and to other men";

(11) "a precipitate of history".

These are very significant points to understand culture of the concerned country and people, their socio-cultural, political and religious behaviour.

As the history of India tells, on the Indian subcontinent humanity dwelt and developed since thousands of years. So the Indian cultural history is also thousands of years old. During different era socio-cultural, political and religious behaviour of Indians remained peculiar towards fellow Indians due to Indian culture. Women, untouchables and tribal were marginalised and became frequently victims of inhumanity committed by majority and this social attitude is inculcated by the culture. This social attitude has not changed even today.

India remained multi-lingual, cultural nation. Graded inequality was/is the culture of India. This social system was/is frequently supported directly or indirectly by religion and governing system. As a result homogeneity in society is always challenged. Even today in the second decade of twenty-first century, each section of society is considered either superior or inferior to another section of society. It is the culture that superior section of society exploits inferior section of society. Even today one section of society is pushed at the periphery and away from the periphery of Indian society. They are Dalits or tribal who were/are unwanted at all culturally, socially, even on humanitarian ground. Even today orthodox Indians are not away from this type of cultural clutch.

India was/is the society of castes. Caste was/is the great threat to India's unity and integrity. Indian culture, in general sense means a culture of mainstream upper castes, no marginalised- Dalits and tribal-were/ are allowed to enter the periphery. In past time a few saintly beings had tried to accept the marginalised on humanitarian ground.

But the major mass remained unwanted, untouchables. After establishment of India as the Republic Democratic nation constitutionally equality is accepted and safeguards are provided to accept the marginalised into mainstream of Indian society. But still even today in the twenty-first century the orthodox upper castes' cultural behaviours towards Dalits have no more changed. Cruelty and injustice to Dalits are still going on. Educated Dalits are writing about these issues. Their writings are the documents of Dalits' saga of suffering, truth about their struggle to get human identity, human rights in India.

As a matter of fact portrayal of facts in Kabir, Phule, and Ambedkarite style is the main characteristic of Dalit writings. Dalit autobiography is nothing but the truth. As a matter of fact Dalit pen doesn't portray fancy but facts. Dalit men's autobiography boldly presents socio-cultural reality of contemporary India. Valmiki's *Joothan* is one of them. In the introduction of English translation of *Joothan,* the translator Arun Prabha Mukherjee has aptly noted in the introduction;

> Dalit autobiography claims status of truth, of testimony....... The concrete materiality of his village and the cities that later inhabits, and the rendering of historical Dalit protest that he participated in or wrote about in the newspapers at a personal cost, give *Joothan* the status of documented Dalit history. (*Joothan*: XLV)

Omprakash Valmiki has emerged from the Chuhra caste, Bhangi caste the lowest among the low castes. But under the influence of Arya Samajists' large scale movement during the early twentieth century, the Chuhra were renamed as Valmiki, the epic poet of the Ramayana. Earlier untouchables could not even accept good names. They could not accept names from the upper castes too. Their names were signifying things like rubbish, meaningless waste. They could not accept good surname or the surnames used by upper castes. Because name and surname the upper castes could/can identify untouchables and keep them away. So at the end of twentieth century, educated Dalits started to change their names/surnames, not to cheat the upper castes but easily merge with the mainstream.

Omprakash Valmiki's name and surname are like upper caste people so the upper castes accepted him many times. On other side he could easily mix with mainstream. The autobiography presents right from the childhood Omprakash struggled got education and government job. With his life struggle Valmiki has presented in *Joothan* the social attitudes of upper castes towards Dalits, upper caste culture towards Dalits. In this autobiography he has also presented Dalit culture.

Joothan can be evaluated from different perspectives but in this paper the text is interpreted from major three different perspectives. The title of the text is very suggestive. *Joothan* means leftover food, after taking meal by the upper castes was given to untouchables out of compassion. Thus, it was believed humanism. And in exchange of that untouchables had to work for upper castes, manually, or as labourers etc. But this practice became custom since time immemorial. In some parts of rural areas it was practiced even end of the last century. For the study of India's culture, India can be divided into three sections: 1. Rural India, 2. Urban India and 3. Metro- India. Each India is different socially, culturally, politically, educationally, religiously, financially etc. But role of caste is very decisive at every level.

1. *Dalits in Rural Areas:* India is the nation of millions of villages. There is the big gulf between rural India and urban India. Still the rural India is lacking infrastructural benefits, educational and health benefits so even in the early twenty-first century the rural culture of India has not changed more. Social attitudes, social behaviour, public mannerisms have not changed even using digital technology. As a result rational culture of India has not still emerged in rural India. Castes control almost major aspects of rural life. Wherever the role of caste comes Dalits suffer a lot. Majority of Dalits in rural India become victims of injustice and cruelty due to caste-based practices, *Jamidaree* and wrong persons getting "Power". Sharankumar Limbale in his autobiography presented the same issues.

The text presents right from the schooling teachers treat the Dalit children with prejudice and inhumanly. Dalits in rural areas are still helpless labourers, either illiterate of little learning. So they can't demand their rights or migrate at the better place. So they have to bear injustice. Omprakash writes about the school at his childhood era;

> Finally, one day I was admitted to the school. The country had become independent eight years earlier. Gandhiji's uplifting of the untouchables was having ramifications everywhere. Although the doors of the government schools had begun to open for untouchables, the mentality of the ordinary people had not changed much. I had to sit away from the others in the class, and even that wasn't enough. I was not allowed to sit on the chair or a bench. I had to sit on the bare floor; I was not allowed even to sit on the mat. (*Joothan*: 3)

In this sort of environment upper caste village children badly treat the author due to caste-based hate. Beating Dalits without any error became practice. And on other hand teachers in school also favour the upper caste students.

In villages even today Dalits are living at the outskirt of villages, doing manual labour in the farms of upper caste people. So rural areas if Dalit goes with new clothes, it becomes a matter of envy and attack on Dalits. Valmiki write thus;

> If we ever went our wearing neat and clean clothes, we had to hear their taunts that pierced deep inside, like poisoned arrows. If we to school in neat and clean clothes, our classmates said, "Abey, Chuhre ka, he has come dressed in new clothes." If we went in wearing old and shabby clothes, then they said, "Abey, Chuhre ke, get away from me, you stink. (*Joothan*: 4)

Hate towards Dalits is already inculcated in innocent minds of upper caste children right from the childhood and school days. This sort of nausea was observed even at end of last century. Abusing and beating Dalits rural areas are reported frequently even today. It shows hate towards Dalits become the part of life.

Dalits exploitation in rural areas was/is frequently reported even today. The text presents many times Dalits were exploited by the farm owners Tagas. They pay very less and Dalits had no any option except working in their farms. With little money they live with hunger.

Whenever there was a marriage ceremony at village chief's home that becomes special event for village. After the marriage feast, leftover was/is given to Dalits out of human compassion. In this text when Omprakash's mother and sister went to Sukhdev Singh Tyagi's place they were bitterly treated with harsh. Both were insulted and abused. The text also presents pigs were very important animal in Dalit houses during that time. To dispose dead cattle in villages were/are still performed by Dalits. The text also presets reality of Bhangi *Basti*. The text presents injustices and cruelties on Dalits were natural social habits of villagers though little change is coming but very slow.

2. *Dalits in Urban Areas:* The writer has realistically presented Dalit's urban life at different places. Dalits' colonies are also separated in urban areas. Generally they are unhygienic and filthy without basic facilities. In upper caste colony to get a house for Dalits is even today challenging.

The writer, for college study goes to Dehra Dun has presented reality of Dalit *Basti* in Dehra Dun at that time;

> Indresh Nagar was settled mostly by the untouchable castes of Bhangis, who worked as sweepers or cleaners, and Jatias, who made and shoes. Bhangis now liked to call themselves Valmikis and Jatias preferred to be called Jatvas......Poverty and illiteracy were the ancestral legacy of both. They all lived a constricted, deprived life in little cubbyholes. Only a few got to eat two proper meals a day. (*Joothan*: 79)

In this sort of area Omprakash started his study. He was also insulted in the school and became victim of ragging. Omprakash first time came into contact of Dr Babasaheb Ambedkar's thoughts and actions.

After getting training in the Ordnance Factory Training Institute, Khamaria, Jabalpur, the writer got a job. Her Omprakash accepted Valmiki as his surname. New surname gave him new identity. Here Valmiki came in contact with Dalit writings. He wrote article in *The Navbharat Times* on Dalit issues. As a result on the base of Shiv Sena supporters' complaint the principal of the institute warned Omprakash thus; "You are the government institution. There could be disciplinary action against you on the base of this article.......Don't do all this during training-you will be thrown out. Go now be careful in the futures" (*Joothan*: 105) as after the publication of article, fellow students' behaviour was changed.

Omprakash was invited at Kulkarni's place on religious ceremony. But when he talked with Professor Kamble he knew about the Kulkarnis; "Maharashtrian Brahmins, especially those are of Poona, don't allow Mahar to touch their dishes." (*Joothan*: 109) He was informed that Omprakash was the Brahmin so he was invited at Kulkarni's home.

After Omprakash's marriage with Chanda, when they came back to Chandrapur, to find a house for them was the problem. After Chandrapur when Omprakash was transfered to Dehradun, finding house was the problem for him. Omprakash was invited in the Dalit Writers' Conference, was held in Chandigarh. Issues of changing surname became hot in the discussion. Orthodox finds out the caste and treats according to the caste. The writer note talk talking place between bus driver and conductor; "Whatever you say, a Chuhra will remain Chuhra. However high an officer he may become, he can't change his caste." (*Joothan*: 151)

Omprakash also writes his experience when both husband and wife were travelling Chandrapur via Delhi, after returning from Jaipur. Fellow traveller was the officer's wife. As the time passed, Omprakash's wife and the officer's wife started talk thus:

> "Bahenji, are you people Bengali?"
>
> My wife replied easily, "No, we are from Uttar Pradesh. My husband is posted at the ordnance factory in Chandrapur" "What is your caste?" My wife's face colour as soon as she heard the question……I replied, "Bhangi".
>
> As soon as they heard the word Bhangi, they laps into silence into total silence. The two families did not communicate during the rest of journey." (*Joothan:* 153)

Thus, the text presents hate and disgust towards Dalit are found everywhere, rural as well as in urban areas. The ways of hating are different.

3. *Dalits' Protest for Human Identity and Equality:* The author is both, writer and activist so he has highlighted Dalit Movement

strongly through his writings. Because of Dr Ambedkar's influence and his active involvement in writings Omprakash has realistically presented different Dalit protests for Dalits' identity. Omprakash is from Bhangi caste, lowest among the Dalit community. The fellows of this caste were and even today are not accepted by the society so unacceptability and caste-based hate the fellows of this caste experience everywhere in society. Valmiki was encouraged and supported by visionary upper castes fellows frequently so his voice was heard through his writings.

The text highlights protest against injustice and cruelty. Omprakash writes when a youth from the *Basti* to refuse to work without wages in his village, at that time farm owner Tagas used constables from their caste, misused the power. Many times this is reported Dalits were/ are wrongly treated by using false or without any reason. Omprakash writes:

> "....Police constables would forcibly take poultry from the *basti*. There was no place to complaint; some Tagas would corporate with the police in this robbery. The moment they saw police, the women of the *basti* would hide inside their homes......two constables came to *basti* and took ten people with them. They grabbed whoever happened to cross their path.......The women and children of the *basti* were standing in the lane and crying loudly. The police had arrested their men for no reason." (*Joothan*: 44-45)

In rural areas, many times for the benefits of caste fellows, dominant upper castes misused even government agencies. They misuse for their own selfish benefits. The writer has highlighted the fact. In this misuse there is no humanity at all.

Omprakash had many questions about the cause of untouchables sufferings, he shared with his *Pitaji*, father, about their caste and attitudes of upper castes. His father told him not to embrace Christianity. But as the protest Omprakash thought thus:

> "Neither am I a Hindu." If I really were a Hindu, would the Hindu hate me so much? Or discriminate against me? Or try to fill me up with caste inferiority over the smallest things? I also wondered why one had to be Hindu in order to be a good human being –

> I have seen and suffered the cruelty of Hindus since childhood. Why does caste superiority and caste pride attack only the weak? Why are Hindus so cruel, so heartless against Dalits?" (*Joothan*: 48)

The writers thoughts show cruelties committed on Dalits by orthodox Hindus. They suffer without their any error. The author has also presented the Dalits' large scale protest and agitation to change Marathwada University's name be changed to Dr Ambedkar University:

> "The state assembly passed the bill for the name change. *Savarna* or upper caste people, had opposed the bill on large scale, and rioting and destruction of public property occurred in several towns and cities. Ahmadnagar, Aurangabad, Nagpur, Sholapur, Bombay, Nasik and Amravati were tense. Marathwada felt the effects of rioting the most. Dalit neighbourhoods were tortured. Hundreds of people died. The news in the paper broke one's heart. (*Joothan*: 123)

Valmiki writes untold history of recent past. He also analysed the issue; "The hatred of thousand years was again visible in its original form.......In their eyes Ambedkar was simply a Mahar, and they could not care less if his scholarship was as vast as the sky." (*Joothan*: 123) The author has also discussed protest against reservation quota in Gujarat. At that time Major cities of Gujarat were badly affected. Dalits suffered a lot:

> The anti reservationists stood under Gandhi's statues in place like Baroda, and Gandhinagar and vented their hatred for Dalits. The harassment of Dalits in government and government-funded workplaces increased. (*Joothan:* 124)

Omprakash Valmiki has skillfully interwoven the Dalits Movement for their human identity and human dignity in his autobiography. While discussing Dalits' protest, he remained very faithful to the facts. He discussed Bhadravati rally. As an Ambedkarite, he knew well the cause of cruelties committed on Dalits. Caste is the major factor, so he writes:

> Caste is very important element of Indian society. As soon as a person born, caste determines his or her destiny. Being born is

> not in the control of a person. If it were in one's control, then why would I have been born in a Bhangi household? Those who call themselves the standard-bearers of this country's great cultural heritage, did they decide which homes they would be born into?... Today caste remains preeminent factor in social life. As long as people don't know that you are a Dalit, things are fine. The moment they found out your caste, everything changes. *(Joothan*: 153-154)

Here the author has presented fact of contemporary India and the significant role of caste wherever Indians are. Caste system also carried with by the orthodox and practiced by them in abroad too.

Considering the various aspects of the text, it shows it is the sincere effort of the author to present socio-cultural reality of contemporary India. He is not so harsh to destroy the system but wishes identity, equality, human dignity, peace and prosperity of Indians, especially marginalised and victimised.

Works Cited

Geertz, Clifford. *Thick Description: Toward an Interpretive Theory of Culture*, in *The Interpretation of Cultures: Selected Essays*. New York: Basic Books, 1973: 4-5. Print.

Valmiki, Omprakash. *Joothan*. New York: Columbia University Press Books, 2003. Print.

23

(Re)Mapping Spaces for a Women Centric Discourse: A Critical Study of Kishore Shantabai Kale's *Kolhatyache Por*

Dr Aparna Lanjewar Bose

Dalit writings have an undeniably vital presence in the literary scenario today. By its very nature it is autobiographical. The publishing industry though wasn't too receptive earlier when these writings started pouring out from Maharashtra its birth place, as also of the whole Dalit movement. Nevertheless, major attempts to bring out Dalit writings into English were made by late Eleanor Zelliot a dauntless Ambedkarite scholar whose laudable efforts came forth in the form of an anthology of Dalit literature which introduced prominent Marathi Dalit poets to the English speaking audience. Poetry then was forceful genre that gave Dalit writings its identity and prominence. This was a generous and propitious attempt in the dreary translation scenario. Then came Dangle's "Poisoned Bread" that brought other literary forms into the foray and several other anthologies followed after that.

Of late, there is sudden upsurge of Dalit writings from all corners of the country. These are becoming the centre stage for debates and theorisations for scholars and researchers on several forums. There is more prioritisation of the autobiographical genre over others but the sad part is the politics involved in publishing them. The publishing industry which was once so hostile to Dalit literature in general, suddenly felt the need to bring out life stories in more numbers, needless to mention the reasons behind. Having said this what is also happening is that these writings which were neglected or at best ignored, and that became marginal more because of the sadist approach than the so-called already were, are to a large extent breaking the regional linguistic shackles and being made available for public consumption. The concerning part however, that still remains is perhaps the politics involved in translating these texts into English from their respective tongues and their depiction as narratives of pain and suffering thereby posing the greatest danger of reductionist stereotyping of these texts being just this and nothing more. This may or may not be less threatening to the non-Dalit translators of the Dalit texts who may or may not preoccupy themselves with its literary value and aesthetics.

Secondly, what is also of my primary concern is, do these texts flooding the markets sensitise the insensitive non-Dalits to the issues of the Dalits at large? Do they at all look beyond reservations and preoccupy themselves with much greater complexities surrounding a Dalit life? Does it concerns the feminists about the Dalit women voices in the lowermost strata waiting to be heard and living a life of debauchery and destitution? The answers may be best left for posterity but what must be said is that the deconstructive process of unlearning must begin and unless the interconnectedness of reading – understanding- accepting and then responding gets established Dalit writings will continue flocking the markets for commercial successes and consumptions as mere sob stories or stories from rags to riches or sagas of pain and poverty. Interestingly, Dalit writings coming from some corners of India to a certain extent lack the profuse social consciousness of writers from Maharashtra. As there seems a general apathy and non-acknowledgement to mass leader Ambedkar and his movement neither is anywhere in the offing the liberatory path of Buddha that he finally accepted. This makes one sit and poses serious questions about their own beliefs and world views before anybody else's. But then these are some exceptions who have gained sufficient publicity as Dalit narratives.

In other words what is to be pertinently understood is to look at these writings unapologetically as something moving beyond squalor and sordid; and something more than the representational discourses of suffering, pain and poverty to prompting resolution for action against inequities and to greater commitment for social transformation. From the literary critical standpoint in formulation of new Dalit Aesthetics and Dalit critical theory that has its initiation and inspiration in the life and works of Phule-Ambedkar-Buddha.

The Indian upper caste/brahminical mindset has developed a willful amnesia of their own ills and evils rather than remorse over the century long perpetrated wrongs. There is a conscious defense of structural polemics surrounding it. Cultural nationalism superimposed the enriched superiority of Indian spiritual and cultural ethos over the material west but gave lip service when it came to the issue of caste and caste violence. The emerging sociopolitical scenario based on newer reforms and legislations emancipated women to articulate their sufferance and voice their struggle with dogmas, conventions and rituals but probably not enough to speak of the sister "other" living at close quarters - a life of penury and destitution. Notionally, they succeeded in showcasing the modern Indian woman but on representational level they were a failure as they couldn't serve as touchstones to understand the live and struggles of women coming from different strata and cross-sections of the society. And this could not absolve them of their participatory stance in the upper caste patriarchy that continued to hold its stronghold on Dalit male internalisation.

There has always been a clear accusation that Dalit autobiographies by men are implicitly masculine self-centred and do not accord much space to their women. That either they are completely absent or then have a subdued presence. Mapping space within the male narratorial tradition the Dalit women autobiographies drew a lot of attention in recent times not just because they presented a women centric world view but in terms of historiography and ethnography too they pronounced, their absence in the male defined Dalit experience and absence and difference both in the female autobiographical tradition in a much more altruistic and pluralistic manner. However, this is not to suggest that the Dalit woman never had space at all in the Dalit male world. On reading Kishore Shantabai Kale's autobiography *Kolhatyache Por* which shook the Marathi literary world with its naked straightforwardness, one gets this impression that it is as much about the writer as it is about his mother as it is about the lives lived by countless other Kolhati women. The un-usuality of the book is in its very title which relates to a distinct identity of being the son of a Kolhati woman rather than a man. Even more unusual and arresting is the nomenclature part where conventionally father's name is used as a middle name but the writer endorses his identity having his mother's name for the middle name knowing full well the circumstances leading to his birth of having a biological father who never claims him as his own. And therefore in his name itself lies a tangible defiance to the very concept of fatherhood and masculinity, a condemnation of a community of men who expose their women to perils of the dancing profession but who fail to protect their women. It is a caustic satirisation of the notion of a family patriarch- a male breadwinner by accepting/ adopting a feminine identity of which there is total assurance and a complete certainty.

Kishore Shantabai Kale's *Kolhatyache Por* has a rare simplicity, remarkable straightforwardness and an unabashed honesty that narrates the journey of young Kishore protagonist from a despised birth to getting into an adulated profession of becoming a doctor. On his voyage we are all voyeurs into the dreary- almost scary world of the Kolhati women, the ways of the Kolhati men, their pernicious practices, beliefs, customs, and rituals of the community. Kale uses the methodology of female surrogacy to mark his scathing attack on male chauvinism and to negotiate space within multiple feminisms. In fact, most of the women presented are opinionated about their defined gender roles and become mediaries of larger concerns of women rights namely, the right over their bodies.

The book is a strong feminist document that puts up the case for the Kolhati women who run the show for their families and who are physically, economically and sexually exploited by the hierarchical caste orders. It vouchsafes for the potent desires and ambitions nurtured by these women, coming from the most vulnerable marginal sections. These women are multiply forced by the greedy and penurious male members of the community against their wishes and aspirations to perform in the Tamasha. Tamasha is a traditional folk dance form of Maharashtra. It is (in) famous for its dancers who sing and perform the Laavni-these are raunchy numbers with implicit sexual undertones, dramatically performed to entertain a live audience which comes from different social strata. Mostly, seen in the Marathwada region, it has gained notoriety and degenerated to a sort of prostitution. The Laavni dance is generally, performed by the women of the Kolhati community- one of the most backward marginalised communities whose survival rests on this folk art form. The girls born in the community are considered assets only because they are eventually groomed up to become Tamasha dancers and subsequent breadwinners of the family while the male members sit and thrive on their incomes and either indulge or vile their time in getting drunk.

Our narrator Kishore Kale then takes us to this infamous underbelly of the societies' underdog to show how his sensibilities grew in this deformed paraphernalia where women, alcohol and money often change hands. How he was a mute witness to the daily trade of debauchery and wretchedness and what made him determined to liberate himself from the mire of abnormality surrounding him. The book stands as a glaring testimony to his undaunted strength, resilience and resolves to transcend extenuating circumstances for a respectable living dedicated to the welfare of his people. Growing amidst several women who influenced his life in some way or the other he saw their untold miseries and labour at close quarters to be thoroughly sensitised and determined to represent their cause. Therefore, interspersed and intermingled in his own narratorial debut is the saga of countless Kolhati women who impacted him and made him for what he was. Be it his mother Shantabai, Jiju the sister to Shantabai's father, a distant relative Madhu Kambikar or aunt Nagin, be they his own aunts Susheela, Rambha, Baby, Shobha or countless other women that appear and reappear in those 116 odd pages.

The uneasy arduous journey holds good for a young boy- for it is a story from desire to fulfillment- to being a dedicated community worker involved in its developmental process- to finally being a well known doctor. Here one finds defiance of not just caste and class but also of rules laid by a community of men-beyond repair, men represented by maternal grandfather Kondiba, his uncles, biological father Namdev Jagtap, his stepfather- Nana who could never appreciate his success or feel proud of his achievements.

Kishore represents a condemnation and violation of every norm pertaining to their so-called assumed "manhood" to which they all hopelessly clung. Perhaps he became a constant reminder to them of their own failings and impotency. In striking contrast to them are men like Ramrao Lonikar, former Member of Parliament who combine the quintessential goodness of thought and action and stand by Kishore when his own people fail to.

The narrative primarily begins with the pathetic story of Jiji, her sacrifices for a thankless and useless adoptive step brother Kondiba i.e. Kale's maternal grandfather and ultimately comes to the circumstances leading to his mother Shantabai's oppression. Her initiation into Tamasha, for which comes the sacrifice of her only dream of becoming a teacher in order to take up the traditional Kolhati caste based occupation of becoming a tamasha dancer. What follows are telling instances of humiliations and body shaming of Kolhati women, the perils and hazards of performing in village after village, the cut throat competitions between different dance troupes for survival. And ultimately the fatal and joyous moment of Kishore's birth through a pernicious practice called "chira utrawaney." (It is a process of sexual initiation of a young virgin Kolhati woman who has attained puberty. She is dressed like a bride ready for the first night for any moneyed person who has paid a price in cash or kind to the family with an assurance that they shall be taken care of in the future. The young woman then becomes such a person's property to be used and abused and can be visited by him as and when his cravings demand. As such there is no legal binding on him and once his hunger is satiated he can abandon and leave her helpless. The poor woman on her part remains loyal as long as she can, sooner or later she gets impregnated and if neglected has to ultimately take to dancing again for a living having very little choices or no choices at all.) (pp. 7-8)

This is then how Kishore our hero is born of a local politician who abandons Shantabai once his hunger gets satiated. The later after a long waiting finally accepts another man named Dharurkar and Kishore's brother Deepak is born. For a while the dancing stops but with the subsequent death of Dharurkar she has taken to dancing again. Thus, the whole journey of start to the finish begins only to restart again in a cyclic manner. Her popularity as an artist, the neck throat competitions between different dance parties for sustenance, the entrapment of the Kolhati woman, the lure for comfort and security besides other social issues are highlighted. The book takes a turn where she eventually meets Nana and the circumstances leading to her elopement and settling down for the quietitude of a family life are all well brought out. The concept of home, family, filial bonding goes for a toss when Kishore spends most of his boyhood days either pining for his mother's presence and love or getting mercilessly flogged, laboriously slogged and ridiculously humiliated by his own people. He bore it all and managed to pass every year.

Kale's deprivation stands on multiple levels as a child begotten from an almost bizarre wedding, deprived of fatherly affection, motherly love or any other love for that matter that comes with (meaningless) blood relations. Back in his boyhood days, staying partly with his mother and Nana and then with his grandfather Kondiba, he only knew too well that nothing was meant to be simple for him. He ran errands for his uncles and aunts and their visitors in the Tamasha. His frank documentation and encounters with thugs, petty criminals, cheats, pimps sluts and all kinds of people is not misplaced. (pp. 77-78) His journey as a young college student bearing his badge of shame as a boy of a Kolhati dancer, the embarrassment of it all and the hurdles faced by him because of his caste. (p. 81) The odd jobs done to meet the expenses of his medical studies since government scholarship proved insufficient; The negative internalisations and low self esteem which, continued in adulthood, only reflect on how childhood trauma can impact the holistic development of an individual and therefore in a way he endorses the need to preserve, protect and create conditions for the psychological well being of children coming from such families. The writer's subjectivity is formed/shaped by the society and its practices. Thus, whenever he is reminded of his lowly birth the facade of his own progress falls flat on his face.

The detailed narration of the ways, practices and beliefs of Kolhatis, their superstitions, self formulated laws of dealing with transgressions (p. 39) and heaping humiliations on such transgressors makes the discourse move towards binaries of the sacrosanct and profane. It brings to the foray multitudinous issues of intercaste marriages, marriage practices in general and intercommunity liaisons; issues of children born out of such imposed weird cultural practices as being nothing less than the tragic mulatoes; of their ill-treatment and of forced child labour. It highlights the issue which many a times gets inadequately handled in male narratives namely, Violence against women (p.74) and their bodies in the name of socio-religious, caste and cultural practices, in the name of filial gratitude, responsibilities, economic reasons. All these tend to render service to patriarchy and problamatises her triply disadvantaged position operating within caste, class and gender.

Kale's women stand a strong moral ground as even amidst degrading circumstances they are strong and poised. Nevertheless, in Kale's mother Shantabai we have a woman who dares to break the jinx associated with the lives of the tamasha dancers by choosing a life of conjugal happiness albeit strewn with marital compromises that too with a much married colourful man. He would batter her at the slightest pretext and disallow her to meet her relatives leave aside young Kishore while she on her part pulled on with his temperament and vices for the choices were hers. She remained loyal to him performing her duties as a devoted wife for the rest of her life. On one hand, by showcasing this aspect of her persona, Kale seems to be disrupting certain myths surrounding the Kolhati women especially in regard to their character, sexual orientation and promiscuity which are wrongly based on assumptions and generalisations made by people. He seems to endorse that the Kolhati women are capable of an unmatched moral integrity, despite a despised living. On the other hand in his own reticent manner he seems to be admoninishing such servitude to the oppressor. Women even if they do make choices are not completely out of the mire. They are as wretched as they were before. It is equally irritant for him to see women defending their men even after undergoing a life of hell. For instance in one particular instance when Kishore in sheer frustration over Nana's wayward ways consumes poison. His mother Shantabai pleads with him not to report the matter to the police. This leaves Kale to comment "Even after all this my mother loved Nana. I saw in her the symbol of an Indian woman" (p.115)

Doesn't somewhere this mother become the mother India? Should not her shaming then be the shaming of the nation? Isn't Kale in his appealing manner making the reader, re-read nationalism and nationalistic discourse in a new light? The wretchedness of this dancer- mother dancing to the whims of drunken men, her wretchedness at home dancing to the tunes of her useless father and brothers, the wretchedness of her life after choosing to live with Nana as his second wife and dancing to his eccentricities and Her utter helplessness especially in regard to her two children Kishore and Deepak, though poignantly delineated, metaphorically endorse "once a dancer always remains so" as she remains dancing to all the men in her life. "A dancer should not love, should not have family, and should not live for her children. Her life is only meant for her mother, father, brother. Is this written in some sacred text of the Kolhatis? Is it a sin to be born beautiful?" (p. 24)

What qualities of Kishore's greatness as an individual is his sense of self-worth and self-respect, (pp. 51-52) his sense of forgiveness. There may be bitterness here and there but that's when he is a commentator and does not prevail on it for long. Though his conception was an unwanted pregnancy for his mother that could not be aborted on time, yet for the community as a whole it proved significant for he stood up for the same woman he knew too well to realise her compulsions of living with a tyrant, and of not being able to openly accept him. He also stood up for other women he didn't knew too well, to imprint that "girls are not for sale." His women characters are not cautiously chosen but they just happen to be so; giving voice to his own angst against things- as they are and as they ought to be. Therefore, there is much given to proselytizing if one may say and to that extent the book is propagandist speaking of an exploitative system where women from the lowermost strata are badly hit.

Practically, women are outsourcing necessities of their community, they are torchbearers of a potent artistic legacy gradually waning, but they are birthing and nurturing successive generations of men and women. Amidst squalor, indignity, notoriety and abuse, preserving and protecting their chastity and integrity while remaining loyal to their men perhaps even more so than what a marriage license could afford, Kale speaks in clear terms the conditions and deprivations of women in his community- Women who kept burning their bodies and feet on the stage so that the fireplace back home could be kept burning.

The book is a strong critique of caste system and its insanely repressive structures. It exposes the hypocrisy of the India upper caste practices where low caste women are not considered fit to become wedded wives as the notion of pollution/purity is strong in their derailed mindsets but the same low caste woman can be had for sexual gratification. It chides a community of men impotent enough to not assume their gendered roles rightfully and who rather send their daughters and sisters amidst leering strangers to dance and entertain and get money home while they the lotus eaters prefer to remain in dazed drunken stupor enjoying their earnings. If someone accidently fell in for any of their women, and wanted to marry her or give her a normal conjugal life; these same community of men would sit to negotiate her price.

The book symbolically culminates on a positive note of the writer's social commitment. Kale the writer donning the role of Kale the activist, helping young girls of his community from getting sold off to vulgar appetites in the name of "Chira Uttravaney." The ambitious yet not unattainable work of selfless social service undertaken along with his friend Shyam Nagarkar of educating people against corrupt practices. On the personal front, his meets, Sangeeta the daughter of Dalit writer Laxman Gaikwad, and the consummation of marriage takes place outside the narrow community lines. He names his son as Prateek Sangeeta Kale with a middle name of his wife instead of his own. All this is borne out of choice while in his case he had none.

The book ends with "I passed MBBS in 1994" suggesting that he fought constraints, survived and achieved but that is not all. There is no finality as the struggle shall continue from there. The sense of fulfillment, satiation is not present and the last part though abrupt, clearly conveys this. In other words even if it was a great achievement for a poor orphaned boy to become doctor, the untouchable self will continue to loom large for the so called touchables. Their heinous attitudes would consistently remind the subalterns of their lowliness.

There is a break with linearity when it comes to narrativisation. This is to imprint that significant change within the community and society is yet farfetched. Therefore, to rupture the assumption of steady progress in the protagonist, the chronological sequence is very often disrupted. This is a stylistic requirement to show that there is still a long way ahead. It is to be understood that there is always a conjunctional link between the self and the community. Individual oppression transcends to voice group oppression and thus, this book speaks for all those like him. The autobiographical genre provides this space to speak for and beyond one's self and creates a praxis that sets out challenging existing literary paradigms.

The writer on his part subverts the mainstream dictum that there is no caste and nothing called untouchability by leaving the book with an open ending. Caste has been and will continue to remain a valid force of social exclusionary practices. The book on the whole stands tall and distinctly apart in the Dalit male narratorial tradition as it has given enough space to the Dalit women and the issue of her identity.

Work Cited

Kale Kishore Shantabai. *Kolhatyache Por.* (Trans. Mine) Mumbai: Granthali.1994. Print.

24

Projection of Poverty and Exploitation of Dalit Women in Laxman Gaikwad's Autobiography *Uchalya-The Branded:* An Analysis

Dr S. Chelliah

> Dalit Literature is one which acquaints people with the caste system and untouchability in India, its appalling nature and its system of exploitation. In other words, Dalit Literature is not a caste but a realisation and is related to the experiences, joys and sorrows and struggles of those in the lowest strata of society. —(Dangle, 256)

Dalit autobiographies have changed the flow of Indian Writings in English and Dalit men's autobiographies have brought a revolution in the society because now the pains and problems of particular person, caste or community have become the problem of many. Dalit autobiographies have been written by male and female writers but the men's autobiographies came to the forefront for the first time.

Laxman Gaikwad's autobiography *Uchalya: The Branded* does not deal only with the problems of only male dalits; it portrays the unheard sufferings and pains of Dalit women of his tribe. Laxman Gaikwad was born in a nomadic tribe and his tribe had no permanent residence and a stable identity. The people of this tribe were just given a brand name 'The Thief.' Thus, Uchalya community was known as a notorious community and it was famous for their skills of pilfering, thievery and pick-pocketing. Dalit men ran their family only by this illegal act and that's why many times these people were unable to provide two times meals to their families. In these conditions many Dalit women had to come forward to run their families. Dalit women also had to embrace the same profession of pilfering and pick-pocketing. Dalit women have made this autobiography so strong that it has become an important document in the history of Dalit literature. Bijender Singh praises this autobiography in the following words, "Laxman Gaikwad's autobiography is a masterpiece of Dalit literature." (Singh, 07)

The life of these Dalit women was very tough as they were from the lowest of the low stratum. Dalits of Uchalya tribe were not given any regard in the society and Dalit women were at the periphery of even these families. Only the bread-winners of the family were given a bit regard in Dalit families but there were some women who also joined shoulders to run their families.

Gaikwad's mother, Dhondabai was one of such women who disliked the dirty way of stealing things. She ran her family by selling milk but she had to face many problems in her life to run her family. She was a very laborious and responsible woman but she was not treated well by her husband, Martand because he did not have faith on her. Martand was very cruel to her. He would beat, bully and tyrannize her. In fact, he had seeds of infidelity in his mind and he thought negatively about her whenever she got late from her milk-selling rounds. He flatly said to her, "You spend your time with your paramour! Saru is not my daughter." (22) He thought that she was a woman of bad character and his daughter, Saru was not his own blood; that's why whenever Gaikwad's sister, Saru came to her parental home after her marriage, his father would not only remanded Dhondibai but also gave her punishment. He would say, "Why do you take her in? Why do you give her a sari and a blouse?" He also forced Dhondibai to do sit ups as a punishment because she had dared to enter Saru without his permission. In this way Dalit women did not have rights for the entry of their daughters. But Dhondibai was a very hardworking woman and she had bought three corrugated iron sheets for her hut by selling milk. Earlier the roof of the hut was made of grass and the bamboo but it was then replaced by iron sheets and a stone wall. She was very caring mother when her son's head was covered with boils. She says:

> This disease seems to be the curse of the goddess. Harlot that I am, I gave up fasting on Tuesdays and so my poor son is afflicted with this dirty disease. She brought ash of the cow dung-cake from the store and prayed, "Oh! Goddess – Mother! Please cure my child of this disease, As long as I don't sacrifice a goat to you, I shall fast both on Friday and on Tuesday". (25)

The women of the Uchalya community were merely the puppets at the hands of their husband and were an easy prey for the upper caste people. Dalit women were merely treated as a commodity. Laxman Gaikwad's elder brother, Dada has brought a woman, Padmini for him to keep her as a wife but he later sold her for two hundred and fifty rupees. They were just considered as an object to satisfy their sexual hungers. Gaikwad narrates a horrendous incidence when he was sleeping in the yard with his sister-in-law. Suddenly somebody came and lay on her forcibly. She could not cry because that man has put his hand firmly on her mouth. He lay by her side and left the place only after the heinous act of sex with a weak and Dalit woman. Thus, the position of the women was not good and their fate was ordained by the men of the village Panchayat. Even the panchas and panchayat had full right to give any verdict for a woman. Here is an instance when village panchayt gives verdict for a woman to get her head shaved:

> At last one of the panchas brought a razor, wetted the women's hair with water and began to shave her head. The woman's heart wept mutely in her agony. The sin of the mother was visited on the daughter. Even while the husband was alive, the panchayat shaved her head clean. Not satisfied with that, the panchas smeared her head with ocher. The bride's mother had pushed the end of her sari into her mouth, lest her weeping be heard. (121)

Thus, the condition of women has been depicted not well in the autobiography *The Branded*. Even Laxman Gaikwad's wife co-operated him very much and she ran her shop in order to run this family and to help her husband financially. She was a fair woman and that's why Gaikwad suspected her and his sister-in-law also filled his ears against her. She was badly beaten also by him. This kind of domination of men over women is clearly visible in this autobiography. Laxman sometimes felt remorseful and guilty after his beatings. Chhabu's grandmother had a hunch back and it was told that the police have broken her back by the beating. She narrates this incidence in these words:

> I had a son, Ram by name. He was a versatile thief. While your wife was still a young girl, he had cut and picked a pocked. He got ten thousand rupees from it. The police came to know of it. About 25 to 30 police constables and an Inspector descended upon our village. They thrashed us all, kicked us with boots, and trampled on our prostrate bodies. They grilled us to tell them where we had kept the money. (143)

The police were very cruel in that area and they would not beat the young ones of the family, they did not spare even the children and the elders of the family. The children were made permanently disabled by them by their beatings. The police would do it because they did not have any fear from this thief tribe. Even the police also exploited and harassed the Dalit women and even the upper caste people used them for their bodies. Women had to sacrifice to get their people out of the jail, "Only then did the police release them without bringing any charge against them in the court. Mother's gold ornaments were kept by the police for themselves. After all, we were thieves by profession; who could we lodge a complaint with." (15-16) The beautiful Dalit women had to live a life of a harlot as there was not much social security for the Dalit women.

It was also seen at many places that the women of Uchalya community worked hard and their husbands were good for nothing. Gaikwad's grandmother, Narasabai was a notorious thief.

> My grandmother, Narasabai ran the household, grandfather being thoroughly useless...My grandfather; Lingappa did maintain our household in heydays, picking pockets lifting valuables and odd things in the markets and fairs. He was a well-known and respected thief in our tribe and area. The Nizam State records mentioned him as a most notorious and dangerous thief. Nobody ever dared cross his path. (Gaikwad, 1)

Gaikwad's grandfather, Lingappa, was a public informer and he had to report to police twice a day about the plans and activities of the thieves of his village that's why the people of his own village killed him. Narasai was not useless like her husband. She was badly tyrannised by the police because of the other members of her family who were thieves.

The women of this tribe were considered just as a commodity and they did not have their independence status. They were merely like the puppets and they did not have a rational thinking. They were conservative and traditional in their attitude as is said, "Dalit women also were under the spell of Hindu rituals, blind faiths due to ignorance and inferiority complex" (Bhave, 16). Moreover their position has been depicted in the following words:

> Condition of Dalit women was deplorably pitiable. They faced dozens of problems simply because they were females. Upper caste people in society always looked at them as consumable commodity. Men and boys teased, molested, seduced them and at time misused their womanhood. Dalit women were treated in a fashion as if they were public property like urinals and toilets. People satisfied their sexual hunger through immoral and forceful relations with them. Girls were sold and purchased like a beast in village. (Jain 9-10)

Another woman, Yellava was also a thief. She would cut necklaces, mangalsutras, Vajratika, Bormaal, trinkets, earrings etc. very deftly with her teeth. She had no fear of her prestige and she stole any sort of material she got a chance. She collected much material after her thieving rounds. Women also had some rights also. If their husbands would divorce them, they were entitled to reimburse the marriage expenses through the interruption of the village Panchayat.

Gaikwad grandmother, Narsabai and mother, Dhondabai had their own ways of thinking. As Narsabai was a notorious thief, police knew her nature very well. Her sons were also involved in this profession so whenever the police were in the lookout of her sons, she was also harassed. Even Gaikwad's mother who was a clean and clear woman, she was also treated badly by the police. Their treatment was inhumanly. The police even did not hesitate to squeeze her breasts and pull her by her hair. Whenever she was found in a good sari, the police would suspect on her, "You harlot, where did you get such a costly sari? Do you have the case-memo for this sari? Show the cash-memo or take off the sari and hand it over to us." (61) She pleaded and begged for mercy but nobody would hear her.

Gaikwad narrates in this autobiography how a Pardhi woman, Hirabai Kale was treated badly by the police soon after her tubectomy. She had undergone a tubectomy operation and she was given an amount of two hundred rupees. She bought half a gunny bag of a Jowar from this money and coincidentally a farmer had lodged a complaint for the Jowar the same time. She was also badly treated by the police.

> The police grilled her: 'From where did you get this half a gunny-bag of jawar'? Poor Hirabai begged and entreated piteously, 'Saheb I've just delivered a child, and I've noting to eat. My husband, thanks to you, is in jail. I got myself operated under the family planning scheme. Out of the Rs 200 they paid for it, I've purchased this half a gunny-bag of jowar. Saheb, I've become so weak that I've no milk in my breasts for my offspring. That's why I've purchased this jowar. (199)

Hirabai Kale tried to prove herself innocent in this matter but the police did not hear anything in this regard. The police would unnecessary harassed these women to grab some money from them.

From all this it can be concluded that Laxman Gaikwad's autobiography *The Branded* narrates the very pitiable plight of women. They had to live a subjugated life and had not had even the equal rights. N. Kanakaratnam, G. Varadarajulu and Surya Raju Mattimalla write:

> Autobiographies interpret repulsive experiences of exclusion of a private and his community. There are the records of out-castes UN agency live in seclusion outside village bounds, on payements, village outskirts yet as those that live in forests and on hills. (3)

Works Cited

Bagul, Baburao. "Dalit Literature is but Human Literature." Dangle, Arjun ed. *Poisoned Bread.* Trans. from Modern Marathi Dalit Literature. New Delhi: Orient Blackswan, 1992. Print.

Gaikwad, Laxman. *The Branded.* Trans. by P.A. Kolharkar from Marathi Autobiography. New Delhi: Sahitya Akademi, 1998. Print.

Jain, R.S. *Dalit Autobiography*. Ahmednager: Ritu Prakshan, 2006. Print.

Kanakaratnam, N., Varadarajulu, G. and Mattimalla, Surya Raju. "The Emergence of Dalit Autobiographyies in India." *International Journal of Multidisciplinary Educational Research.* Volume 4, Issue 9(3), September 2015.1-8.

Phadke, S.D. "Dalit Literature: A Minority Discourse." In Aston, N. M. ed. *Literature of Marginality: Dalit Literature and African American Literature.* New Delhi: Prestige Book, 2001. Print.

Singh, Bijender. Dalit Resurrection in Laxman Gaikwad's *The Branded. Indian Scholar: An International Multidisciplinary Research E-Journal.* 1.1. (2014): 49-55.

Index